Scent of an Orange

The Story of Our New Life

Revised Edition

TERESE DRON

BALBOA
PRESS

A DIVISION OF HAY HOUSE

Cover design by Jennifer Black

Balboa Press books may be ordered through booksellers or by contacting:

Balboa Press
A Division of Hay House
1663 Liberty Drive
Bloomington, IN 47403
www.balboapress.com.au
1 (877) 407-4847

Because of the dynamic nature of the Internet, any web addresses or links contained in this book may have changed since publication and may no longer be valid. The views expressed in this work are solely those of the author and do not necessarily reflect the views of the publisher, and the publisher hereby disclaims any responsibility for them.

The author of this book does not dispense medical advice or prescribe the use of any technique as a form of treatment for physical, emotional, or medical problems without the advice of a physician, either directly or indirectly. The intent of the author is only to offer information of a general nature to help you in your quest for emotional and spiritual well-being. In the event you use any of the information in this book for yourself, which is your constitutional right, the author and the publisher assume no responsibility for your actions.

Any people depicted in stock imagery provided by Thinkstock are models,
and such images are being used for illustrative purposes only.
Certain stock imagery © Thinkstock.

ISBN: 978-1-5043-0509-9 (sc)
ISBN: 978-1-5043-0510-5 (e)

Print information available on the last page.

Balboa Press rev. date: 10/31/2016

In memory of my parents,

Anna and Paul Dron

For my brothers and my children,

And all our children,

to remember

CHAPTERS

PROLOGUE

My daughter Karen often made business trips up the coast, and one time she had taken me along. After going as far as Grafton on the coast, we travelled inland to Armidale. We didn't talk much.

Driving along the New England Highway, we passed through some towns faster than I could think to say, "Are we stopping here?" Karen had one more stop to make at Tamworth.

As we travelled through the New England towns and farms, a rainbow appeared, and it reminded me of when I was a little girl living on a farm in Germany during the war. Seeing the green grass parrots on the edge of the road, I thought of the time we first came to Australia.

I said to Karen, "This part of the country reminds me of the time we left Germany and came to Bonegilla."

"Why *did* your parents come to Australia?" asked Karen.

She knew little about her grandparents. As their eldest child, I am the only one who knows the story or their journey from the war in Europe to a new life in Australia. Even my two younger brothers don't know very much; one was a baby when we came to Australia, and the other was born here. My parents didn't like to talk about the war, or their life in Poland.

Mother kept everything to herself. Sometimes I would find her crying, and I'd ask what was wrong. "Oh, nothing, I don't know", she would say. She wouldn't open up, but from things she said over the years, and from overhearing things that I shouldn't have, I put the pieces together. Now I know why she cried. She had lost her whole family. I don't know if her refusal to talk about it was because she didn't want to upset me, or because it upset her more to remember.

I couldn't get close to my mother, and in some ways, it's the same with Karen and I. I remember one day when Karen came home from school. They had been reading a book called *The Silver Sword*. Karen said one of her teachers had said Hitler was a good man. I threw up my hands and shouted "How dare you say something like that!" My anger had stopped any conversation about it there and then.

I looked out of the car window at the farmland. Some of it was green with crops. Other parts had been ploughed and were ready for planting.

"Mum?" said Karen beside me. I realised that I had been lost in my own thoughts, and hadn't answered her question. "Mum!" she said again. "You should write down what you know about the family."

Karen was right. I had to tell my children, and their children, about my parents' life. I had to set the record straight!

THE DRIVE

After her father passed away, my daughter Karen phoned twice a week to see if I needed anything. She often made business trips up the coast, and one time she offered to take me along.

"We'll be leaving at six in the morning, Mum. Will you be ready?"

"Yes," I said. "I'm looking forward to this trip."

"I'll see you in the morning, then," replied Karen.

I hadn't seen much of Karen since she left home at the age of twenty. At that time she had a morning job at Cessnock McDonalds, and an afternoon job at Cardiff Workers' Club. She put in sixteen hours a day and had little time to see me. After ten years she progressed to a full-time job with Subway, working as a director. Her job now is to audit the books and to see that everything is running smoothly in each shop she calls on. I was glad to be travelling with Karen; it would give us an opportunity to talk.

The next morning, Karen picked me up at my house in her company car. The car had bucket seats for a comfortable ride, and a car phone. It was like an office on wheels. To speak on the phone, Karen only had to press a button. She didn't need to let go of the steering wheel. We drove from my house at Beresfield towards Hexham. We crossed the Hunter River on Hexham Bridge, and travelled north to Raymond Terrace. Not a word had been spoken. As we came to Raymond Terrace, I broke the ice by saying, "Your father and I were married in this town, just up the hill in the street on your right. Saint Bridget's Roman Catholic Church." There was no need to say the town was rich in history, but I didn't know how much of its history Karen appreciated.

As Karen drove, I enjoyed the countryside. We passed the huge lake at Grahamstown, the reservoir that supplies water to surrounding towns. We travelled through the forest, and passed a sign on the road that said 'Look out for Koalas.' We crossed small creeks, and then a sign saying 'Swan Bay'. Karen said, 'Remember the one and only family holiday we had at Frank's weekender at Swan Bay?"

"Yes, I do. That was a long time ago." I said...

'Anthony was nine, and I was ten,' said Karen.

Frank used to deliver bread to our house. He owned a weekender cottage at Swan Bay, and he let the cottage to us for two weeks in the May school holidays. Frank, his wife Pat, and their son Bruce came up on Friday evening to stay for the weekend with us. Frank brought a boat with him.

"Frank, Dad and I went out in the boat fishing on the river," said Karen. "The boys were left at the house. They were going fishing with Frank the next day. I caught the biggest fish – a small shark. We got so excited. I can't remember if Dad or Frank caught any fish that day."

Karen opened up. "Dad was in his glory those two weeks, lighting the fuel stove every morning and going fishing for a while."

"More like killing time,' I said, 'waiting for the club to open. After he came back from the river, he would drive to Karruah RSL for a drink and a chat with the local chaps."

"Dad really enjoyed the two weeks at Swan Bay. While he was at the club, you had us collecting rocks for your garden, Mother! You nearly caused Dad to have a heart attack when we were packing to leave. You told Dad that the pile of rocks we collected was to be put in the trailer to take home. I laughed at the expression on Dad's face. I could see what he was thinking!"

Karen laughed. "Mum, I couldn't live like you do; scrounging things and bringing them home to clutter up your garden."

"What else could I do?' I said. 'We never had money to spend. I found a hobby that I enjoyed and didn't have to spend much money on. Most of the time I get cuttings from friends. I need to have some interest."

Karen was silent for a moment. She gathered her thoughts, and picked up where she left off. "When we came home from Swan Bay, Dad started planning for the next year's holiday."

"Yes, I remember going to the big retail store with your father to buy the tin boat.'

Karen laughed. "A boat! It was a bath tub!"

"It was all we could afford, Karen. Your father was on an invalid pension. That didn't leave us much to spend and we knew nothing about boats. I realise a bigger boat would have been safer. But then your father couldn't handle a bigger boat by himself."

"Dad and Anthony went out together fishing on the Hunter River at Hexham, said Karen. 'Anthony told me they fished under the Hexham Bridge. I remember the day Dad and his mate, Ray, went fishing. They came back within an hour. I said, "You're back early Dad. What happened?" Dad was so mad! He said, "The stupid bastard! We were putting the boat in the river – he couldn't get into the boat quick enough. Didn't listen to what I had to say, the stupid bastard, standing up trying to paddle the boat like it was a gondolier! He must have thought he was in bloody Venice on the canal! He tipped the boat over, lost all the fishing gear and then jumped into the river to retrieve it all! The stupid bastard got wet so I had to bring him back home!" Anthony overheard this, and decided that his fishing days with Dad were over."

"Who could blame him?' I said. Anthony had more sense."

There was silence. Karen put on a prayer tape.

Then Karen asked, "Do you see Frank at all these days?"

"Yes,' I said. 'Frank is a carpenter now. I call on him when I need repairs done to the house. Sometimes I see him at the social dance."

We travelled towards Bulahdelah, a town nestled beneath the mountains. The town is surrounded by bush and water.

"This is where your father and I spent the first night of our honeymoon,' I said. 'We stayed at the hotel and had hamburgers for tea; that is all we could buy. The publican prepared a room for us with a bottle of sparkling wine and some funny comics for the evening's entertainment."

"Some wedding night, Mum!" Said Karen.

As we drove into the Bulahdelah Forest, I felt the cool change of the trees. They are so tall and straight, and big tree ferns grow under them. I opened the car window to hear the sound of the bellbirds. The winding road climbed higher into the Bulahdelah mountains. Although the scenery was lovely, I felt nervous. This part of the road was notorious for horrific accidents. Thank goodness it wasn't raining. Karen put on another prayer tape to put me at ease. Once we were over the mountains, I could breathe a little easier.

The car phone rang. One of the girls from the shop in Newcastle needed Karen's advice. The shop had been broken into overnight. "Is there much damage?" Karen asked.

"Only the lock on the door,' said the girl. 'I have notified the police. They came and took finger prints. The police said the thief must have been disturbed when breaking in."

"Call the locksmith,' said Karen. 'Have the locks changed and ask them to send the bill to Subway'"

Coming into Taree, we stopped at McDonalds for breakfast. Karen had worked for McDonalds as a store manager, and it was a big help in getting her present position with the Subway Company. I had trouble getting out from the low seat, and was a little wobbly on my feet stepping out of the car.

We only ordered coffee. I drank my coffee slowly. "Don't take too long,' said Karen. 'I have a few shops to attend today."

I tried drinking the coffee faster, and that caused me to have a coughing spasm. We left the restaurant. Karen carried the coffee out for me. Seated in the car again, I put on the seat belt, and Karen passed the coffee to me.

"Don't spill the coffee, Mother." Said Karen.

When Karen is impatient with me, she calls me Mother.

"I will do my best not to, Karen." I said.

She got in the car and we drove off. When Karen was impatient like this, I wondered if it was because she missed her father. She had taken care of him in his last years, although he was living on his own. Karen went to see him, and took him to the doctors whenever it was necessary. She had his prescriptions filled, and visited him in hospital. She had attended to all his needs.

We passed the Big Oyster on the roof of a restaurant as we were leaving Taree. Breaking the silence, I said, "It seems that the business people like to advertise their products in a big way in New South Wales and Queensland."

"When we reach Coffs Harbour you will see the Big Banana,' said Karen. 'We'll be stopping at Port Macquarie next. Have you been to Port Macquarie Mum?"

'Yes, twice. The first time with your father. It was part of our honeymoon. The other time was with friends. Six of us spent a week's holiday in Port Macquarie. We had a wonderful time!"

'I'm glad you enjoyed yourself Mum.' Then she asked, 'Did you bring water with you?"

"No, I don't drink when I am travelling a long distance. I'll get a drink the next time you stop." I replied.

"I'm only stopping at Port Macquarie for a short time. Don't walk too far away from the car. I will bring a drink out for you." Karen said.

At Port Macquarie, I had to get out and stretch my legs, and move about a little. My joints were stiff. We still had a long way to travel.

After a long drive, we arrived at Byron Bay. Karen was lucky to find a spot to park her car in front of the Subway shop. She handed me the keys and said, "My work will take about two hours. Take a walk and see the town."

I walked towards the beach. I thought I would collect shells for my garden. As I came to the end of the street, I saw teenagers hanging about near the public toilets. They looked to me like they were off the planet. I would have to go past them to walk to the beach. I changed my mind.

Deciding to go window shopping instead, I walked up and down the street, browsing through the shops. I wandered into an antique shop to look around. To my surprise, I found a salad bowl that matched a set I had at home. The set was imported from France, and had been a wedding gift to Bryan and me. Over the years, I had broken the middle-sized one, and this one in the antique shop was just the size I needed! I bought it.

It started to rain. I walked back to the car. Wanting to open the car door, I pressed the wrong button and set off the car alarm. I dropped the keys. "Help, help me!" I screamed.

People stopped to look. Karen ran out from the shop to see what was happening. She saw me standing next to the car. "You've pressed the wrong button, Mother!"

Picking up the keys from the ground, I shouted back at her. "We didn't need gadgets like this in our young day!"

People in the street started laughing. When I got over the shock, I laughed with them. I didn't mind. It had broken the boredom in the street, and maybe it would be something to talk about with the family at the evening meal: "the dear old lady that didn't know what button to push to open the car door.'

I sat in the car waiting for Karen to finish her work.

We were back on the highway, on our way to Coolangatta. Karen said, "I can't imagine what a dull life you must have lived back in the fifties and sixties!"

"We had good movies and good songs,' I said. 'There was soothing instrumental music on the radio stations in our day. I liked reading Readers' Digest books. There is one story that is still in my mind, a story I read of a doctor working in China as a missionary. He made his home there. He said he could be a very wealthy man in Australia, but he was content to stay in China helping the poor hard working people. They paid him with eggs and vegetables, and poultry. He said he wouldn't have it any other way."

Changing the subject, I said, "Your father and I spent a day of our honeymoon at Byron Bay. We had a lovely time. Your father stopped the car at Cape Byron light house to show me the most eastern point of Australia. We could see spectacular views of the coast surrounding the light house. The goats kept the grass down. They have been on that hill from the time the Cape Byron light house was built."

I started to laugh as I remembered a conversation Bryan and I had heard between two men as we walked around the light house. I told Karen how one of the chaps said to his English friend that Byron Bay was the most eastern point of Australia, and that there should be a law passed that every cat west of Byron Bay be shot. "The Englishman was horrified. He was obviously a cat lover. He said, "You don't really mean that do you?"

"That's Aussie humour, Mum." Karen laughed.

"I found Byron Bay and the entire coast interesting,' I said. 'I was seeing parts of Australian history and visiting the places that I learned about at school. Your father told me that Captain Cook named Byron Bay after an English sailor who was the grandfather of the famous poet George Byron."

"Hmm,' said Karen, 'a little more exciting than reading comics on your wedding night."

I took the hint. Karen may have been bored by this conversation. I said no more.

The tape was on again. By the time we had listened to what the Lord had to say to us through the minister, we were close to the Queensland border. Karen said, "I am taking you to a good Indian restaurant at Coolangatta."

"I have never eaten Indian food. You will have to order the meal for me. Will we have time to change?" I asked.

"No, Mum. We are going direct to the restaurant. I'm running late and we don't want to miss out on our meal." Karen answered.

"I would have liked to change and refresh myself so I would look and feel good."

"I wouldn't worry, Mum. You always look good, even in the clothes you choose to wear."

"I dress according to my style, size and age. I am happy with that, Karen. Anyway, if you put it that way, the dress designers must be walking about with their eyes shut. They don't see the average woman in the street. They design dresses for young Twiggies. That is what they see in their minds, but I don't see many Twiggies walking about in the street, do you Karen?"

"OK, Mother, you've made your point."

Karen stopped the car close to the restaurant. We walked in the door just in time to be seated. The Indian waiter was neatly dressed in a white long sleeve shirt and black trousers with a red cummerbund. He pulled the chair out for me, and moved quickly to the other side of the table to do the same for Karen. Then he bowed, excusing himself. I appreciate good manners. It is very nice when people are polite. It makes life worth living.

We were the last customers to be seated. The waiter came back to see if we wanted to order drinks. Karen asked for two glasses of water. There was no need to look at the menu. Karen knew what to order. She placed the order with the waiter before he left our table. The waiter came back with the two glasses of water, and asked if we wanted a drink with our meal. I asked for a lemon, lime and bitters, and Karen asked for a glass of wine.

Our meal of sweet chicken curry arrived. While we were eating, I looked around the restaurant. The windows and doors were shaped in the Indian style. White lace curtains screened the lower half of each window. No-one from the street could see in to the restaurant. Chandeliers hung from the ceiling, giving the room a soft glow. The atmosphere was cool, clean and inviting with its white table cloths, crystal wine glasses and silver cutlery. The blue napkins looked good on the white tablecloths, and matched the blue carpet on the floor. Soft dinner music was playing. I felt relaxed, and took time to enjoy the meal. I felt like a VIP.

"Would you like sweets?" asked Karen.

"The meal was delicious,' I said. 'I may finish on that and leave the sweets out."

Before leaving the table, I thanked Karen for the wonderful evening and said it had been a long time since I was treated like a VIP. As we left the restaurant, the waiter bowed and opened the door to let us out.

We walked to the car. The soft breeze blowing on my face and through my hair felt so good. I love walking in the evening. It is so pleasant to smell the trees and shrubs release their perfume into the evening air. I wished the car was parked further away so the walk could be a little longer.

"We are going to a motel at Tweed Heads,' said Karen. 'I stay at that motel every time I make a trip this way. It's away from the main road, no noise from the traffic. It's only ten minutes from here."

Arriving at the motel, Karen got the key and opened the room. I smelt a mixture of smoke and room deodoriser. "Could we leave the door open for a little while?" I asked.

"That's OK,' she said, 'I have some paperwork to finish. I'll leave the door open till then. You use the bathroom first, Mum. This will take some time. When I finish I'll leave the window open all night."

After I'd had my shower, Karen said, 'I start work at nine in the morning, so I don't have to get out of bed before eight.'

I didn't know how I was going to sleep with the continuous buzzing I get in my ears. I usually listened to a radio under my pillow. I could have switched on the radio in the room, but I had to think of Karen. She needed her sleep. As soon as Karen laid her head on the pillow, she was out like a light. I must have done the same soon after.

In the morning, I was the first to wake. I heard lorikeets outside the window greeting the new day. I dressed quickly and left the room quietly so as not to wake Karen with the "ooh" and "arrh" from my back pains, and my morning ritual of sneezing and coughing.

The morning was a little fresh. I walked to the river and watched the sun rise. I like to look at peoples' houses and the plants in their gardens. All these things give me pleasure. It's food for my soul and mind, a complete rest, and the walking exercise is good for my back. After the sun had risen I was not alone in the street. Young people were jogging, and older women and men were walking their dogs. Everyone said 'Good morning' as they passed.

I got back to the motel at about a quarter past seven. Karen was still sleeping. I didn't want to wake her. I made coffee. When she woke up she said she appreciated the extra time in bed. It's not often she gets the time to sleep in.

After breakfast, we went to the Tweed Heads shop. Karen said, "I will be here for two hours. Don't get lost – I won't know where to find you."

"I will be back in time. You should know that by now." I assured Karen.

I walked to Coolangatta, not realising how far it was. It was rather a long walk, but it was no trouble for me to walk that distance. I looked at the building which had been in the early stages of completion when I was here on holidays with the dance group some years back. On the ground floor were very exclusive shops for ladies' wear, jewellery and antiques, things that I could not afford. I couldn't imagine who would pay such prices. I looked at my watch. Time was up. I had to take a bus ride back to the car because I had misjudged the distance from Tweed Heads to Coolangatta. Karen had finished just as I arrived.

Our next stop was the Subway shop in Grafton, and Karen said she would be some time. I looked around the town, but the shops were closed. When I returned to the car, Karen was still working. When she finished, we drove to a motel. This time we had a shower and dressed for the evening meal at the motel restaurant. She told me that here in Grafton she had found the dress for her wedding.

The next morning, before Karen woke, I went for a walk. After our breakfast, we went to a bridal shop. Karen wanted me to try on some of the dresses she had in mind for me to wear at her wedding. Karen and I don't see eye to eye on dress sense. I didn't argue and went along with her and put on the dress she had picked out. I tried three dresses Karen had chosen for me. Somehow I didn't look like what she had in mind. A short tight skirt above the knee was not flattering for a big and middle-aged woman like me. I thanked the sales lady for her assistance and we walked out of the shop. Karen was disappointed, and said "You choose what you want."

"I bought some lace years ago when we were in Malaysia,' I said. 'I'll have that made into a lovely top to go with a circular skirt in soft material."

We began our journey back home, going inland to Armidale. We didn't talk much. Travelling along the New England Highway, we passed through some towns faster than I could think to say, "Are we stopping here?" Karen had one more stop to make at Tamworth.

As we travelled through the New England towns and farms, a rainbow appeared, and it reminded me of when I was a little girl living on a farm in Germany during the war. Seeing the green grass parrots on the edge of the road, I thought of the time we first came to Australia.

I said to Karen, "This part of the country reminds me of the time we left Germany and came to Bonegilla."

'Why *did* your parents come to Australia?' asked Karen.

She knew little about her grandparents. As their eldest child, I am the only one who knows the story or their journey from the war in Europe to a new life in Australia. Even my two younger brothers don't know very much; one was a baby when we came to Australia, and the other was born here. My parents didn't like to talk about the war, or their life in Poland.

Mother kept everything to herself. Sometimes I would find her crying, and I'd ask what was wrong. "Oh, nothing, I don't know" she would say. She wouldn't open up, but from things she said over the years, and from overhearing things I shouldn't have, I put the pieces together. Now I know why she cried. She had lost her whole family. I don't know if her refusal to talk about it was because she didn't want to upset me, or because it upset her more to remember.

I couldn't get close to my mother, and in some ways, it's the same with Karen and me. I remember one day when Karen came home from school. They'd been reading a book called *The Silver Sword*. Karen said one of her teachers had said Hitler was a good man. I threw up my hands and shouted "How dare you say something like that!" My anger had stopped any conversation about it then.

I looked out of the car window at the farmland. Some of it was green with crops. Other parts had been ploughed and were ready for planting.

"Mum?" said Karen beside me. I realised that I had been lost in my own thoughts, and hadn't answered her question. "Mum," she said again. 'You should write down what you know of the family."

Karen was right. I had to tell my children, and their children, about my parents' life. I had to set the record straight.

ROOMS

My earliest memory is me sitting on the floor in a room, alone. A tree branch tapping at the window attracted my attention. The branch was covered in pink blossoms. Butterflies and bees came to rest on the blossoms, and then off they went. I sat and watched until the day faded. It was a long time that Mother was away. When she came back, I remember that she washed me, fed me and put me to sleep. The next morning, Mother fed me, gave me a kiss and off she went. I was alone in the room again.

I watched the branches in the window every day until the flowers were gone and green leaves grew on the branch. I watched birds hopping about.

I started to become aware of the door that Mother closed when she went out. I took more notice of the room and things around me. I saw something blue, with pretty things attached, hanging on the wall. My idea was to get it down but it was too high for me to reach. I pushed a little stool from the corner of the room across to where the pretty blue thing was hanging. I stood on the stool and fell off. I got up and again stood on the stool, pulling at the pretty blue. It was soft, like chiffon or silk. It ripped off the nail.

Mother returned from work and saw her only good blouse lying on the floor, torn. I felt her hand smacking my bottom.

Sometime later, I had a baby brother to look after. I don't know what age I was. I remember Mother saying to me before she left for the day, "Terese, my little kitten, listen to me very carefully, and try to remember what I am saying to you. I am going out and won't be back for a long time. Feed your brother Wladek when he cries."

Mother made some things for him to suck on and showed me what I must do. She said,

"Put this into the bowl of milk." She took it out of the milk and put it into his mouth. "You have plenty to feed him with until I come back." I did as much as a child could do for a little baby brother.

One day, Mother took us outside. The vast blue sky above me was so bright. The trees across the road were in bloom. The ground was brown. It had just been turned over, ready for planting. We were living on a farm. It looked like paradise. Everything was big. I was given a small basket to pick blueberries with Mother. I ate more than I put in my basket. I remember being given a stick to help another little girl chase the geese into their pens, but the geese chased me, pecking at my head. They were bigger than me.

From then on, we went outside regularly, but before we went, Mother always spoke to me. "Terese, listen to me," she said, "and pay attention. It is very important that you listen to me. When you hear the boss whistling a tune, it means you must run to him. Will you do as I tell you?"

I nodded my head.

"If you don't do what I say, you will be taken away and not see me or your brother Wladek again."

The boss played the game with me. When I heard him whistle the tune, I ran to him, and he hid me in many places on the farm. Sometimes I was taken to the kitchen cellar and put in a cupboard, and told to stay and not make a noise until the boss or the cook came to let me out. One time I was put in the corner of a pig pen with the pigs. The boss said, "You must not be frightened. Be very quiet. I will get you out soon."

Sometimes I was hidden in a spring well behind a wall. Again I was to be quiet and not to make a sound no matter what I saw. The well was underground. A brick wall was built around three sides, with steps going down to the spring. It was where the farm labourers came to drink. Where the water sprang up from the ground it was only ankle deep. There was no danger of me drowning. The water flowed away into a stream.

At other times I was sent to the field of poppies. They were very tall, and I had to stay there until the boss whistled.

One day my little brother and I were left in the pram under a tree in a field where Mother was working. A plane came, spraying bullets at the labourers working in the field. The bullets whistled as they passed Wladek and me sitting in the pram. Later, I picked up the bullet shells that were left lying about, and gave them to the boss.

After a long stay on the farm, we were put on a wagon with other people and moved to a place in the mountains. I remember that Wladek was at the walking stage. On the way, we saw a farm house on fire. Mother said to me, "Watch that house. Don't take your eyes off it. The house will fall down any minute." Just as she said it, the house fell. The woman sitting next to me said, "Remember this child. This is war."

It was a long journey by horse-drawn wagon to the mountains. The sun had almost set. We were shown the way to the horse stables. Three men tended a fire, making ready our tea. One of the men was my father. I remembered him from when he had come to see us a few times at the farm. Wladek and I were fed and then laid down to sleep. I don't remember if there were other children with us.

Early in the morning, the stable door was opened wide. It was foggy and cold. By the time we had eaten our breakfast; the sun was rising and peering from the mountain top. The fog lifted, and revealed an orchard of trees covered in blossoms. It was pretty to look at, and I felt happy. The day was sunny, and Wladek and I played with Mother. She didn't have to work that day.

When the sun set behind the mountains, it got cold. Men working in the orchard lit a fire. We had tea and were again laid down to sleep on the straw in the stable.

I woke up in total confusion. I was not in the warm stable. I was lying beside Mother on a wooden bench. There was a dreadful smell, and something dripping on me from above. The woman on the bench above us had just died. Her bladder and bowels had let go and I was drenched in her excretion. This unbearable stink made me vomit. I was sick and cold, upset and crying, clutching to Mother in this strange place.

There was some uproar from the women in the hut. My crying had upset their sleep. Mother tried to comfort me. She grabbed the smelly blanket of the dead woman and threw it on me to cover my putrid wet body, and said, "Cuddle into me to keep warm." Mother couldn't cuddle me because she was cuddling Wladek, who was lying in front of her. We had to lie on the long hard benches until Mother said we could get up and put our feet on the ground. When I got up, I saw women climbing down from benches above us.

We left that smelly hut and went out into the open. Outside, the stink was just as bad as it was inside the big hut. It was a foggy morning, and when the fog lifted I saw a terrible filthy place with high wire fences all around. It was nothing like the orchard we had been in the day before. I didn't know where we were.

Wladek and I walked with Mother to a place in the open where women were cooking, or washing. I was only a child, so I couldn't tell what they were doing. I saw steam rising from big drums. We were brought to this open space so Mother could wash the putrid smell from us. She dipped her hand into a puddle of dirty water, and washed our face and body the best way she could. She dried our bodies with a piece of smelly cloth.

A soldier in black grabbed Wladek from Mother's arms, and pulled me. She didn't want to let go of us, but it was difficult for her to hold on. She was whipped until she let us go. I clung to her dress as they pulled me away. Mother cried out to me, "Cuddle Wladek! Take care of him!" I heard Mother's voice crying out for me to take Wladek's hand. Her hand stretched out to us as we were put on a truck.

I was petrified. I don't remember the journey to the big building. There were other children inside a big room. We were all terrified, crying for our mothers. I clung to my Wladek like a big sister does to comfort her little brother. We were stripped of our clothes and stood naked. I took my brother's hand for the short time it took to get to a door where the other children had gone through before us. After we were examined, my brother and I were separated. I was never to see my baby brother again.

I was then taken to a bathroom. A nurse bathed me. Then I was taken to a room with a bed in it. There was nothing else in the room, only me sitting on the bed crying for Mother and my baby Wladek.

The door opened and a nurse came in with a bed on wheels. She put me on that bed and wheeled me to a room with big lights hanging above me. Monsters lifted me to a bed under the lights. They were not people like my mother. They had no faces, just eyes showing, and they had shiny things on their heads, and funny hands.

They poked my ribs and stomach, and gibbered to one another. Alongside me, I saw a big long tank holding water. The monsters put me on my side, holding me down with force so that I couldn't move. They jabbed something into my hip, and I yelled out with the pain. That is all I remember.

I woke up shivering in a bed, in another room.

I don't know how many times I was taken to the room with big lights. Maybe it was two or three times a week. I know it was not every day.

A monster came in with meals every day; that is how I knew the difference between days. The monster brought porridge every morning. It was like glue. A child has to be very hungry to eat porridge with no milk. In the afternoon, I was given boiled spinach, nothing else. It was always served on a white plate with a red rim. There was no milk to drink, only some mixture in water. It was as clear as mud and tasted as bad.

All the time I was in that place the monster spoke only one word to me: "*Essen*," which meant "Eat".

Every day I cried for my mother. Every time the door swung open, I lifted my arms, wanting someone to pick me up and carry me back to Mother. But no one did. It was only the monster, taking me to that room where pain was inflicted on me again and again.

I realise now that the monsters were nurses and doctors with masks on their faces and gloves on their hands, dressed to perform operations. They were injecting me with large needles. Up until my early twenties, I still had scars on my hips from these needles.

Things changed. I was no longer taken to the big room. The monsters came to my bed every day with small injections. Each time the door opened there was another jab in my bottom. After every injection, the walls of the room moved. My head was spinning. When I closed my eyes, my head spun even more. I felt like I was tumbling in mid-air.

My sleep was constantly interrupted. When I finally drifted off, I felt as if I were tumbling like a weed. This kind of nightmare would wake me. My body felt like it was on fire. I was thirsty. No-one heard my cry for a drink of water. There was no-one to clean me from vomit. There was nothing to cling to for comfort, not even a rag to hold onto. I was sick, in pain and very much alone. Every time I fell asleep, it was the same: tumbling like a weed.

In the morning, the monsters came again with the injection. My bottom, arms and the tops of my legs were pricked like a pin cushion. My stomach was the next target.

My finger nails were never cut. I peeled them off with my teeth. No-one combed my matted hair. No-one spoke to me all the time I was in that cold and lonely room.

I cried for my mother. I missed my Wladek, my little Wladek. He must have gone through the same horror as I did. I cried day and night for Mother to come and take me away. I cried for days and months, until my tears literally dried up.

The only comfort I got was from nature herself. Sometimes the moon shone through the window and lit up the room. Some nights I heard the sounds of a cuckoo bird in the tree that grew near. Before daybreak I heard birds chirping. On some mornings, the sunrise came through the double glass door and brightened the room.

I was very ill, unable to move any more. I remember being on a trolley pushed quickly, turning corners. My face was covered, but I could feel my body swaying from side to side. I was lifted off the trolley and the cover was taken off my face. I was put into a small enclosure. It was warm inside. The ceiling was not the same as it was in the room. I was in something small, like an oven. The heat must have overcome me. I don't remember anything after that.

I opened my eyes briefly. I saw Mother standing beside me, crying. My eyes closed again. I didn't cry. The lonely feeling was gone.

I was not able to keep my eyes open for long, but I knew I was in a different room. The door and the window were not in the same place, and the smell of the room was pleasant. The ladies entering this room were dressed in long dark dresses, and wore veils on their heads. I could see their faces. They were not like the monsters. Years later I learned from Mother that these were nursing nuns, and this was an Anglican private hospital. The nuns propped me up with pillows so I could sit up to be fed. When my health improved slightly, a nurse carried me outside in her arms and walked around the garden.

One day the door swung open. A strange man stood in the doorway. He was different to the people I saw every day. He wore a soldier's uniform, and his skin was dark. I know now that he was an American soldier. He threw something round and bright onto the end of my bed. A nun came in and picked up the bright round thing. She peeled the skin away from it, and a lovely scent filled the room. The nun then split it into pieces, and put the pieces on a plate. "*Essen*," she said.

I understood, but was too weak to move my arm. The nun picked up a piece and put it to my mouth. I sucked the sweet juice.

It was the first orange I had ever tasted, although I did not know it as an orange at the time. Nor did I know that this moment represented the beginning of a new life for me and my parents. All I knew then was that the scent of that orange filled the room, and filled my senses. It was as if I were being brought to life. It was the sweetest taste I had ever known.

But the doctors said that there was nothing more they could do for me. They did not expect me to live through the night. Mother asked if she could take me home to be with her. I was now the only child of our family. My brother Wladek was gone. She wanted to hold my weak little body. She wanted me to die in her arms.

Father brought me to a house they shared with other families in the town of Schwabisch Hall. Our room was in the attic. I opened my eyes for a brief moment. Through blurred vision

I saw Mother sitting at the side of the cot. I tried to keep my eyes open. They were sore and swollen. I could only open them momentarily.

Mother leaned over the cot, crying as she brushed my forehead. Her tears fell on my face. She said something to me I didn't understand. My eyes closed again.

When I opened my eyes again, it was morning. I saw Mother's face drenched in tears when she bent over to kiss me. I wanted to lift my arm to touch her face, and to say "Mamma", but there was no strength left in my body.

I was a living corpse lying in the cot. I couldn't even hold a bottle to feed myself. Breathing was very difficult. Every time I coughed, blood oozed from my mouth. When Mother changed me, I whimpered like a weak kitten. To relieve my cough and to nourish my little body, Mother made up an old remedy that was used in her young days: onion boiled in goat's milk, then mixed with a teaspoon of butter and a teaspoon of honey in half a cup of milk. This mixture was given to me four times a day. I was also given chamomile tea to relax me, and relieve me from pain. Chamomile and herbal tea brought down my temperature and settled my upset stomach. Father brought me bitter herbal medicines from the local bio chemist. There was no other medication for me at that crucial time. Mother hung damp sheets on the wall to help my breathing.

Mother was always with me, kneeling at my side with rosary beads in her hands, and praying. The minute I opened my eyes, Mother put down the rosary and gave me the mixture that was keeping me alive. While Mother prayed, Father whittled a flute in his spare time, hoping that he would teach me to play tunes on it one day.

Father did not live with us at the house because my illness was contagious. I was suffering from tuberculosis. Dad was working with the Americans, defusing unexploded bombs that were still in the ground, so he lived in the Allied forces camp. The army health authorities had put our room under quarantine. Mother was not to leave the house, and not to have close contact with other people in the house. Father came to the house every day and stood at the door just long enough to see the progress I was making, and to leave the groceries and ingredients that Mother needed. The only time he saw Mother was when he left the medication at the door and whistled a tune to let her know that he was standing beneath the attic window. Mother waved to him from the attic. As my health slowly improved, the half cup of milk increased to a full cup of milk.

Mother's home remedy treatment was working. Over months my health slowly improved with help from the doctors and the herbalist. I was able to sit up by myself, supported by pillows, and eat solid food. The military doctors came to examine me and see for themselves that I had recovered. They were astonished to see me alive and sitting up. The doctors advised Mother to make an appointment for me at the hospital for further treatment. Some weeks later, when the weather had changed and warmth was in the air, the military doctors came back to see how my health was progressing. They lifted the quarantine.

I said my first word: "Wladek."

Mother's eyes filled with tears when she heard me. I didn't know if the tears were because she was glad to hear me talk, or because she was sad about Wladek. Maybe the tears were for both. She kissed me and said, "He is not with us. The angels have taken Wladek to Heaven. We will not see him again."

Sadness came over me knowing I was not going to be with my little Wladek, but there were no tears left for my brother. They dried up in the room of that horror place.

My visits as an outpatient to the hospital doctor were progressing well. Cod liver oil was added to my treatment. It gave me a boost. I gained weight and grew stronger. I remember waking up in the early hours before sunrise, and Mother giving me a black currant jam sandwich cut into strips, with the crust cut off. I could only eat soft things. This became a ritual every morning.

As months went by I was able to sit at the attic window and watch the weather change from sunshine to rain, from autumn to winter. I loved watching the clouds in the sky change every day. Some were big, white and fluffy, and then came the grey clouds taking over the white.

There were days when the sky was just grey all the time. When I looked at the clouds I thought of Wladek, and hoped that I would see him sitting on a white cloud with the angels.

The trees lost their leaves in autumn, and eventually snow fell, covering the bare limbs. The trees looked like sculptures in the winter landscape. The houses across the street looked crisp and clean and long icicles hung from the windows. Dad said the icicles were long enough to play tunes on.

The house was at the end of a street, near a cemetery and a park. Occasionally, a dog ran past the house, leaving his paw prints in the snow. Mother taught me to count the prints. My visits to the hospital were put back until the snow melted and days warmed up. When spring arrived, I was well enough to make a trip to the dentist, which was a must. There was snow on the ground that day. Father pulled me along on the toboggan he had made for me. It was only a short ride up the street to the dental surgery. In a garden across the street, I saw snow-drop flowers appear from under the snow.

My teeth needed attention. I had already lost the front teeth. Some of my back teeth were very loose and had to be extracted. When my teeth were pulled I screamed and my dear dad fainted. He had to sit at the surgery for a while before he could take me home.

Dad said to Mother that he could not bear that I should suffer more pain. "When I heard Terese scream," he said, "I felt a sharp pain in my heart."

By summer, I was strong enough to walk a small distance, and eh hospital visits were resumed. It was only a short walk through the park and the cemetery. On one of those visits to the hospital, we were walking through the park and Mother remembered that she had left her money purse in the house. She said to me, "Stay here on the track. Watch me run back. You can see the house from here so don't be afraid."

I was alone in the park. The wind blowing and rustling through the treetops, and squirrels jumping in the trees, made me uneasy. Seeing monstrous red slugs crawling across the track petrified me. I couldn't move. I was shivering and stiff with fear by the time Mother came back. She realised the effect it had on me, and she never left me alone again.

On my routine visits to the hospital I often saw two black horses with plumed black feathers on their heads, pulling a beautiful glass carriage. It was very impressive. The carriage was prepared for funerals. One day, coming back from the hospital, we saw a woman with a child in a pram in front of a house that was partially destroyed by bombs. The German woman offered Mother the loan of her pram.

Most of the time, I stayed in the room. I was playing with my small doll when a bird flew in through the open window. Mother caught the bird and it stayed under my cot all that day. I looked several times under the cot, hoping that the bird would come to me, but it stayed in the corner of the room, not moving at all. The next day, Mother said I should let the bird go. "His mother is missing him and he is hungry," she said.

Mother picked the bird up and put it in my hand so I could have the pleasure of letting it go. She opened the window and the bird flew out of my hand. That was one of many little pleasures in life.

I loved living in that house. For the time we lived there, Mother cooked lovely meals. The taste is still in my mind: crumbed pork chops and potato salad she made every Sunday. That was the last good meal we ate before we left that house.

During the summer, on Sunday afternoons, we walked in the fields at the back of the house to enjoy the warm sun. In the distance, I saw grazing cows with bells on their necks. All this was new to me. Wild flowers grew in long green grass. Everything in the fields was beautiful.

Father thought we would live in the house for some time. He started working on a vegetable garden. While digging, he hit something hard in the ground. He had found a trunk full of crockery. He got excited and yelled out to Mother to come and see what he had dug up. Everyone in the house heard Dad, of course. Women were running, pulling things out of the trunk. Father managed to grab a few pieces of the crockery before Mother came down. I still have the big coffee pot; that is all that is left of my mother's crockery from that chest.

I remember the time we went to the cemetery, not far from the hospital, for the unveiling of the Polish memorial. It was a warm day. When the ceremony had finished, people went looking at the graves. I wandered along with the crowd. Walking along, I felt the warmth on my body from the rays of the sun and enjoyed being outdoors. On my way, I picked up a cigarette lying on the ground. I would give it my dad. The people from the house found me and took me to my father. I was so thrilled that I had a cigarette to give him.

Dad took the cigarette from me, and said that it was good of me to think of him, but that I must not get lost again. I didn't know I had been lost. "You do understand what I am saying to you, don't you?"

I nodded my head to say yes. I still did not talk at that stage. I was not aware that I had been lost and that my parents had been looking for me.

DISPLACED

We lived in the house at Schwabisch Hall for eighteen months. Then we were moved to a displaced persons camp. We were driven by army truck to a bleak and dismal wooden barracks located somewhere at the edge of the forest. This camp was one of many camps for displaced people in Germany after the war.

My parents couldn't believe we were in a camp again. Mother began crying and said to Father, "Why did this have to happen to us now coming into winter? How are we going to cope through the cold days and freezing night in these huts? I am terribly worried about Terese. How am I going to keep her warm through the winter in these huts? Back at home we had better stables for our animals."

"Maybe with some luck we won't be staying here too long," said Father.

This camp had been an Allied prison camp during the war. The walls inside the huts were not lined. One couldn't imagine how cold it was living in these dwellings through the wild winter surrounded by snow. Sometimes the temperature would plunge to minus fourteen Celsius.

Each person entering the camp was issued with blankets, towels, sheets and parcels from the Red Cross. The parcels for men contained two packets of cigarettes, a tooth brush, tooth paste, soap and personal necessities, and vitamins. The women and children's parcels were much the same, but, instead of cigarettes, included two chocolates for women, a jar of peanut butter, two packets of jelly, a chocolate block and four rolls of fruit life savers.

The American military ran the International Refugee Organisation (IRO) camps for displaced persons. Germany had been divided into four zones: American, English, French and

Russian. We were fortunate to be in the American zone. The Americans were very helpful, and were obliging in every way. Some of the American soldiers were from Polish-American families. The American soldiers (and possibly Canadian soldiers as well) who could speak Polish were chosen to work in the administration and medical sections in the camps. That made it easier for our people to communicate with them when problems arose.

There were people arriving from different countries with different nationalities and class distinctions. We all needed clothing, food and housing. We were thrown together into one camp and there were many problems. The authorities tried to make life easier by placing people of the same nationality together in one hut. It was easier for refugees to share huts with people from their own country and traditions.

We shared with two single women, two orphaned teenage boys, two young married couples and a family with one little girl about my age. Her name was Eva. We were fourteen people all together in the one hut. The single women's beds were positioned in each corner at one end of the hut. The teenage boys' beds were positioned in the corners at the other end of the hut. One of the young married couples had drawn their single beds together next to our three beds in the centre of the hut against the wall. The other young couple's beds and the other family's beds were in the same position opposite us.

Old blankets were hung from the ceiling to divide the hut into bed 'rooms', allowing us some dignity and privacy. There was just enough room to walk around the beds. There was one table, a few chairs and a small stove in the middle of the hut. It barely kept the hut warm. Living in the hut like that was depressing. It looked like a wash day in the laundry with all the blankets hanging in the room and undergarments hanging on a line over the stove. A chap in the hut was taking a seat at the table when a bra hanging on the line brushed his head. He looked up and sang out "Hallelujah! This is the first time I have been propositioned from above."

The most important building in this camp was in the middle of the compound. Every man, woman and child living in the camp had to use it: the communal latrine. It is one of many nightmares that have haunted me for most of my life, adding to the ones my mother and I already had.

The latrine hut consisted of two long benches in the middle with about twelve holes for sitting on each side. The seats were positioned in such a way that you were sitting back to back as well as having someone sitting next to you, and no partitioning in between. It was the only latrine in the whole of the camp. It disgusted me and I could not use it without Mother's help. The stench made me vomit every time. Mother would only use the latrine when I was ready to go. She couldn't bring herself to go in more than was necessary.

People suffering dysentery were unable to make it on time, missing the hole in the seat. Their waste spilled on the seat bench and in winter it froze almost immediately. There was vomit on the ground. Some people had no paper and would slide off the seat to try to clean themselves, leaving their waste behind on the latrine seat. By the end of the afternoon there was not one seat left clean. Some people relieved themselves on the ground. When you walked into the latrine you had to look where to put your foot and dodge all that filth. Going into the latrine was a living nightmare, and it was humiliating. It was embarrassing to see a man with his pants down as we walked in, and you had to be quick getting down and on with the job before your bottom froze from sitting too long.

I missed the house we had been living in. I missed Mother's cooking, I missed the warmth and comfort of the room in the attic, and I missed the bathroom, the clean toilet and the laundry that were inside. We didn't have to go out in the bitter cold like we did in this camp.

There was no harmony living in the camp. It was overcrowded and tempers ran short. Some people were still sick from being in concentration and labour camps. People who hadn't experienced those camps had no understanding of those who were still suffering the effects of the horror. The war was over but there was little contentment in our camp. There were many disgruntled people.

Meal time was not one of our pleasant memories. I can remember my mother complaining about the cooks from the Baltic countries spoiling the food with their excessive use of paprika and caraway seed. Our meals were mainly soups and no-one in our hut could tolerate eating that kind of food. It wasn't the authorities who were to blame for not supplying enough food; it was the people from the camp working in the food store and kitchens who traded on the black market. They were stealing food from us.

The people living in our hut were young and there was some fun in our barrack. The men loved to play jokes on one another and sometimes Father would play his harmonica while the rest of the gang sang folk songs. Sometimes things turned into comedy. A chap was sitting on a chair. He stood up to reach for something, and in the meantime a young boy whisked the chair away from the table. When the chap went to sit back into the chair he fell. The expression on his face was so funny when he hit the floor that we all broke into laughter, especially us two girls and the young boys. That was real comedy.

From time to time a Jewish lady was one of the single women in our hut. The men couldn't resist playing jokes on her. She was secretive, always going places, leaving the camp at breakfast time and returning late in the evening. She tried her best not to make a sound entering the hut. To avoid waking anyone, she took off her high-heeled shoes, and never turned on the light. One evening, the men gathered cans from the kitchen, strung them together and tied them to the door knob before going to bed. We waited. In the dark, the lady pushed the door open, making the cans rattle, and everyone in the hut broke into laughter.

The same joke was not repeated; the fellows had to think of something different each time. After a few weeks, the women in the hut had their turn by shortening the sheets in the lady's bed. It was rather funny listening to her struggling to get into her bed in the dark while everyone in the hut was quietly killing themselves laughing. For the woman to get into bed she had to turn the light on and rearrange her bed.

The last prank played on our friend the Jewish lady happened not long before we left the camp. The young women filled a small cellophane bag with water and put it between the sheets. But the joke didn't work. The old lady had become wise to the tricks and searched out their joke, pulling the water bag from her bed. That poor woman didn't stand a chance on her own. She asked, "Why do you treat me like that? I try hard to keep out of your way."

"That's right lady," said one of the men. "You make us feel as if we are not good enough to be in your company. You don't stay one night with us to join in and play cards. You dress in good clothes and put on your fur coat – possibly from Paris – and all that gold jewellery you are wearing! We can see you have not spent time in concentration or labour camps during the war like some of us. We do this to break the boredom and hunger that we live with every day. We include you as you share this hut with us, if only for a few hours at night, and we hope you are a good sport and able to take a joke."

"Alright, you have your fun," she said. "But you can't blame me for not staying in this camp all day when I have things to do in the village, and have friends to stay with in the evening before I retire for the night."

As a child, I too had noticed that this woman was different. She was bigger and older, her hair was wavy and neat, and she looked different from the women in the hut. She was dressed in lovely clothes and wore gold chains on her neck and beautiful rings on her fingers. Every time I saw her she was dressed ready to go out. I couldn't take my eyes off her hands and the big ring she wore on her finger. The lady left the hut every morning as Eva and I were getting ready for school in the camp.

I was nearly seven years of age. It would soon be Christmas, and the priest in the camp organised a party for the children to celebrate the feast of St Nicholas on the 6th of December. I had no recognition of Christmas or birthdays. For me these events didn't exist; I had been locked away.

A week before the party my father came back from work with a sable fur coat to keep me warm through the winter. Dad had bought a fur jacket from a Russian pilot for a few packets of cigarettes and had the jacket made into this coat especially for me. It was slightly big because it was to fit me for some winters to come. I had a new cuddly fur coat to keep me warm and was able to wear it to the Christmas party.

The party was held in the class room hut. Children were excited playing games waiting to see St Nicholas. I was shy and sat quietly with Mother, watching the older children playing and having fun.

I remember the St Nicholas entering the class room. It was our Polish bishop playing the part. He was dressed in ceremonial clothing and carried a staff in his hand. Two altar boys walked beside him. Their faces were smeared with charcoal, and they carried sacks of gifts with them. We said a prayer before the presents were given out. When a child's name was called, that child approached St Nicholas and kissed the ring on his finger. St Nicholas spoke to the child. His helper then handed the gift to St Nicholas, who gave it to the boy or girl.

The children were excited opening their presents. For many, it was the first present they had received in their life. The gifts were all the same: two pairs of underwear, a pair of mittens to keep our hands warm, a beanie to keep the cold from our head and ears, a chocolate, a bag of sweets and a small toy. Each toy was different. In addition to the gift, an apple was given to the children who had behaved through the year, and a branch of birch tree to the children who had misbehaved. It was our tradition of fun. The birch tree branch was mainly given to big boys. I didn't know it was a game. When Dad told me the story I believed it to be true and took the game seriously.

When my name was called, I froze and could not move, frightened that I would get the branch of the birch tree, and that St Nicholas would know the secret I was burdened with. St Nicholas came to me and said, 'There is nothing to be frightened of. I am here to give presents to children like you. I know you have been a good girl through the year.'

St Nicholas then handed me the gift and gave me a pat on the head. He said, "Go and open your present." His helper handed me an apple. I was so relieved that my secret was safe. I walked back to my mother and opened my gift to see what toy was in my parcel. I pulled out a black and white Mickey Mouse with legs that moved.

I had started to live a life finally freed from that dreadful disease, tuberculosis. The cough had eased and I could breathe without much pain. If my secret was exposed I would want to die. It wouldn't be too hard for me to do that; my health was frail and I was finicky about eating food. All I had to do was to stop eating. But I didn't really want to die. Life was very important to me. I was starting to be aware of things around me and my aim was to be on my best behaviour all through the year. If word got out, the embarrassment of wetting the bed would be too much for me to bear.

A child at my age wetting the bed was a disgrace. Women and children would be pointing at me and yelling out, "This girl wets her bed!" they would say, "Shame on you!" Living in camps, one came across all kinds of people, but if anyone was caught doing something wrong, that was the way they were treated by people in camp.

The teacher asked the children to bring their toys to school in the morning for show and tell. I hadn't been going to school for the last month, as it been too cold for me to leave the hut. But now I had my cuddly fur coat. Mother said I could go the next morning for a little while, so I could show my Mickey Mouse to the children.

The teacher used my Mickey Mouse in the class. The teacher walked him down a sloping plank. When Mickey stopped in front of a child, the teacher turned him to the child and asked a question. These games were fun and an easy way to learn our lessons. This school was not a school. We had no pencils or exercise books. It was merely to keep the children together and learn to socialise. There were not many children in this camp. Most of the people were young adults, and single.

The school closed for the Christmas Holidays. Mothers had to keep their children in the huts for most of the winter. It was very very cold. The only time the camp looked good was when a blanket of snow covered it. The ugly mess and the hut and windows were decorated with icicles. These miserable dwellings looked like the scene of a white forest on a European Christmas card.

I walked out from the hut one frosty morning, and down the wooden steps. They were covered with ice. I slipped and fell, spraining my wrist. I was taken by my mother to the medical centre that was provided for the people in the camp. We walked into the surgery and there was no-one waiting. We sat down. It was nice and warm in the waiting room. Everything was so efficient, spick-and-span. There was a place for everything, and everything was in its place. The soldier behind the desk, speaking to Mother in English and using his hands in sign language, asked her to come to the desk. We walked to the desk and he said to Mother, "*Name please.*"

Mother answered in the German she had learnt in the labour camps, "*Das ist meine kindlein Terese,*" pointing to me at the same time.

"How old is Terese?" he asked. Mother understood the soldier. The words were close to the way German was spoken. She answered, "*Sechs Jahre,*" showing six with her fingers.

The soldier asked, "Where was Terese born?" He mentioned some countries: Ukraine, Russia, and Poland. Mother answered, "Poland."

He wrote down the information, then walked to the door and knocked. The door opened and a man stood in the doorway, dressed in military uniform with shiny buttons on his chest and shoulders, and coloured ribbons on his uniform. He took the papers that the soldier handed to him. The man looked at me and said to me in Polish, "Terese, come in."

We walked into the surgery and the door closed. Then he said, "I am a doctor." He was very polite in greeting us. "How can I help you, Terese?"

I pointed to my hand.

"It hurts, does it?"

I nodded my head and said "Yes" softly.

"How did you do that?"

Mother had to speak for me, explaining what had happened. I couldn't put sentences together.

"Let me look at your hand and see how we can make it better for you."

He picked up my hand very gently and examined it with care, so as not to hurt me. He asked me, "Can you move your fingers for me?"

I could manage to do that.

"That's a good girl," said the doctor. "Your wrist is not broken. I will wrap your wrist with a bandage so it won't be so painful, and an extra bandage to keep your hand warm."

While I was in the surgery I coughed constantly. The doctor said that he didn't like the sound of my cough, and he examined my chest. "How long has Terese had this cough? he asked.

Mother told him how I had been found in a German hospital after the war, and how I had not been expected to live. She told the doctor how I had recovered slowly with herbal medicines.

"Yes," he said. "I can see that she has been traumatized. I have heard of this case. You are a remarkable woman, Mrs Dron," said the doctor. "It is a pleasure to have met you. I will keep a close eye on Terese."

He got up from his chair, walked into the next room, and came back carrying bottles of medicine to ease my cough, a bottle of cod liver oil and a packet of vitamin tablets. Handing them to Mother, he said "Give these to Terese three times a day. Try to keep her warm. Don't let her out in the cold. Of course, you already know that. Bring Terese back in a week to see me."

It was then that Mother mentioned the neglect of the latrines, saying, "How can anyone get better using those horrible amenities?"

The doctor said that he would attend to this problem immediately, and he did. There was vast improvement in the latrines. An attendant was present every day, all day, to clean up immediately any accidents that occurred, and there was plenty of paper. That was an improvement to life in camp.

The Jewish lady in our hut was going out, as she did every day. It was a cold morning and I was sitting close to the stove. I looked at the lady and her hands before she put on her gloves. She looked and spoke to me for the first time. We had never had time before, as I was getting ready to go to school when she was going out.

"You like pretty things?" she asked.

I nodded my head and softly said "Yes."

"I saw you looking at my rings. Would you like a closer look at my pretty rings?"

I nodded my head again.

She said, "Come and sit at the table with me."

I liked sitting next to the lady. She was nice to me and appeared to be a good person. There was a lovely smell about her. She took the rings off her fingers and let me handle them.

'Which one do you like the best?" she asked.

I picked up a particular ring that I liked. It had a large circle covered with rubies. I had a good look at it, and handed it back to her. She lifted the circle and said, "See, it's a watch. It keeps time so I know when to be at the station on time to catch the train. I brought this ring from Poland with me. It brings back memories of Poland and the way things were when I was a little girl like you are now. Europe has changed so much in the last eight years. I hope you will grow up in a better world."

The lady stood up from the table and said, "I am going now. I will see you in the morning." And she walked out the door.

The next day, before she went out, the lady again sat at the table with me. She said, "I have something for you. I am sure you will like it." She passed a small box over and said, "This is for you."

At first I was hesitant to open the box. I thought it may be a trick like the men played on the lady. She must have read my mind and said, "This is not a trick."

I looked at her, then opened the box very slowly and pulled out a gold ring with a single ruby set in the middle. It was lovely. I was surprised.

The lady asked me, "Do you like it?"

I could not show my appreciation. I was shy and didn't know how. All I could do was to nod my head and say a soft "Thank you," just like a small child does when she is learning to talk.

We survived the freezing winter in the hut by going to bed fully clothed and wearing three pairs of socks on our feet. One could die during the night, with chilly winds blowing through the gaps in the hut and almost burying the buildings in snow. The temperature dropped below zero. I had to sleep with Mother in my fur coat on a single bed so the heat of her body would keep me warm through the night. It wasn't comfortable for Mother or me, but that was the sacrifice she made to keep me alive through the winter.

We changed our clothes after a bath once a week. It was not possible to take a bath every day. Not only was it freezing, but the camp was built for men only. There was only one shower hut and a limited amount of warm water. A roster was drawn up for men and women to take a shower once a week. However, with my mother's small bathtub, we managed to have a good wash in our hut every day, and to change and wash our undergarments, hanging them up near the stove to dry.

Living in these cramped conditions was not easy. The lack of food and sleep, and the odour of sick people made people angry. Sometimes people seemed to yell at each other for no good reason. One has to experience conditions like that to understand. Sometimes I wonder how we survived.

The oncoming spring was most welcomed. The snow had melted away and the grass was growing again. We were given orders to move to another camp. The little girl Eva and I were sitting on the wooden steps while our parents stood for the roll call and waited for the truck. I twisted the ruby ring on my finger. Eva asked me to take it off so she could try it on. I took the ring off and handed it to her. She put it on her finger, admiring it, and said, "One day my father will buy a gold ring for me."

As she slipped the ring off her finger to give it back to me, it fell on the step and bounced into the long grass. We searched frantically, looking for over an hour but could not find it. I had lost my ring, never to see it again. Our parents came for us and we were lifted into the army truck and transported to the nearest railway station.

We arrived in front of a huge building. The men jumped off the truck and lifted children and women to the ground. The Military Police showed the way through a door to a big place with a glass dome above it. I asked Father, "Where are we? What is this place?"

Father said "This is a railway station. I will tell you all about it when we are told what place we are to go to."

The military authorities pointed to the far end of the platform and said to take a seat, the trains will come soon. Sitting and waiting for the train, again I asked Father where we were.

Father said, "We are at a train station. See the big engine pulling these carriages? That is a train, and we will be on one of them soon, going to a faraway place."

I saw trains coming into the station. There were so many people on the platforms. Some were getting off the train and others were running against time to catch the moving train. This was the first time I had experienced the outside world. Everything was big and frightening to me. While the authorities organised the train, I sat with my parents, watching and learning about life outside the camp gates.

Our train pulled into the platform. After a very long time of waiting, we were finally allowed to board this train provided for us, the *auslander*; the foreigners. We were not welcome in Germany. Some of the German people, especially the upper class, were not at all polite towards us. We were treated with contempt in public places.

At the time, no-one knew that this train was to be living quarters for us for over a week. On the first day everyone on the train received a package from the Red Cross, much the same as in the camp before, but this time containing extra necessities for the trip. The children's parcels were much the same, with a little extra chocolate and two packets of chewing gum in every parcel.

We travelled from one end of Germany to another, stopping only for emergencies, like toilets and the hot food that was organized for us once a day. The train stopped far from the main station, at platforms used only for goods trains. When we arrived, the Red Cross ladies were on the platform with a change of nappies, and milk in bottles for babies and children.

The military cooks were ready and waiting on the platform with hot meals for us. We lined up to take the food trays as we passed the temporary kitchen tent. The food was served with a smile and a cheery *"Bon appetit!"* I said *"Thank you,"* in English. The cooks turned their heads to one another and laughed, and made some comment about what I said.

My father had taught me the most important words to start me speaking English. They were *"please"* and *"thank you."* He said, "Those magic words will get you a long way. When you are lost, you say *'please'* and *'thank you'* to show your manners. People like to be spoken to with good manners."

We ate the meals out in the open because hot food was not permitted in the train. There were tables and chairs set up under a tarpaulin. We were fortunate there was no rain that week. At the other end of the tarpaulin were two drums of hot water. In one drum we put the trays and into the other the cutlery when we finished eating this lovely food. The military soldiers were good at cooking meals. It had been a long time since we had eaten good cooked meals.

The train stopped for a good few hours and we were able to stretch our legs. Father always managed to find a shop close to the station and buy bread rolls and cut meat for our breakfast next morning. He always returned long before the train whistle blew for us to board the train again. We were given fruit and a packet of cereal to take on the train to carry us through to the next day.

After a few days, this routine was interrupted. We were picked up from the station by military trucks and taken to a camp for an evening meal and a shower, and to sleep one night in a bed. The next morning we were examined in the camp by a team of military doctors. We stayed one more night in the camp, and then were moved back onto the train going to God knows where.

This journey was not a joy trip. There were no spare seats on the train. The men had to stand during the night to make room for their little children bedded down on the seats. The women sat on the arm of the seats all night. Some older children slept on the floor. After the second day the little children were crying, cramped in one seat all day. The mothers became anxious not knowing when the train journey would end. People were uneasy. Men were asking each other, "Does anyone know where this train is going?"

Some young smart-alec who had no idea of life in concentration camps yelled out "*Auschwitz!*"

With this one word he created panic in the carriage. Women started to cry. Everyone in this train had possibly lost a husband, a close relative or even a child. My mother had lost her son, my little brother, and most of her family in one of those horror camps. Some men in the carriage got hold of this young fellow, held him down, and gave him a punch or two, and a few kicks that he would not forget in a hurry. He was lucky there was no rope available. The men would have hung him and torn strips off him. The Military Police rushed over and intervened to stop the beating. They put the young man in a different carriage.

When things settled down, Dad followed the MPs to the carriage where they sat. Dad knew some English that he had learned when he worked for the Americans in Schwabisch Hall.

Father came back with a blank look on his face. He sat down beside me, looking out the window for some time without saying a word. That was nothing strange. It was impossible to hold a conversation with the noise of babies crying and restless children whingeing. Mother was quiet. I sat next to the window, watching towns and the landscape passing by. Occasionally I turned my head from the window to look at my mother, and saw her sad face. She was saying her rosary in silence after the incident of the young fellow's Auschwitz remark. Dad's face looked like he was trying to work something out. I turned my head to the window, nibbling on the breakfast cereal until it was dark, and I finally fell asleep.

The next morning, when we left the train to get our meal and were alone, Dad said to Mother, "I went to see the authorities on this train yesterday to find out when this journey will come to an end. No-one seems to know."

Dad told Mother of his conversation with the MPs. He said he had asked them if anyone had some information on when we would reach our destination, and why we were on the train for such a long time. Father had told them, "The women and children are upset; we have not changed our undergarments for days. The entire luggage is in the back carriage. We were not told that this was going to be a long one."

One of the officers had spoken, but offered little help. He had said, "No information has been passed on to me. I can only check on what's happening next time the train stops. When I came on this train my orders were to keep peace on the train and get off at the next stop, wherever that may be."

Dad said to Mother, "I have been thinking – and what else is there to do on this train but think? – And wondering why this is such a long journey. I have come to the conclusion that the camps are all full. There are no vacant camps for us. That is the logical reason why we have been on this train for so long."

"Maybe they have forgotten about us," said Mother.

"No, we are not forgotten. The authorities are taking care of us. The hot food and the Red Cross people are on the station every day. No, we are not forgotten. The soldiers are going back home every week. There will be a camp for us soon, I am sure of that."

Father was right. At the next lunch break there was an announcement made that we would be sleeping in beds that night: "The train will be stopping at the city of Stuttgart. The trucks will take you to a camp at Ludwigsburg.

LUDWIGSBURG

Luitpold Kasrine was a former German military camp outside the town of Ludwigsburg, about 25 kilometres from Stuttgart. When we arrived at this camp, the signs of war were still evident. Burnt-out tanks and trucks stood in the middle of the compound. The buildings and work sheds along the walls were damaged, the roofs and walls ruined by bombs. The debris had not yet been removed. This had been a high class camp with a swimming pool that was now half-filled with rubbish. The two-storey brick buildings that had housed soldiers were still intact.

Again we were sharing dormitory rooms, and once again blankets were used as dividers. The living conditions did not change. We were still cramped in one room. The toilets and wash rooms were at the end of each floor of the building. I heard two young women in the toilet room having a conversation. One of them said, "What an improvement these toilets are. We don't have to leave the building. I can sit in privacy and take my time to relieve myself in the cubicle with the door shut and not be embarrassed by a man walking in on me, and without fear of my bum freezing to the seat in the winter."

"Who knows where we will be by next winter," said the other woman. "We can hope and pray that this journey will have a happy ending."

Like all military camps, the showers were outside in a separate building. Rosters were made for men and women to have showers on alternating days. It was difficult living in one big dormitory with strange people. No-one was happy about that situation. However, we were better off than some of the Germans in their own country; at least we were provided with food and a roof over our heads.

Some people were difficult to live with, like a family with one son named Janek. Janek's parents were disgruntled. They had something to complain about every day and made sure that everyone in the room heard about their disappointment at having to live in a dormitory with people like us. Janek was a few years older than me, and he was spoilt by his mother. In her eyes he could do no wrong. He was one of the bullies in the camp, and he teamed up with Mihal, the son of Mila, a woman who would become my mother's close friend.

The two boys made life difficult for me, mocking and teasing me, especially when we received parcels from the Red Cross. They would trip me, and when I fell down, they would kick me. Janek said that they would stop kicking me if I gave them my sweets and chocolate. I nodded my head to say yes. The adults didn't stop to help me. I heard one woman say to the other, "What do you expect from an idiot like her? She will have to learn to defend herself."

I had to save myself from these bullies. When I got to my feet I went to the dormitory to get a small chocolate and a roll of lifesavers for the greedy boys. There was hardly had anything left for me. The next morning I was sore and bruised, and could hardly move. Mother saw the bruises on my body and asked me, "How did this happen?" I was reluctant to say; being frightened of the boys. Mother got very angry with me. She wanted to know how I got these bruises on my body. Finally I had to say that Janek and Mihal were the culprits.

It was hard for me to cope, learning to communicate with children of all ages. I found it difficult to put words together to make a sentence. I could speak a few words of German and a few words of Russian that didn't make sense to outsiders. I was mocked. I was looked upon as an autistic child. Coming to this camp was a sudden shock for me. I had to grow up quickly, both physically and mentally.

I remember the time I had a pair of shoes made. I was sick at the time, so Dad had the cobbler come to the dormitory to measure my feet. The cobbler carried samples of material with him so Mother could decide what material and style to choose for my shoes. While she was looking through the samples and discussing each one with the cobbler she was rudely interrupted by

Janek's mother, who said, "You would think that your daughter was a princess the way that you are fussing over her shoes, knowing that she is not normal in the head."

Mother and Dad carried on the conversation with the cobbler, ignoring her remarks. Dad whispered in my ear, "Don't listen to that green-eyed dragon. You are Mummy and Daddy's princess and that is all that matters to us." Then he said, "I would have made you a beautiful pair of shoes myself. I will tell you a story after the cobbler leaves."

When the cobbler left, Mother said to Janek's mother, "I am sick of your remarks and listening to your complaints. You are better to concentrate on your son and tell him to keep away from my Terese. If I see bruises on her body again I will personally deal with you by tearing your hair by the roots from your head. I will say this only once so you'd better remember that." My mother was naturally a quiet woman, and kept very much to herself, but she would stand up for herself and her family if provoked.

When things quietened down I was hoping that Father hadn't forgotten about telling me the story. To remind him I pulled on his sleeve.

"I know you want me to tell you the story now," he said,

"Yes?"

So he began. "When I was living in Poland, and had finished school, I took up a job learning to make shoes. I was to be a cobbler in my village, but things didn't work out as I had planned in my life. I will tell you a story of the green dragon that once lived in Poland.

I remember my Grandad sitting me on his knee when I was a small boy, like you are now, and telling me stories. The one I remember well was that of the green dragon. Long, long ago, before the Castle and the Cathedral were built on the Wawel Hill in Krakow, there was a small village by the river Vistula. The people who lived there were hard working, happy people. They sang folk songs while they worked on the land and attended their flocks of sheep, goats and cattle. They kept hens and pigs to put food on the table.

On Saturdays, when work was done and the sun had gone to sleep, the people gathered around the fire to relax. They sang songs, and the old men told stories of years gone by. One of the stories was about the dragon that lived in a dark cave in the side of the Wawel Hill. The hill was overgrown with thick vines, long grass and weeds. No one would dare go near the entrance to the cave where the dragon was sleeping.

Now, the young boys listening to the story didn't think it was true, and one day they went out to the hill. They cut their way through the vines and the grasses until they reached the entrance to the cave. Shining their torches into the cave, the boys could see nothing, but they heard deep breathing.

Slowly they went deeper into the cave. Suddenly, in front of them was a huge body, like a big rock covered in green scales. It was waking up. The boys got a fright and ran away as fast as they could. They heard the bellowing and roaring of the creature behind them, and felt its hot breath on their backs. The boys fell, and rolled all the way down the hill to the bottom. They looked up and saw a huge green dragon breathing fire from its nostrils.

After its long sleep the dragon was angry and hungry. It came down the hill. The ground shook with every step. The dragon headed directly to where the sheep and the cattle were grazing. The people saw the dragon grab one of the little lambs and take it back to the cave. No-one was safe out in the open. The villagers were frightened. They locked themselves and their children inside the houses, and watched through the window. The dragon took a lamb or a goat and sometimes a cow. There was no more happiness in the village. The boys were ashamed of what they had done.

Now, Prince Krakus in the village was a good and wise man. He took care of his people. When a child or anyone in the village was sick, he would mix herbs for the sick so they would get well again. He didn't like to see his people living in fear so he said that he would give his daughter's hand in marriage to the brave knight who could kill the terrible dragon.

There were many brave knights who tried, but their primitive weapons could not cut the thick scales of the dragon. A young village shoemaker asked the Prince for some herbs. The Prince wanted to help, so he gave the herbs to the young man. The young shoemaker filled the skin of a goat with a mixture of the herbs and sulphur. He carried the goat half way up the hill while the dragon was sleeping. He left the goat close to the entrance of the cave.

When the dragon woke up, it was pleased to see that someone had brought food. After eating the goat, the dragon got very thirsty. It came down from its cave to drink at the river. People watched the dragon and waited to see if the mixture would work. After drinking the river half dry, the dragon suddenly exploded and burst into flames. People ran out from their houses singing, "The dragon lives no more!"

"You see, Terese, if I was a shoemaker back in those days, it may have been me that married the Princess and you would be a real Princess of Krakow."

"Or you may have been a princess of the Baltic Sea," said Mother. "Maybe I should tell you the story that my grandfather told me, but I will save it for another time."

I pulled on Mother's dress to let her know that I wanted to listen to her story. Mother often suffered with headaches and needed peace and quiet. She sometimes wouldn't talk for days, so I wasn't letting go of the opportunity to hear Mother tell me her story.

"So you want me to tell you the story?"

"Yes," I said quietly.

"Alright then," she said. "A long time ago my grandfather's father was a young fisherman. He would go on his boat out to the Baltic Sea to catch fish. It was dangerous work. The seas were often rough and a small boat was tossed about from side to side like a toy. In the early hours of the morning, when the seas were calm and the boat was full of fish, Great-grandad was on his way back to the shore. He told my grandfather that he often saw mermaids come out of the water and sit on the big rocks singing while they combed their long blonde hair in the glow of the moonlight. Great-grandad saw the mermaids and never thought much about them.

There were times the fish nets were empty. Great-grandad had been on the sea every night for a week and had caught nothing. He wondered whether he should stay longer or return home with an empty boat again. That would be a disaster: no fish for the people in the village.

He thought of the mermaids and wished that one night he might be lucky enough to catch a mermaid in his net. Deep in thought, he felt the boat tip to one side. He was surprised to see a mermaid sitting in the boat. He wondered what he should do.

"You don't have to do a thing," said the mermaid. "Just sit and talk to me. I have watched you fishing many times. This morning, your boat is empty. Just talk to me and you will have plenty of fish before you go home."

"What do you want me to say?" he asked the mermaid.

"Tell me what you do with all the fish you catch."

"I sell them at the village market. This is the way I earn my living."

"The mermaid said, "I will fill your boat with fish before you go home."

"Will I see you tomorrow?" he asked.

"Not until the full moon," answered the mermaid.

"She flipped over and out of the boat into the sea. Great-grandad's net was full of fish that morning. After that, he often thought of the mermaid while he was fishing. He made up his mind to ask the mermaid to marry him before the fishing was finished for the year. During the winter it was too cold to be on the sea.

The next time Great-grandad met the mermaid, it was the same as before. She came out of the sea and into his boat and before he had a chance to speak, the mermaid knew what was in his mind. She spoke first, saying, "I will be very busy. It is time for the elections. We have a big festival to prepare for and I have to make sure the invitations are sent out to the four corners of the sea before the blue moon. That is the time for the election. Poseidon, the King of all the oceans, will sit on his throne and all the fish from the seas and oceans will meet the king. Then the election will take place. Every important fish is given a different position to the one it held before."

"When is this blue moon?" asked Great-grandad.

"The mermaid said it is when the full moon shows up in the sky twice in the same month. Before Great-grandad had a chance to say something, the mermaid flipped out into the water. She said, "I will see you after the election in the next blue moon, when the night sky is bright."

"My great-grandad looked out for the mermaid. She never came back to meet him. She was a princess, the grand-daughter of the great Poseidon. You see, Terese, if Great-grandad had married the mermaid you would have been a princess of the Baltic Sea!"

I wanted to say to Mother that I was glad she wasn't a mermaid. I didn't like water; I didn't like my skin to be constantly wet and cold.

I was seven years old, and still needed medical care. Dad, Mother and I left the camp for a few days, travelling some distance to the Black Forest to see a herbalist.

It was a long and tiring day. First we had to catch a train and then we walked the rest of the way to the edge of the Black Forest. We walked past many small farms. It had been a long time since I had seen farm animals. I knew what the animals looked like but I didn't know the name of a cow or a pig or a horse. As we were walking along, Father named the animals so I would know. After a long walk we finally reached the herbalist's place at the edge of the forest. Many patients were already waiting. In those days, there were no appointments. People had to wait their turn to see the herbalist.

While waiting for my turn, we filled in time by walking in the forest. Father pointed out the woodpecker bird pecking at the tree, and the red robins flying about. I saw squirrels in the trees. They were lovely little furry animals with bushy tails, running from one branch to another. Father showed me the strawberries growing in the wild. He picked one and passed it to me and said I could eat it. I amused myself looking for more of the plant with the sweet little red berries. What else was a little girl to do in the forest? It was my first time in a forest, and it was wonderful seeing the birds and animals, and listening to sounds I had not heard before, and ending the day with my mum and my dad, the two people I had grown to love.

It was late in the afternoon when the consultation was over, too late to go back to camp. We stayed in a guest house in a small town overnight. When we walked into the room there were two chairs in each corner of the room. The beds were built in the wall, a single bed on one side of the room and a double bed on the opposite side with drapes to be drawn across when it was time for sleep. It was cosy sleeping with a feather quilt in that lovely soft bed. In the morning, the room was bright with sun shining through the window. The room was neat and tidy, different to the way we lived in camps.

As soon as the displaced people were settled in Luitpold camp, the Priest, with the help of the men, started work on building a church along the back wall in the camp grounds. Keeping our Catholic faith was very important to us Polish people. Although we had experienced the catastrophe of the Holocaust, faith was, and still is, much in our lives. Our faith nourishes our spirit and wellbeing. While in the concentration camp, when hope was gone and there was nothing, there was faith to cling to. Mother had faith, and had believed that the end would come to Hitler's brutal regime, and that the gates of Hell would open before the end came to our countrymen.

Everyone who was able put in some time to work on the church. They used the part of the camp building that once was a workshop. It was damaged but not completely wrecked. The men cut and joined some of the timber from the debris that was left. Mortar was scraped off the bricks that were not broken so they could be used again. The church began to take shape.

Before our church was built, Father, Mother and I walked all the way to a cathedral that stood on a hill in the town. There were two cathedrals close to one another. The first was a Protestant cathedral, which we entered. I don't know if Mother and Father had been in a big cathedral before. Having lived on a farm in a village in Poland, they may not have recognised a Protestant church. Mother and Father made the sign of the cross and genuflected before entering the pew. The parson came and said to Father, "This is not a church for Roman Catholics. The Roman Catholic church is the one on the top of the hill."

In those days Catholics and Protestant were very much apart. God forbid that one would attend a church service or marry outside one's own faith. It was not acceptable to enter each other's church. We walked to the top of the hill and entered a beautiful cathedral. Statues stood in hollows in the church walls. Stairs led up to a small platform where the priest stood during the Mass to speak to the people. The sun shone through the stained glass windows. It was beautiful. My eyes were dazzled with the colours on the church windows. I was only a child but I felt joy in my heart. That was the first time in my life I had entered a grand structure like a cathedral.

When our little church was finished, the Polish bishop blessed and opened it by saying Mass. This honour was followed by a procession in the grounds. People had built this church with love and pride. We were devoted to our church, the place where God's spirit dwelt among us as we prayed together at Mass. The church was special to me. It was where I took part in the wedding of one of Mother's friends, and where I made my First Holy Communion. Later, when my brothers, the twins, were born, they were baptized there.

The camp was like a little Poland in the midst of Germany. This was where we could freely exercise our faith and belief without infringing on the local people. The grounds were big enough to have our holy day processions. I loved the procession with its colourful banners carried in front. Walking behind, girls carried baskets of flowers, spilling petals on the ground. The priest carried the Eucharist, walking on the carpet of flower petals. We had many processions in this camp celebrating holy days and saints' days. Walking in procession and saying prayers was a way for the priest to keep the people together in harmony.

There was plenty of work in Germany after the war had ended. There was a great need for housing, and Dad worked as a labourer for a German company building high-rise apartment buildings for German people to live in. In June, the company held a picnic day with games to entertain the employees' families.

Dad was young and energetic, and entered every game that day. He won the wheel-barrow race. The first prize was a balloon and an ice-cream voucher. Father handed the balloon to me and I jumped with joy. To have a balloon was something special in those days. Dad also won the pole climbing race. The prize was two men's hankies and an ice-cream voucher.

The ice-cream vouchers were given out with every prize. To buy the ice-cream we had to go to the ice-cream factory next door to the picnic ground. Dad said, "Follow the children to the ice-cream factory and give the voucher to the lady. She will give you an ice-cream."

This was a special treat. After the war, not many people had money. Coupons were the currency used to buy clothing and food, but there were no coupons for ice-cream. There were more important foods to buy. One was lucky if things didn't run out in the shop while waiting in the queue.

At the end of the picnic day, every child going home from the picnic carried a balloon on a string. We were walking back to the camp when I said to Father that I was tired and could not walk anymore. I hadn't fully recovered from sickness yet. Father picked me up and carried me on his shoulders. I loved my dad. I was so proud of him. No-one in the camp compared with my dad. He was a man who loved music and fun, and he got on well with people.

As we came close to the camp gates, Dad lifted me off his shoulders and I walked into the camp holding my red balloon. The children came running towards me, asking me if I would let them take turns holding the balloon. Mihal ran up and grabbed the balloon off me and let it go. I watched my red balloon drift into the grey sky. My heart was filled with sadness watching my balloon going to the heavens where my little brother Wladek was with the angels.

I did not cry, but stamped my feet like a little child. Everyone laughed at me. Suddenly the sky changed, and lovely colours appeared.

"Look Dad, look at the sky!" I cried out.

"The colour you see in the sky is a rainbow. You haven't seen a rainbow have you Terese?"

"Is it always in the sky?" I asked.

"We can only see the rainbow when it is raining and the sun is shining at the same time," said Father.

While I was watching the rainbow, Father got hold of Mihal, screwed his ears and gave him a lecture on how a boy should behave. Mihal stayed clear of me for some time.

I learned that children like Janek and Mihal were naturally aggressive. Aniela, a girl

I played with, was another bully. She hit me with her skipping rope for no reason that I could understand. I felt I had no chance against people like her. I ran over to the half-finished church, but she followed me. I thought I would find safety in the church. She came running in after me, screaming and lashing me with her rope, yelling "I want to play with you!" I felt cornered. I told her that I would give her a chocolate if she left me alone.

Some women were working in the church, making flower vases from bottles for the church altar. They didn't chastise Aniela for the way that she behaved. One of the women said to me, "You are stupid! Why don't you pick up the bottle and throw it at her?"

I couldn't do that. I had never raised a hand to hit anyone. It was not my nature to inflict pain to anything or anyone.

I had to find a safe place from the bullies. It was summer and most of the women were crocheting and knitting outside, enjoying the fresh air and the warm sun. I found a safe haven with them. They didn't mind me hanging around. One of the women was Mother's friend Jusza. She asked me if I would help by holding the woollen garments while they pulled them apart. Used clothing was sent to the camp by various charities, possibly from overseas. The boxes of clothing and shoes were left out in the compound for everyone to take what they needed for themselves and their families. The knitting circle women took the knitted garments and pulled them apart, rolling the used wool into a ball to make children's jumpers, beanies and mittens for the coming winter.

I picked up a crocheted pink bed jacket. It was the pink that drew my attention. The colour was so delicate and pretty, and the garment was soft and warm. I fell instantly in love with pink. The clothes we wore at the time were old and drab. The pink lifted my spirits, and I wore my bedjacket every day. I only took it off so it could be washed.

Jusza said to me, "Terese, if are going to be with us you'd better make use of the time and start to knit."

She handed me knitting needles that her husband Stefan had made for me. They were bicycle spokes cut down and sharpened to a point at one end. I was given scraps of wool, and the stitches were cast on for me to start knitting. At first I had to learn to hold the knitting in my hand. It looked easy when the women did it. It wasn't so easy for me, but I had to try. It wasn't a question of whether I wanted to knit or not; it was considered a sin to waste time and do nothing, or to be lazy. The women were good at knitting. There were no knitting books in the camp. The women learned to memorise patterns and exchanged them with one another.

I had an appointment to see the doctor in town. While there, Mother bought skeins of blue wool and asked Jusza to knit a cardigan for me. Jusza chose a nice pattern. Knitting with new wool, she took care and pride in every stitch she made. When the cardigan was finished, it looked lovely. I was happy with the cardigan made especially for me, but it was not so pleasant to wear. The wool was prickly and made my sensitive skin itch. The problem was solved by wearing a dress with long sleeves. Jusza also knitted a pink short sleeve cardigan for cool summer days. I had been wondering what had happened to my pink bed jacket; it had become a cardigan!

I enjoyed listening to the adults talk. The men working on the church sometimes sat and talked with the women while waiting for the building material to arrive. The conversation was camp gossip, news of the world and politics, and what they had heard about new things like "picture radios" (meaning a television) and cars that could drive themselves – all the driver had to do was to turn the wheel. They also talked about things one could buy on the black market. I remember talk about gold Swiss Omega wrist watches, with an expensive price tag. It was every young man's dream to own one of these wrist watches. The men and women also talked about how Germany was getting on its feet again, with America giving aid to German industries. I was an inquisitive little listener, eager to learn, and taking in everything that was said.

The conversation led to the subject of a man who was missing from our camp for some weeks. When he left the camp he didn't let anyone know where he was going. People were concerned for him. The rumour was that the missing man may have been killed and sold as pork meat on the black market. The rumour was that young single people without families would be targeted. I remember people talking of another chap coming to sell pork sausage in the camp, and when the rumour of the missing man spread, this chap stopped coming.

I heard people say there was not much food in Germany, especially in the cities, and that anything was possible. At the time there were six million displaced people in Germany, and more coming every day, escaping from the communist countries. If someone went out and they had no-one close to let know where they were going, it would be difficult to find them. Listening to the adults talk like that frightened me. My father left camp every day. He worked a few kilometres from the camp. I didn't want something like that happening to him.

On weekends, Father took Mother and me for a walk. Sometimes we went window shopping in the town. We came to a toy shop window. My eyes opened wide, looking at the beautiful doll and lovely cane prams. I asked Mother if Father would buy a doll and a pram for me. Mother's answer was that I must wait until we were settled in some place where our home would be. There was no place for a thing like that in the dormitory.

On the way back to the camp we walked to the park not far from Father's place of work. We stopped at a small ice-cream shop. There were tables and chairs outside the shop. A waitress came to take the order of people who could afford to sit at the tables in the sun and enjoy eating ice-creams. Dad stood in a queue and bought us ice-creams, and we sat on the grass in the park to them. (I must say that German people made wonderful ice-cream!)

During the summer we went out every Sunday after church. One Sunday, Father suggested that we take a look at the town from the tower. When we came closer to the tower, I nearly fell back looking up. It was so tall it almost touched the clouds in the sky.

"Dad, I can't walk all the way up," I said. "It's too far."

"No," said Father. "We don't walk. We take a lift all the way to the top."

I had no idea what a lift was but I trusted my dad. Without question, Mother and I went along with him into the small square room. Father pressed a button on the wall and the door closed and the room moved upwards. "Why is the room going up?" I asked.

'This is a lift. It takes people up. This tower is very high and the lift is the way we go up," said Dad.

It seemed a long way up before the room stopped and the door opened. We walked onto something that looked like a balcony all around the tower. I'd never been far up in the sky. Father held my arm as we walked closer to the edge and said, "Look, there is the city at your feet my little princess!"

There was that word again: *princess*. I didn't know what it meant but it must have been good. Mother would have chastised him if it wasn't proper. I was overwhelmed with the view, to see the houses so tiny, cars and trams moving around the streets like little toys no bigger than ants. In the distance was the river with little ships sailing. I felt I was someone special standing up high above the city looking down on small things.

"How did all those things get small?" I asked Father.

He laughed. "No Terese, nothing is smaller. This tower is very high up off the ground – so high that it makes things look small in the distance."

"Dad, I love this place! I would like to stay here forever!"

"No one stays here. This is just where people come to look at the town. We must all go back down to the place where we live."

When we were back on the ground I felt just a little person again, like the rest of the people.

There was a variety of places to go to in Ludwigsburg for entertainment, and most places were within walking distance of the camp. It had been over two years since the war ended. Germany had made progress in many ways, and my health had improved. On occasion, we had an afternoon at the opera, which was held in a palace in Ludwigsburg.

Inside, the palace was big and grand. The walls and ceiling were beautifully ornamented and it was a pleasure to walk into a building like that. While Father bought the tickets, I had a good look around and admired the splendour of this building before we walked over to the seats. The orchestra played as people took their seats. The beautiful music made my body tingle with excitement. Although I didn't understand what the story was in the opera, I loved watching the people on the stage dressed in beautiful costumes, dancing and singing to the happy music, and all against the background of a mysterious and enchanting forest. It was a pleasure to watch the lady coming out from the house to dance with the man waiting for her at the bottom of steps. My heart burst with happiness to see this lovely show, and I became a hopeless romantic. That was how I wanted my life to unfold: to have lovely clothes and shoes to wear like the ladies on the stage, and to have a house to live in. The story of the opera stayed in my mind for days afterwards.

At other times on the weekend, we walked to an evening dance. I can't be sure, but I think it was held in the palace grounds that were open to the public just outside the town, close to the camp. Boats rowed young people out to a dance floor floating on a lake (or perhaps it was a river). The girls were dressed in lovely flowing dresses and high heel shoes. The young men were dressed in their best suits. I loved watching the young people dance with romance in their hearts.

In the grounds there were several vendors, one with frankfurts and rolls, another with sandwiches and rolls filled with all types of delicious German sausages, hams, cheeses, herrings and gherkins. Drinks were bought for a few German pfennigs. Coca-Cola and Pepsi were the most popular drinks. We sat at the water's edge eating the rolls that Father had bought for us, and watching the dance. We didn't stay too long. I was tired so it was 'to bed' with me. I enjoyed walking back to the camp in the summer moonlight. The flowers in the garden were more fragrant in the evenings.

I remember one time Father took Mother and me to see the townhouses that had just been built in areas around town. Maybe they were looking to buy, not knowing at the time what decisions they were going to make. Or maybe they were looking for a place to rent.

We passed a house with a garden. A man had his head down, working in the garden. I stopped to take a closer look at the bleeding hearts and fuchsias. The man in the garden stood up. He happened to be one of the men who worked with Father on the building site. Father introduced us to his workmate, who opened the gate for us to come in. He showed Father the vegetable garden growing in his backyard. He said to me that I could help myself to the gooseberries that were growing on the bushes neatly in a row. They were very good to eat. I always liked taking walks with Mum and Dad, learning about things that I saw for the first time. Everything was new and exciting to me.

With new arrivals in the camp, there were enough children to start school lessons for two hours a day, and to prepare them for First Holy Communion. The Priest and the camp commandant tried to find a suitable building for a school house. Most of the buildings were damaged and had to be repaired. There were no school teachers in the camp as yet so the first lessons were held by our camp priest, Father Bonkowski. Our first lesson started with the story of the first chapter in the Bible. Father Bonkowski taught us the lesson of the creation.

I learned that God created heaven and earth, working for six days. He rested on the seventh day and made it holy, the day of rest. God made all the living things on earth. There was no rain, but a mist rose from the earth and watered the surface of the ground. God made a man in His image from dust, and gave him the breath of life and named him Adam. God put Adam in the Garden of Eden to look after the things that He created. Adam was given the privilege of naming all the creatures on Earth.

God saw that Adam needed a companion. He put Adam into a deep sleep and took a rib from him. From the rib of Adam, God made a companion. When Adam woke and saw that God had made a creature very much like himself, he named his companion a woman, and he gave her the name Eve. She was the Mother of all living things. God said to Adam and Eve that they could eat fruit from every tree in the garden but not the fruit of the tree of knowledge that grew in the middle of the garden. If they touched the fruit of that tree they would die!

A serpent hanging about in the forbidden tree tempted Eve to take the fruit from the tree of knowledge, saying to Eve, "Take the fruit, you will not die." The fruit did look good to eat. Eve trusted the serpent and picked the fruit, took a bite and gave it to Adam. Adam, trusting Eve, took a bite of the fruit and from that moment they both knew that things had gone wrong. The serpent had lied.

Listening to this story at the age of seven, and seeing a picture of the snake in the tree terrified me. I didn't want to know things like that! I had troubles of my own, coping day to day. When the lesson was finished for the day I said to Mother that I didn't want to go back to school.

Mother said, "Terese, it's very important that you should go to school. There are things you must learn in life whether you like it or not. These lessons that you are taught are to prepare you for the journey of life, to help you cope with difficulties and make decisions that will arise later in life. You must go to school."

More people arrived in the camp, some with tertiary education, and they took over from the priest, teaching and adding more subjects and more hours in school. Father Bonkowski continued to teach the Bible lessons about the Ten Commandments that Moses brought down from Mount Sinai. Father Bonkowski said we must not forget that we were people of Poland. It was important for us to remember that we were Ambassadors of Poland, whatever country we would make our home.

One of the new arrivals at Ludwigsburg was a woman named Janka. Mother knew her from the concentration camp. They had been together in the same hut. Mother spoke to her but she didn't respond. Janka's husband said, "She hasn't spoken a word since she was released from that dreadful camp. That was a living hell."

Seeing Janka in this state, Mother was very upset. When Dad came home from work, Mother was crying. She told Dad how the SS monsters had broken Janka's spirit. "That's what the monsters were very good at – beating and torturing defenceless, helpless and sick women. There was no-one that could help us against this brutality. She must have been tortured to the point where she was driven mad. That poor poor man! He survived the camps only to be burdened with two sick children and a wife."

I made friends with the children, twin girls named Renia and Marisha. Like me, they had been with the monsters. Marisha was slow like me. Renia was moreso. The two girls were still sick, recovering slowly. Renia was the weaker of the two. She didn't or couldn't talk. Although the girls were sick they were not confined to bed.

The twins' parents didn't have the money for the girls to get the special treatment I was getting. Their father couldn't go to work. He had a full-time job looking after his family. Janka could do absolutely nothing for herself. One time I went to their dormitory to see Renia when she was sick in bed. Her mother was sitting on the bed and never said a word to the girls or me. She sat in the same position and didn't move the whole time I was in the room.

Janka's husband did everything a wife and mother would do for a sick family. He learned to do the work of a woman. Washing clothes wasn't easy; everything was washed by hand. He learned to darn and knit socks.

Mother said to him, "Bring Janka outside. We will take care of her. She will be alright sitting with us women." His girls and I always played together, and Mother was on hand if she was needed. He took the opportunity to go fishing with the men at the river not far from the camp. That was the only time he could get away. I remember when he cooked the fish he caught. The smell of the fish cooking would make anyone hungry. The fish were only small and I was given one. That was the first time I had eaten a fish; it was good to eat.

On warm afternoons when Janka came to sit outside, she didn't speak to anyone. The women spoke to her, but she didn't respond. She sat until she started to get agitated. Her husband knew the signs and attended to her needs. I heard women talk, saying to one another that the war had ended, but the battle was not over for that family. I heard adults say, 'Children will grow up and forget the horror. Children have ways of forgetting. They get over tragedies and grow to live a normal life.'

What did they know about children? How would the adults know what effect it had on us children? We were ripped from our mothers' arms by the monsters with no regard for human life. We were just babies, separated from our mothers. We were frightened and alone. I remember Mother crying out to me, "Look after your brother!" when he was pulled from her arms.

Death was still at our heel. Now we faced life with our minds scarred from the horror years, traumatized. Disabilities robbed us of the development that a child learns when growing. No-one understood that we were tortured by nightmares. Waking in the middle of the night, we were told it was only a bad dream and to go back to sleep. How could we sleep? Our nerves were shattered.

Stripped of my childhood

Denied my sweet dreams

Frightened to fall to sleep

Accompanied by nightmares

Night after night

Tumbling and tumbling like a weed

A jerk wakes me

I am in a lonely dark room

I feel things crawling over my body

I scream for someone to help me

No-one hears my cry

I cry for my mother

She hears her children's cries

From behind barbed wire

Keeping her away

From children she loves and yearns for every day

We needed help to heal our unseen wounds. We needed to be released from the pain of purgatory. There was no treatment for us. No-one wanted to know about the frightening loneliness we faced. "The war is over," they said. "It's no good looking back and talking about the past."

The children endured suffering and death the same as the adults, and maybe hundreds of thousands of children died like the adults. Children like Marisha, Renia and me, who lived through the horror and survived, were often told that we were the lucky ones. I wonder.

Renia's little body couldn't cope with the pain. She suffered a mental breakdown as well as suffering from tuberculosis. Eventually the girls' father came with us to the herbalist, paying for the consultation with cigarettes, chocolates and some tinned food that he had managed to save. The verdict from the examination was that there was some hope for Marisha, but little for Renia. Her lungs were in a bad way; it was only a matter of time. Renia never complained of pain for the two years she lived with us. Maybe it was the constant prayers said for Renia that gave her two years of comfort in life while we were together.

The twins' father wanted his family to start their new life in America, but there was little chance of that. Displaced people had to be in good health and well educated before they were accepted into the country of their choosing.

There were partly ruined buildings at the back of the camp. We three girls played in one of those buildings at the far end of a corner wall, near a chestnut tree, keeping away from the adults and other children. There were many loose bricks and we used them, putting up a wall three bricks high, making individual rooms. We swept the dirt floors with our hands and made it our house. We sat in our rooms, but we were not alone for long. Mihal and the boys joined in our play house.

The boys cleared bricks to make more space to play. We were given some old dresses for dressing up. Mihal was director, telling us how the play should unfold. We had no idea what we must do, but we loved playing out the stories we were told. Mihal had a good imagination. He showed us the play he made up.

He showed us other games. Using a pocketknife, he drew a big circle and divided it into six parts, a piece of "land" for each of us. We each took a turn throwing the knife at the circle from a distance and grabbing part of our neighbours' land until the whole circle was owned by one owner. That was Mihal. He was good at that game, and he was good at winning marbles. He won all the marbles we girls had received in the last Red Cross package. This area was our place to play and be happy. We played in that part of the building through the summer months. In winter time our play area was covered in snow.

This was not a healthy camp. There was a big problem in the camp keeping the toilets clean. One had to go in the morning just after they were first cleaned because by the afternoon they were overloaded. When the chain was pulled the putrid contents of the bowl spilt over onto the floor. It was disgusting to live like that. Inconsiderate people, perhaps teenage boys, used our play area for dumping their bodily waste. Our playhouse was fouled by faeces. We children were of no importance to people who lived like animals.

Children were sick with mumps, measles and diphtheria. I remember that one of Mother's friends was taken to the hospital suffering from typhoid. She lost her hair and was close to dying. People prayed for her recovery, and she got well. Her hair grew strong, beautiful and wavy. I heard the women talk of her remarkable recovery. I said I would like to lose my hair and grow lovely hair like that. Mother was furious. She gave me a hiding. Hours later, when we were back in our room, I asked her why she had hit me. She said, "You know why." But I didn't know. All through the years I have wondered why I was punished that day, and it is only now that I understand how Mother must have felt about me losing my hair. Only two years before, she had been told that I was about to die.

LEAVING LUDWIGSBURG

In February 1948, Mother came back from hospital with twin baby boys. A new arrival in the family is joy. I was so thrilled to see Mother come back from the hospital with two babies. I missed her so much when she was away. Friends of my parents were happy for them. There was much shaking of hands, congratulations and pats on Father's back, and a lot of talking that I didn't understand. I remember giving the school teacher a description of the babies' heads and their tiny fingers, and saying that the babies were like small dolls. Mother and Father named the boys Czesiek and Zdjeszlaw.

Having to live with two new babies in the dormitory was too much for Janek's parents. They never stopped complaining to Mother, telling her to keep the babies from crying. Mother could not bite her tongue any longer and said to Janek's mother, "You have been making more noise ever since you came to this dormitory than the two babies put together. Put in a complaint to the camp commandant, why don't you!?"

It was very difficult for Mother to live under those conditions. She had to be up at odd hours during the night trying to feed her babies in the dark so as not to disturb others, and trying to keep the babies warm. Father would have one baby in bed with him at night and Mother took the other. They kept the babies close to their bodies through the cold winter nights. There was nowhere for the babies to sleep in the day; there was no room in the hut for a pram. Father brought in a large cardboard box from the camp kitchen to be used for the babies' crib. He put it at the end of my bed. We lived like this for some weeks until the authorities of the camp could arrange something to accommodate our family.

There were some private rooms in the camp where the camp commandant and the higher ranking personnel lived. The priest occupied two rooms. He lived in one room, and used the other as his office. When the church was completed, the priest's office was moved to the church, and that gave my mother the opportunity to request that we move in to the priest's former office. As soon as the room was vacant, the authorities let our family move in. That was living in comfort: a room with a toilet, all to ourselves! The window in the room faced the street, and the sunshine kept the room warm. I could see the outside world from this window. Dad bought a small table and hotplate for Mother to warm the milk and cook our food.

The mornings were cold and thick with fog. Walking to school one morning, I slipped and fell, bruising my knee. I didn't think any more about it that day, but the next morning, my knee was swollen and very painful. I didn't want to go to school but Mother insisted that I go. By the time I had walked all the way to school, the pain had got worse. I had trouble walking up the steps, slowing down the children behind me. Someone pushed me and I fell down the steps, hitting the ground. The pain shot through my leg. My knee felt like it was on fire. I yelled out with pain. A woman teacher and the other children stepped over me like I didn't exist. Some of the girls in my class helped me to my feet, and I was sent home. I stayed away from school for a week.

Spring was coming. The teacher suggested we work on a garden and learn to grow flowers from seeds. The camp swimming pool was filled with soil and used for this school project. The boys dug up worms, picking them up and throwing them onto the girls. I shrieked, showing I was frightened of these horrid things. The boys saw the way I reacted and put worms on my head. I went into hysterics, unable, in my mind, to separate the worm from the snake in the Bible. I went into a shock and could not speak. I was taken to Mother.

The incident affected my health. From that night I started walking in my sleep. Mother was concerned and locked the door to keep me safe in the room. Not able to go to the toilet during the night, I wet my bed in my sleep. Mother couldn't tolerate me wetting the bed again, and she smacked me. It was a disgrace at my age to be wetting the bed. My sleep was constantly disrupted. The bad dreams got worse and from then on I had recurring dreams of snakes. I didn't go to school for some time after that incident.

I sat in the room watching the military cars and trucks going past and helping Mother with the babies, sitting on the bed holding one baby while Mother fed the other one. I was happy sitting at the window watching German children playing on the footpath outside the camp. I got to know them and learned to speak a few words of German. As the weather got warmer, the German children playing on the footpath asked me to join them in a game of hopscotch.

We had been living nearly twelve months in the Ludwigsburg camp. The Red Cross issued the children with new clothing and sandals. The cardigans for the girls were made all the same, and all the dresses were made in the same floral material and in the same style. On Sundays, Marisha, Renia and I wore our new dresses to Mass. After lunch we walked up the street to the park. Sometimes we walked all the way past the American military camp. Just outside the gates there was a fruit vendor with plums, peaches and beautiful big black cherries. We stood at the fruit cart working out what fruit we had eaten in our lives. We recognised apples, pears and oranges because sometimes we had them at the camp with our meals. The cherries looked very good.

An American soldier came walking out to the fruit cart. He bought three bags of cherries while we were standing there and he handed them to us three girls. This soldier remembered how tough it was for children. On the way back to camp we passed private houses. Women standing in their home gardens talking saw us three girls dressed alike in our new dresses. They walked to the gate and asked if we were triplets.

I remember the first time the greengrocer came to the camp with fruit in season: plums, cherries, grapes, gooseberries and a strange thing that was shaped like a moon. I ran to see Mother, telling her that the man outside was selling moons and may I have one. Mother humoured me and gave me money to buy this moon I wanted. I brought it back to her to see what I could do with it.

"First you break the top off and peel the skin like this," said Mother. Then she handed it back to me and said, "Now you can eat it."

I took the first bite and then I had no trouble eating the rest. It was good and filling and tasted like firm custard. My belief that I had eaten the moon bothered me, and then I thought that maybe there are more moons in the sky. That evening I ran out several times to see if any moon was in the sky, but I saw none. Dad saw that I was anxious, running outside several times.

"What is upsetting you Terese?" he asked. "Are you sick?"

"No," I said. "I went out to see if the moon was in the sky. Dad, I can't see it. There will be no more moonlight at night. I have eaten the moon!"

"Don't worry," he said. "The moon will be back. What you ate today was a banana, a fruit that grows on the trees in Africa. The moon is still in the sky. Tonight it's hidden by the rain clouds. That is why you can't see the moon."

I was relieved when the clouds cleared and I could see the moon shining again.

Easter was near. The week of Lent started with a Mass on Ash Wednesday. Each school child donated a potted flower for the church. Marisha, Renia and I walked to the florist's shop not far from the hospital. Trading two cakes of personal soap and a chocolate, we each bought a flowering plant in a pot. Mother wasn't happy that the two girls had each got cineraria, and I only got a polyanthus! The Easter Holy Days started on Holy Thursday with an evening Mass. On the morning of Good Friday, we prepared a basket of food, and dyed hard boiled eggs. Mother made patterns on the eggs with wax, then boiled them with onion peelings. I asked Mother why we did this.

"The story of painting the eggs goes back, a long way back," she said. "When Jesus was taken away by the Roman soldiers from the garden of Gethsemane to be tried by Pontius Pilate for treason, it was said that Mary carried a basket of eggs to Pilate to ask him to release her son. As she passed the courtyard where Jesus was whipped, a drop of his blood fell on the eggs and coloured all the eggs in the basket. The story was told to me when I was a little girl like you. That became the tradition of painting the eggs on Good Friday and having the eggs and food blessed at Mass on Saturday for the celebration of Jesus' resurrection on Sunday."

Dad took us to see the Passion of Christ played out in a quarry. To me, it was like stepping back in time to the year Jesus was living on earth, as if we were watching the real crucifixion taking place in the Holy Land. I asked why the feet were crossed and only one nail used. Mother said that a gypsy took the other nail. He was sorry for the wrongs done to Jesus, and took the nail, hoping that Jesus would be spared if there were not enough nails to crucify him. Father said that the people of small villages were tolerant of the gypsies taking a chicken or some eggs because they believed in the story of gypsies trying to save Jesus from crucifixion.

The priest was respected, and played an important part in our everyday life. The door to the priest was open any time of the day or night. He was there to help solve problems and to boost morale. If there was something beyond his reach and he couldn't help, he would accompany the person to the church and say prayers with them.

Father Bonkowski suggested to Mother that I should go back to school, if only for two hours a day, to get used to it. The priest continued teaching lessons on religion two days a week, preparing the children for the sacrament of Holy Communion. We were constantly repeating the Ten Commandments and the Seven Deadly Sins. "That is something you must never forget," said the priest. "Our lives are based on these laws that God has written on the tablets Moses brought down from the mountain of Sinai. We should learn to keep to the laws of God."

The priest and the camp commandant worked hard to keep the boys active. They set up a games room and a kiosk for young people so they wouldn't have to leave the camp for entertainment. The priest also managed to get the children together for a church choir, working hard and practising for months. Later, when the children were in tune and harmony, they sang Christmas carols in our church.

Father Bonkowski taught the stories that were important in Polish history. One was the story of the Black Madonna of Czestochowa holding her child Jesus. The religious painting of her is a very important icon to the Polish people. Father Bonkowski said this painting went back to the time Christianity began. It was painted by the Evangelist Luke on a table top that Jesus made when he was an apprentice carpenter to Joseph, his earthly father. As a little girl, I didn't know the history of the painting and why it was called The Black Madonna. While writing this book, I found out more.

The story goes back to the third century AD, when Constantine the Great was a soldier. He had a vision of Christ and wanted to unite the Roman Empire. He wanted to replace the many pagan cults with just one religion, Christianity. Constantine was the first Christian Emperor to reign over this great Roman Empire. His mother, Helena, (now St Helena), was moved by her son's sincerity and strong belief, and she also converted to Christianity. Helena travelled to Jerusalem, collecting relics from the time Jesus Christ and his Apostles lived in the Holy Land. Searching for many years, she found what was to be the true cross. She found the nails and the spear from Christ's crucifixion, and the painting of the Madonna holding her child Jesus. The painting had been hidden from the Roman soldiers by the Apostles at the time Christ was crucified. Helena brought these relics back with her to Constantinople and gave them to Constantine, who built a shrine to house them.

Later, Constantinople was attacked and overrun by the Saracens. The painting was hung on a city wall and prayers were said to the Madonna and her son Jesus until the Saracen army withdrew from the city. It was believed that the painting had saved the city from destruction. In the ninth century, the painting of the Madonna and child, and the spear from the Crucifixion, were in the possession of Charlemagne the Great. He was the first Emperor of the new Holy Roman Empire.

Charlemagne gave the painting to Prince Leo of Ruthenia (in Hungary) for his military services. The painting remained at the royal palace of Prince Leo until the eleventh century, when Ruthenia was invaded by the Bohemians. Prince Leo prayed to Our Lady the Madonna to help his small army. Darkness descended and in the confusion the troops attacked one another. As a result, Ruthenia was saved. Fearing that the painting would be destroyed, Prince Leo handed it over to the Prince of Belsk for safe-keeping, where it was protected in the castle chapel. The boundaries of countries changed over the centuries, so it is difficult to say exactly where this castle was, but it was somewhere in the Carpathian Mountains.

In 1382, the Tartars attacked the castle chapel. During the attack, one of the Tartars' arrows landed in the throat of the painted Madonna. A mysterious cloud surrounded the chapel and the invaders fled. Prince Wladislaw, defending the castle, feared that the painting might be destroyed, so he escaped with it during the night. He was guided in his dream by a divine messenger to take the painting to a small village that no-one would know. He stopped at a Polish village named Czestochowa, and handed the painting over to the Pauline monks. They kept it in the small church.

In 1386, King Jagiello II and his wife, Queen Jadwiga, built a cathedral around the small church and the monastery to ensure the safety of the monks and the painting. The cathedral is on Jasna Gora (Bright Hill) at Czestochowa.

On the 14th of April, 1430, the Bohemians attacked and looted the cathedral. One of the thieves attacked the painting by raising his sword and striking the Madonna's cheek twice. Before he could strike it again, he fell on his knees in agony and died. The looters took the painting with them, but their horses stopped at the village boundaries. Whipping them was no use; the animals wouldn't move. The looters dropped the painting, and the horses then moved on their way. The monks found the painting some distance from the monastery, lying in a field, covered in mud and blood. The monks picked up the painting, and from that very spot water sprung up from the ground. The monks cleaned the painting before taking it back with them to the monastery.

In 1655, Poland was again at war, this time with a Swedish King. Czestochowa was overrun. The monks defended the church and the monastery with prayers, the rosary and weapons. They defeated the Swedish army in a six-week siege. Eventually, in 1660, the Polish were able to drive the invaders from their land. The next year, King John Casimir II proclaimed the Madonna as the Queen of Poland. At a special ceremony, the Black Madonna was crowned and dressed in jewelled robes, and placed in a gold and silver frame. On the 9th of September 1661, Czestochowa became the spiritual capital of the nation.

Poland defended herself from attack over the next three centuries. Eventually, Poland was divided between Austria, Prussia and Russia, but Polish people remained undivided in their faith to the Queen of Poland. In 1920, on the 15th of September, the day of Our Lady's Sorrows, Soviet Russian troops fought their way to the banks of the Vistula River and threatened to attack Warsaw. According to legend, the image of the Madonna appeared in the clouds over the city. The two cuts and the arrow wounds were visible on her face. Seeing the image, the Russian troops withdrew from battle. This victory was called "The miracle at the Vistula." The Madonna of Czestochowa had again come to the aid of the Polish people.

The painting is called the Black Madonna because for centuries it was venerated with candles constantly burning around it. The wood absorbed the soot from the candles. Exposed to the elements, the painting turned very dark over centuries.

In another story, Father Bonkowski taught us a lesson on discipline, morals and self-control. He told us a story of his friend and colleague, Raymond. Father Bonkowski and Raymond had studied for the priesthood together in Poland before the war. Raymond's parents were devout Roman Catholics, but Raymond, like most boys, was mischievous and larked about. On one occasion, Raymond's mother didn't approve of something he had done, and that had embarrassed the family. His father lectured him about his behaviour, and sent Raymond to bed early without supper.

As he was saying his prayers, Raymond remembered his father's words and realised how embarrassed his parents must have felt at the way he had behaved. In his prayers he asked Mary the Mother of Jesus what was to become of him. Mary appeared to Raymond in a vision holding a red crown and a white crown. The white one meant that he should persevere in purity and the red one meant he would become a martyr. Raymond accepted both crowns. He believed this vision would shape his future actions.

Raymond had wanted to become a soldier and fight for Poland. He went to Rome, and realised that the world was much bigger than Poland. In his heart he felt that he could do more for people as a priest, so he entered the priesthood to study philosophy and theology. He took the name of Maximilian Kolbe.

In his early twenties, Maximilian Kolbe suffered tuberculosis. When the Second World War broke out, Father Kolbe harboured Jewish and Christian refugees from Hitler's regime. He was arrested by the SS and taken to Auschwitz.

In Auschwitz, a Polish soldier, Sergeant Francis Gajowiczek, was told to stand forward with nine other prisoners condemned to death as punishment for one prisoner's escape. Father Kolbe stepped forward and asked if the soldier could be spared, and offered to stand in his place. The Polish soldier's life was spared.

Father Bonkowski had only given us a brief story about his friend. We were children, and the teaching was simply that we should follow the example of Father Maximilian Kolbe. Pope John Paul II declared Father Kolbe a saint on the 10th of October, 1982. Former Sergeant Francis Gajowicdzek, the soldier spared from death, attended the ceremony of his saviour. Maximilian Kolbe truly was a saint, wearing the two crowns that he accepted in his dream.

At the school we had a new teacher and the first school lessons were the Polish alphabet, arithmetic, times tables, and poems. A few notes were added to make them into folk songs. Later in the year we were taught Polish history. That was my favourite subject. I wanted to learn everything about Poland. I was hoping that in time we might go back to live in the country of my birth. My hope was to go back to where my parents were born and had lived, to walk the city streets of Poland and hear people speak in their mother tongue. I was hoping to visit the city of Krakow to see the second oldest university in Europe, where the famous Polish student Copernicus (Koperniak) studied astronomy. He caused an upheaval in astronomy and religion by proposing that the planets orbited the sun, and not the other way about.

I wanted to see the bones of the dragon hanging in the cathedral, a reminder of the legend of the green dragon that Dad had told me. I wanted to see where the Kings of Poland were buried and I wanted to see the ancient Wawel Castle. In the centuries of war, Wawel Castle was destroyed many times by invaders and each time it was rebuilt. During the Second World War, Hitler's SS troops used Wawel Castle as their headquarters.

I would also like to have seen the church in the town of Czestochowa, and the painting of the Black Madonna. But none of this was possible. Poland was taken over by the Russian communist government. My parents, knowing about the communist regime, had no desire to return to Poland. The borders were changed. The iron curtain shut out western countries for over fifty years. No visitors or tourists were welcome.

The big day for the school children arrived. The 23rd of May was chosen as the day we were to receive the sacrament of the First Holy Communion in our little church. We had been preparing for this for over twelve months. It was a very important day for us children. We rendered our heart and spirit to God. We were now at the age of reasoning, to know and understand the commands of God, and the moral code of right from wrong; to make the most of our lives as we grew to the rules that we had been learning; and to keep the spirit of our body strong, guarding ourselves from weak moments of temptation.

Unfortunately, my First Holy Communion was memorable for another reason. In the ceremony, we held lighted candles in our hands. As I stood up from kneeling, my long dress became caught in my shoe. As I tried to free myself, I tilted the candle too close to my head, and my hair caught fire! Someone sitting in a pew close to me jumped up and beat the fire out with their hands. I was just one of those children: if something happened, it would be me!

I remember the excitement in the camp every time wedding bands were announced in the church. The most exciting was the wedding of Mother's friend, who was also Czesiek's godmother. (Unfortunately, I don't remember her name.) Before any plans were made, the bride and groom had to have a blood test. The ceremony was performed in a registry office followed by a church wedding if that was the wish of the bride and groom. Most young people had a church wedding, and most of the camp weddings took place on a Sunday.

The women in the camp prepared for the big day. The bride's dress was stitched by hand from silk parachutes used during the war. Not every woman getting married wore a veil and a white dress. They may not have had the money, or may not have wanted to. Arum lilies were ordered for the bride to carry on her arm as she walked down the aisle. The flowers for the church altar came from the camp garden. There was no need for cars in the camp; we all walked from the barracks to our little church. As the flower girl, I walked in front of the procession, throwing flower petals on the ground so the bride and groom could walk on a carpet of flowers.

The wedding was open to anyone in the camp who wished to join in the celebration. At that time there was no big feast of food, just a sip of wine for the bride and groom. Mother's fine china egg cups were used for this occasion; they were more appealing than the camp kitchen mugs. There was music, dancing and singing. My father entertained the wedding party by playing his mouth organ and dancing the Cossack dance. Most of the young Polish men liked to dance. One was not considered to be a man if one couldn't dance.

Janek and Mihal were always into mischief. One time Janek was trying to impress some young boys who had just arrived and were jumping off the back of the truck. Janek was carrying a billy can of boiling hot tea from the kitchen to the dormitory for his parents, swinging the billy can around over his shoulder and head. He did this repeatedly as he was walking from the kitchen, saying to me that I couldn't do the same. I could sense the danger and said to him, "The tea will spill out and you will get burnt."

"I won't get burnt. I am not stupid like you!" said Janek.

Maybe he wasn't stupid, but he didn't anticipate that someone would run into him and that's just what happened after I warned him. Janek was badly burnt on the leg. He screamed with pain. For months he lay in bed, not able walk or play, or to go to school.

Sickness raged in the camp: chicken pox, mumps, diphtheria and typhoid. The camp was quarantined. No-one was allowed in or out. My two baby brothers were taken ill with measles in the first week of September. The younger of the two, Zdjeszlaw, had to be taken to the hospital. They said he had pneumonia in his lungs. He didn't recover. He died two days after being admitted to the hospital. He died alone in hospital during the night. In those days the rules were different. Parents were not permitted to stay in hospital to sit with their dying children. Mother and Father never had the chance to hold their son to say goodbye before he died. Zdjeszlaw—our little Zdiszu—was only seven months old. He was the second child my parents had lost.

I could not believe my baby brother had died. The next day I went to the hospital with my two friends, Marisha and Renia. We looked for my brother. The sister at the hospital came to the door and said that he was not in the hospital, and that I should go home to my parents. They would tell me where to find him.

I knew that Zdiszu had died, but I just didn't believe it. I hoped that it wasn't true. I was sent out to play as if nothing had happened. I wasn't in a playful mood; we had just lost our baby. A loss for my parents was a loss for me. My heart was breaking just the same as Mother's and Father's hearts. They didn't understand that I, too, was grieving for our little boy.

Our baby's funeral was held in the chapel at the Ludwigsburg cemetery. When we walked in, the casket was open. Zdiszu was laid out in his blue baby suit. Mother and Father stood by the casket, taking a long look at our little angel lying there as if he were sleeping, his eyes slightly open. That is how he always slept, with his eyes opened slightly. I stood on the opposite side of the casket and saw the sadness in my parents' faces. Tears streamed down their cheeks. Father stepped forward first to say his goodbye. He kissed his tiny son's forehead and lifted the tiny hands, taking his time to kiss each one of them, and then stood back for Mother to say her goodbye. She first brushed each side of Zdiszu's cheeks and picked up his hands and kissed each one of his little fingers. Then she brushed her hand gently down his legs and touched his tiny toes one by one. They both stood back to have the last look. Dad supported Mother, holding on to her shoulders so she wouldn't fall.

All I could do was to kiss my baby brother on the forehead to say goodbye and stand aside. I had no tears. Since the time I was near death in the house at Schwabisch Hall, I had not cried about anything. After the prayers were said, and the casket closed, I felt as if a door had been shut on me. I was in darkness. The sun was shining but there was darkness in my mind. Father picked up the little casket and carried his baby son to the grave site. The priest said prayers and our little angel was lowered into his grave. Mother and Father both had to be supported by the babies' godparents.

In the cemetery chapel

My baby brother lies in an open casket

Mother's and Father's eyes are fixed on our little angel

Their hearts fill with sorrow

It is hard to say goodbye to our little sparrow Zdiszu

The white casket is closed

With a heavy heart Father lifts his baby son and

Carries the tiny body to a final resting place

After the funeral I was sent outside. I wanted to spend time on my own. The only peaceful place I was able to find was among the heap of rusty tanks and trucks that were still left in the camp grounds. I found one of the military vehicles in an upright position. We children had been told not to play in the wrecks because it was dangerous. For the first time in my life I was disobedient. I sat in the truck, and stayed there until it was time to go for tea.

A black cloud hung over me for days. Again I went to sit in the truck. I felt no danger; this was a comfortable place for me. I had been warned once again not to go near the wrecks because I might get hurt. Somehow it didn't matter to me. That was the only place I could be by myself.

I was kept inside for the next week and in that time the wrecks were removed. Bricks were laid around that spot for a flower bed to be planted in the next spring. At that time I didn't realise that I was suffering from depression. I don't think anyone had even heard of the sickness in those days.

After the long dark winter, I had an appointment in the city hospital to see a specialist. On the way back, Mother took me to the Ludwigsburg Fair. She wanted me to experience some pleasure in my life. We both needed to lift our spirits after the loss of our baby.

I had never seen so many wonderful things. It was like walking into a wonderland. I wanted to take a ride on everything I saw, but I was only allowed to take three rides. My first choice was the bullet train. Mother tried to talk me into taking a ride on the merry-go-round but I insisted on the bullet train. Mother gave in. She had to come on the train with me. After the fast ride for about one minute we both came off sick. My head was spinning and I felt like I wanted to throw up. Mother was annoyed with me and said, "Don't tell me your troubles! You insisted on the train ride. We must go home." Mother and I couldn't walk straight; we wandered from one side of the path to the other like we were a couple of drunks.

For my final visit to the doctor's, Dad walked me to town. After we left the surgery we walked a little distance to a shop. Dad bought a small machine to make his own cigarettes. He put them in the silver cigarette case he always had in his coat pocket. We came to the street crossing and waited for the traffic to clear. Father was holding my hand. Suddenly I pulled my hand away and bolted across the busy road into the traffic. I heard wheels screeching. A big car just touched me as it pulled to a sudden stop. An American soldier jumped out from the car to see if I was alright. He was mighty angry, cursing at me for being so stupid. I don't know what made me pull my hand away from Dad.

In the summer evenings, the twin sisters and I sat on the garden brick wall listening to the older teenaged girls telling us fairy stories. I remember the story of the princess and the frog, and the story of the wolf, the nanny goat and her kids. Marisha, Renia and I had no understanding of make believe at that stage of our lives. We believed they were true stories, and they sounded so sad. For the first time, I cried. I felt sorry for the mother goat's kids being taken by the wolf. I was sorry for the mother goat losing her children, as I remembered being left on my own for a long time in the war years. The three of us were broken-hearted hearing the story.

The older girls told us to stop crying. They said that the story was made up, like many other stories we were told while sitting on the brick wall watching the sun set.

People in camps were constantly on the move. Some months after Janeks' foolish act of burning his leg, he and his parents moved to another camp. They were going to America, if accepted, to make their new home. I had heard people talking and most of them wanted to start their new life in America. Maybe Janek would get a job in Hollywood doing stunts for movies and making lots of money, or maybe he would go to South America to work like a monkey and be paid peanuts.

As I was writing this part of my story I was asked to be in a film to train young nurses at a university. I was to play the part of a crippled old woman being helped from a car to her front gate. The chap shooting the film said it would take about one hour to shoot, but that we may have to take more than one shot.

"Take as much time as you need," I said. But I was a natural in the part! We only made one take; shooting was over in five minutes. The payment for my acting was a packet of chocolate, and written on the packet was "Koala Pooh". How is that for payment to a star? No better than Janek's peanuts!

At about this time, Marisha and Renia also left the camp. I wasn't sad. People came and went all the time. I didn't expect anyone to stay long. After they had gone, Mihal joined me and two brothers, Staszek and Zbeszek, I was hanging around with. The brothers were a little younger than me. My mother was friends with their mother. Mother kept an eye on them while their parents were working, and I was like a big sister to them.

Every day, the three boys and I were sent to the bakery just around the corner from the camp to buy bread for making sandwiches for our parents to take to work. Once a week, we were rewarded with money to buy ourselves a frankfurter each at the butcher shop on the way back from the bakery. Mother gave me extra money for Mihal's frankfurter. She had a soft spot in her heart for Mihal because he had no father. Friends looked after one another and helped out in times of need.

Across the street from the shops was the town prison, surrounded by an orchard. It was fenced off from the footpath by barbed wire. Mihal was always into mischief, and he saw that the fruit was ripe and ready for picking. He was tempted to go into the prison grounds, and he tried to entice us to go in with him.

"I am not going with you," I said. "Mother says it is wrong to steal, and the guards are watching you from the tower, and I am going to tell your mother on you."

That made no difference to Mihal. "Go and tell my mother! See if I care, you tittle tat!" he yelled out.

Mihal and the older brother, Staszek, had no fear. It was a big adventure for them. They crawled under the wire into the prison grounds. The younger brother, Zbeszek, and I stood on the other side of the street watching. I am sure that the guard walking back and forth with a rifle on his shoulder saw the boys crawling under the wire fence and turned a blind eye. Mihal had picked up a pear from the ground and taken a bite. He nearly choked when the guard yelled out from the tower. Zbeszek and I ran towards the camp. Mihal and Staszek wet their pants with fright and ripped them when they got caught on the barbed wire. They ran flat out past us towards the camp gates.

The MPs saw the two boys running with their pants ripped and wet, and picked them up by the scruff of the neck. The MPs asked what they were running from. The boys were too frightened to speak. I was the one trying to tell the story. The MPs said to the boys, "It's not the fruit of the tree that you have to worry about – it's the pear on the ground in the forbidden orchard. That's where the trouble began. Take note and remember this in future when you grow up to be men."

After the MPs had had their joke, they let the boys go, knowing that the embarrassment of ripping and wetting their pants was punishment enough.

A tragic incident happened to Mother one morning. She was going to church and she passed the storage building as she had done many times. This time, something made her turn back. She got such a shock to see a man's face in the cellar window of the building. She screamed. People came running to see what had happened. Mother couldn't talk. She pointed to the window and to the man's grey face, his tongue hanging from his mouth and a red cord around his neck.

Mother ran to the safety of our room in a state of shock. I could see the despair and sorrow in her face. She fell down on her knees to pray. What could a little girl do to help? Only go down on my knees with her and say the rosary. That was the only comfort I could give my mother. She cried so hard, saying to me, "What have I done for this to happen to me?"

This incident happened on the anniversary of our little boy's death. The horror was too much for Mother, who was still grieving. I discovered later that this date was also Mother's birthday.

She fell ill. She was not Mother as I knew her. She seldom went outside and could hardly cope on her own. School days were over for me. Mother relied on Father and me to help. I stayed home to look after my brother Czesiek through the day and Father helped Mother with the washing after he finished work. Mother never went out alone. I still went to the concert and choir rehearsal. It was a long time before Mother got better.

In the days leading up to Christmas 1949, the priest organised the camp's Polish school children to make a recording of Christmas carols in Stuttgart. The recording would be broadcast on air for the people in the camps to bring cheer on Christmas Eve and during the season's holy days. Dad came home carrying a package wrapped in brown paper and tied with string. He put it on the table, untied the string and pulled aside the brown paper to reveal a black box with a glass front, knobs at the bottom and holes in the back.

'What is that?" I asked.

"It is a magic box," said Dad. "It talks and plays music. I bought it so we could listen to the recording that your school choir made for Christmas day."

"How does it work?" I asked.

"You see those two wires at the back? They are antennas. I put them out the window to catch the sound from the air. I put the plug into the electric power point, turn the knob and listen to the radio box talk. Terese, isn't it wonderful to have a box that brings music to the room?"

I was a little puzzled by all this, but then I was puzzled by many things. There were a lot of things I had to learn.

"Every day after work Dad came home and put on the radio, listening to the news so we could learn more of the German language. We did not know at that stage where our new home was going to be; it might even have been Ludwigsburg.

A week before Christmas, we were busy rehearsing for the Christmas concert to be held in the camp. Every school child and teenager in camp had a part to play. We had so much fun rehearsing the play and learning to sing the Christmas carols. We had no fancy costumes. The girls playing angels dressed in something white. Most of us, including me, wore our own white flannelette nightdresses, with blue sashes around our waists. We tore up old blue dresses to make the angel sashes. The boys wore men's shirts to play Joseph, the shepherds, and the Three Wise Men. Women's old floral dresses were ripped up and used for the boys' head gear. The boys objected to putting old dresses on their heads, but we girls enjoyed seeing the boys get what they deserved for the cheek they gave us.

I was given the part of one of many angels needed for the nativity. Being a small girl, I was to be placed on the roof with another small girl. Dad got carried away when he was making angel wings for me. They were big and awkward, and he had used heavy wire. Putting them on, I nearly fell back. Everyone was in the stable taking their part. The big boys who were helping had a job getting me up on the stable roof. The timber on the roof creaked and the stable started to sway. I was frightened I was going to fall.

"Get me down!" I yelled.

Mary, Joseph and the shepherds scattered, running off like rats from a sinking ship and leaving the baby behind in the manger.

The priest sang out, "What about saving the baby?!" (It was only a bundle of material.)

"Jesus can take care of himself!" cried Mihal.

"Mihal!" said the priest. "You have just lost the part of Joseph!"

I was not getting up on that roof again. I only wanted to *play* the part of an angel; I wasn't dying to *be* one! A spot was allocated for me behind Mary in the stable.

I am sad to say that after the concert, tragedy struck. On Christmas Eve, the mother of the two brothers I played with, Staszek and Zbeszek, was killed at her work. She was cleaning the office windows when she slipped and fell from the second floor of the building, hitting the footpath. People in camp mourned her death. I felt very sad and my heart ached for the boys, especially because little Zbeszek had cried and begged his mother to stay with him that day. There was no festive celebration at camp that Christmas, only the service at midnight to celebrate the birthday of Jesus. The funeral was held after Christmas.

Sometime in that new year of 1950, Dad came back from his English lesson with the American soldier. He grabbed Mother by the waist, sweeping her off her feet and swirling her around the room. "Anna! We are going to *Australia*!"

After he put Mother down, he said, "I have been talking with the soldier who teaches me. He said that he has been in Australia, in Sydney and Melbourne, and he said he liked the country. The people are friendly and obliging and the weather is warmer. It's a good country and there is plenty of land. The people in Australia are mainly from British background. Living is much the same as in England. It's a good place for growing children." I said to him "Your word is good enough for me! Put our name down for Australia. I am not changing my mind."

Father received a letter telling us to be at the Immigration Office at the appointed time and to bring photos for the passport. When we arrived at the office, the clerk asked Father some questions and filled in papers. I was old enough to take in the information that my mother, Anna, was born on the 8th of September in 1919 at Grabownica, in the County of Dobromil. My father, Pawel Dron was born on the 30th of June in 1920 at Byble, in the County of Pszemysl. I was born at Grabownica, now Miasto, on the 1st of January, 1940.

Then we were asked to sit in the waiting room before we went to see the big chief of immigration. After a few minutes the door opened and we were asked to come in. The immigration officer spoke to Father in English through an interpreter, who spoke very well in Polish. He said that we were on the list of people emigrating to Australia. The interpreter was dressed in military uniform. I couldn't identify whether he was Canadian or American; the uniforms were much the same to me. The immigration officer looked through the papers and said, "If everyone in the family is in good health there should be no problem to be accepted for immigration to Australia."

"Everything is OK," said Father. "I have a certificate from a specialist to say my little girl is recovered from sickness and is in good health."

The officer stood up from behind his desk and shook hands with Father, saying, "I wish you good luck for your journey to Australia." The officer sat back in his chair, gathered all the papers together and passed them to Father.

I stood up and said "*Thank you very much*" in English to the immigration officer.

The officer nearly fell off his chair with laughter. The others in the office also thought it was funny. The officer said to me, "You'll get on little one. That is a good sign. You will make a good Australian citizen. Good luck to you all."

When we came back home, Mum and Dad started to weigh up the pros and cons. "It is a big decision we have to make," said Father. "Australia is far, far away from Europe. We know very little about the country. Once we go we can't come back."

As they discussed what was to be settled, Mother told Father about the letters some people had received from their friends living in Australia. "One of the letters said that Australia is hot during the day and cold at night," said Mother. The friend wrote "We should have brought some feather eiderdowns with us. Australians don't have eiderdowns, only blankets."

"Then Stasia said that in a letter she received, she read that people who die in Australia are burnt. The ground is too hard to dig a grave. Her friend Olga wrote that she hadn't seen rain since she arrived in Australia. It is very dry, not a patch of green grass to be seen.

"Helena said "What country is this? No rain, no grass?"

"Then Stefka said that in the letter she received from Australia, her friend wrote that her husband works mostly at night, crocodile hunting in the river and they have to watch for poisonous snakes and spiders."

Then Zbeshek read his letter out to us. He said, "Listen to this, my friends. Ryszard says he hunts crocodiles with the black people. In the letter he says the first day he started working, the blacks showed him the way hunting is done. When the work was finished in the morning, the friendly blacks invited him to come along with them to their camp to share their food with him."

Mother continued to recount Ryszard's letter. Ryszard said his new friends got him to undress and sit by the fire. Ryszard wrote, "I was put in an embarrassing position. Here I am, a white man, sitting in the nude, eating with the men, and women walking around me. Not only did the men share their food with me, they offered to share their women too. What's a man to do?"

Then Helena said that her parents had received a letter from her older sister in Belgium. The letter said that they are returning to Germany. There is no future for them in Belgium. There is no work, and what little work there is, it's in the coal mines. It is hard work for little money. Living in Belgium is difficult for newcomers with no family for support, and living is very expensive.

I listened. Mother's telling of the letters that friends received and spoke about made no sense to me. I spoke up. "I don't want to go to Australia. I don't like what I am hearing. Mihal told me that snakes in Australia live under the house and they have to be fed six bread rolls a day."

"Don't believe Mihal," said Father. "He is making it all up. Listen, I will tell a story that is much better than what Mihal is telling you. Back in Poland when I was a small boy we lived on a farm. In our house, behind the fuel stove, during the winter, lived a snake. No-one knew about this, only my sister's little friend. She came to the house every day to feed this snake a few crumbs that fell from the bread she was eating.

But my sister's little friend was sick and didn't come to the house for a few days. The snake got hungry. One evening, it came out looking for food. Everyone in the house screamed when they saw the snake – in Poland snakes are rarely seen. Grandad picked up the poker and killed it. When the little girl got better and came to the house to feed the snake, she couldn't find it. She asked Grandad to look behind the stove. To humour the girl, he looked behind the stove and was surprised to find a small golden crown, not quite finished. The snake had been making the crown for the little girl to say thank you for her kindness. The little girl was very sad and went home crying as she had grown fond of the snake."

"I like your story Dad," I said. But I still wasn't convinced about going to Australia to live. "Why can't we go back to Poland?"

"It is not wise to go back to Poland," said Father. "That country does not belong to the Polish government now. The Russian Communist Government has taken over."

"Why can't we stay in this country? We have to leave our boys, we can't take them with us,' I said.

"No, we can't. The boys have a place in Heaven with the Angels. Mother has reasons for not staying in Germany, explained Father.

Mother interrupted and said, "I want to go to a place where my bones won't freeze in the winter, a place where it's always hot, and a country that is in peace."

I voiced my opinion, saying "I want to go to America!" Everyone wanted to go to America. It was a rich place.

"No Terese, said Father, we can't. The books on immigration to America are closed. We can go to South America – Argentina, Brazil..."

"Do they speak English in Argentina?"

"No, they speak Spanish.

"We can't go there," I said.

"Why not?" asked Father.

"You don't speak Spanish, you speak American."

"We could go to South Africa – they speak English."

"No," I said, "I don't want to go to Africa and live with the monkeys and gorillas and elephants."

"You will have lots of bananas to eat," said Father.

"No! The monkeys and the elephants eat the bananas. There will be nothing left for me!"

"What do you know about Africa?" Father asked.

"We had a lesson in school on Africa and the animals. There are big snakes that jump from the trees onto people, and coil around and squeeze them to death and eat them. I don't want to go to live in Africa to be eaten by a snake," I replied.

As soon as Dad got word from the Immigration Office that we were accepted for immigration to Australia, he brought scrap timber home from work and made two crates for our belongings. Father and Mother went shopping in the town and came back with feather eiderdowns and pillows to keep us warm on cold winter nights in Australia. Father walked in looking very smart in a new trench coat and carrying a big suitcase wrapped in brown paper. He unwrapped it to show a crocodile skin suitcase, then opened it to show Mother the interior lined with black and white check material and pockets sewn in each side.

"It looks a first class expensive suitcase," said Mother.

Father was so happy owning a suitcase like that. He picked it up and walked around the room. Putting it down, he ran his fingers over every bump and ridge of the crocodile's lumpy back.

Watching him, Mother said," Pawel, your hands are all over that suitcase like it was a woman."

"There are other things in life besides women that a man has interests in," said Father. "This is a fine suitcase, wouldn't you say Anna?"

I was thinking that Dad had fallen in love with a dead crocodile. Father opened the suitcase again and said, "Terese could sleep in this comfortably."

Now I was in trouble; Father was suggesting I should sleep in the belly of a dead crocodile.

"Did you have to say that?" Mother spoke harshly, with a stern look on her face.

"Oops! I said something to upset mother," said Dad, looking at me and lifting his eyebrows to make a face.

"What concerns me," said Mother, "is how you are going to carry this big suitcase when it's fully packed."

"Don't worry Anna, I will manage, Father replied.

Mother opened one of the other packages and lifted out a red eiderdown. She wrapped herself in it and said, "Terese would be more comfortable sleeping in this, wouldn't you say?"

"Oh yes," said Dad. "That looks good with you wrapped in it, the red is so inviting!" He grabbed Mother and threw her on the bed. This was the first time I had seen Mum and Dad having a little fun together. It was good to see them being happy.

After a little while, Mother went back to packing the eiderdowns away and started sorting out the clothing. Not that she had a lot to choose from: "This dress is too old," she said. "It will do for washing days in the Australian bush."

"We are not going to live in the bush!" I cried.

"Most of Australia is the bush," said Mother.

She wasn't too far from being wrong.

Some of the people were going back to Poland, among them my parents' friends, Jusza and Stefan. Mother begged Jusza to reconsider, saying, "You know that Poland is under the communist government – why do you want to go back?"

Jusza believed that things would change for the better in time. Jusza and Stefan had made their decision and nothing that Mother or Father could say would change their minds. We went to the train station to say our farewell to them. My parents were very sad to be separating from their dear friends after all the years they had known each other, from the time before the war had taken them all away from their homeland. The two women cried.

"I hope we made the right decision, going back to Poland." Jusza said.

Jusza and Stefan hugged and kissed Czesiek and me before embracing Mother and Father. They couldn't let go, knowing they would not see each other again.

I walked away from them and stood with my brother. I couldn't bring myself to wave goodbye. My heart was saddened. I felt like I was being abandoned by the two people I looked to as my aunty and uncle.

Boarding the train, Jusza said, "I hope I am right in believing that life will change for the better in Poland…"

Jusza and Stefan were full of the hope of finding their family waiting for them at the other end.

Walking away from the station there was sadness in our hearts. Not a word was spoken between my parents until we arrived back at camp. Father broke the silence and said, "If your wish is to go to Poland, just say the word Anna."

"No!" Mother yelled. "Are you crazy Pawel?! Did you forget the plans we made?"

"No, I'm not crazy. I haven't forgotten the plans Anna. I thought that you may have changed your mind," Father answered.

"We have spoken on this before Pawel. I don't want to go to a country that is governed by communists. We are going to Australia. I know it's going to be difficult for us going to a country we know little about, and learning a new language. I am counting on you to help me Pawel. I want to be free. I don't want a communist to run our lives. I want Terese and Czesiek to have an education and I want the choice to go to church and pray any time I wish. There will be no more talk of going back to Poland."

These were Mother's final words on the subject.

It was time for us to leave Ludwigsburg and Luitpold Kasrine. I had loved living in the camp for two years. It was important for me to be in one place for a time and have the stability I needed, to bond with my parents, and to learn and develop mentally. Before, when we were moved from the house to the first camp, there was tension. I had to be out of the way and sit quietly for hours with the baggage. I grew tired waiting for my parents while papers were checked and transport was arranged. That kind of life is not for growing children.

Depending on what country they had chosen as their new home, people from Ludwigsburg were scattered to camps all over Germany, one step closer to their ship journey. In a few days, my family was on a train going to the Immigration Commission camp at Augsburg.

AUGSBURG TO BREMER HAVEN

The train pulled slowly into Augsburg station. Although it was raining, I could see through the window that the station was neat and clean. We stayed in Augsburg for two nights and it rained the whole time. The camp grounds were well maintained; it was a pleasant place to stay. I wished we could stay longer. I would have liked to walk through the streets with my Dad to observe this lovely city, but this was only a stopover camp. In no time at all we were pushed through the process of health examination and inoculations. ID papers, passports and all important certificates were processed and given to us and we were sent on our way to the next camp, Wildflecken.

Our train travelled through a lovely part of the country. The houses had attic windows on high roofs and everything looked clean and tidy. The train went through tunnels and around winding mountains, pushing its way to the picturesque villages and green valleys. It was like a train trip through fairyland, or a place you would see in the story books. But things didn't turn out the way they should have. My little brother had a bad reaction to the inoculations. Mother was angry and worried, complaining to Father that there was nowhere to lay her little boy down, no medication for him. Mother and Father had to take turns in nursing Czesiek in their arms or on their lap. There was no one to call on for help.

The journey to Wildflecken was to be only a few hours, but we were taken all the way to a camp at Aurich, in the far north east of Germany. We arrived late in the evening. I was tired and don't remember much about that night. The next morning I woke up in a dormitory on the second floor to the sound of clip clop, clip clop, clip clop. I was puzzled by this sound coming from the open window that faced onto the busy street. I jumped out of bed and looked out of the window. I was surprised to see two big horses pulling a long open wagon loaded with vegetables. It was the horses' shoes on the cobblestones making the sound. What a delight to see this wonderful town of mediaeval charm.

We had arrived in Aurish at the end of the week, and nearly everyone in the camp went to the soccer game the next day. Soccer was the most popular sport in Europe and my Dad was one of those people who loved watching a good game of soccer.

Mother wanted to be alone with her sick little boy, so she asked Father to take me along with him to the games. Walking to the sports oval we passed a big lilac tree covered with large heads of pink flowers. The perfume was unforgettable! I instantly fell in love with its blooms and their heavenly smell.

The soccer must have been a big event that weekend. People must have come from all over the country to see these games. There were crowds of spectators when we walked through the gates. There was entertainment on the grounds for children and adults before the games and at half time. Soccer in Germany was fast. A big wave of people yelled out and the crowd went wild whenever the ball hit the net. I enjoyed the afternoon games with my Father. Walking back to the camp we passed the beautiful lilac tree again.

The sounds and smells have remained with me all these years. One recent Saturday morning I was lying in bed in my house at Beresfield, and I heard horseshoes in the street. Two girls were riding their horses past my house and the sound brought back the memory of Aurich. Another time, I was taking a shortcut to the shops. Passing a house garden, I could smell lilacs. I thought this was strange, as I had not seen lilac trees in Australia before that. Was I hallucinating? I turned and walked back to the house, and there in the garden was a lilac shrub by the fence with small blue flowers. I will never forget the lovely memories of the time we spent in Aurich, but it was only a short stay. In a few days the camp in Wildflecken was cleared for us.

There was often trouble getting us from one camp to another. We stayed on the train longer than expected when there was a snag somewhere in the plan: the ships not running on time, or some ships developing engine troubles on their way back from the last voyage. Other ships on the way back to Europe were diverted to the islands in the Far East to bring passengers back home. With the threat of war in the air again, some IRO ships had been diverted to transport Allied troops to South Korea. The authorities had to leave the displaced people on hold wherever they were until a camp was cleared.

The train arrived at Wildflecken in the late morning. Ladies on the platform with hand puppets tapped at the windows, giving a smile and a welcome gesture to entertain the children as the train slowly pulled into the station. Everyone had to stay on the train until the medical officers came through to see if there were sick children or adults. They were taken off the train first. My brother was one of the sick children; he and Mother were taken directly to the camp hospital for further examination. The rest of the passengers stayed in the carriage until we were given a number that coincided with the number of a truck and a barrack. That was the military way of doing things. Father and I were transported to the barrack only two buildings from the hospital where Czesiek was admitted. When we were settled in our dormitory, Father and I went to the hospital to bring Mother back.

Mother was allowed to visit Czesiek every day, but children were not permitted to visit the hospital. I made friends with a Lithuanian girl named Meta. She lived in the same building on the same floor. The two of us hung around the hospital hut every day; I was frightened that Czesiek might die like the other two boys we had lost. Meta and I were at the back of the hospital, feeding our faces on raspberries that grew wild in the fields beyond the back door of the hospital. I watched the window, waiting to see if Czesiek would stand up in his cot. Nurses came out in their lunch break and joined us in picking raspberries. I asked them about Czesiek. They assured me that he was getting better every day and that it wouldn't be too long before he could leave the hospital.

Wildflecken had much the same living conditions as the camp in Ludwigsburg. This camp was at the foot of the mountains about 240 kilometres from Frankfurt. It was a holding place before we proceeded to another camp, one step closer to our journey on the ship. Wildflecken was big; there was a health clinic and a dental surgery and a small hospital. There was also a small station wagon and driver to take people with more serious illnesses to a hospital in town. There was a kindergarten for the children, mostly for toddlers up to five years of age. It was well set up for the children.

After Czesiek had recovered and was returned to us, Mother asked me to take him to the kindergarten. She hoped that I might stay with him. I walked to the hut and knocked on the door. When the door opened, I saw that the inside was like the cottage of Snow White and the Seven Dwarfs. Everything was made for toddlers: small beds, small tables and chairs, lots of lovely toys. I wished I could stay and play, but older children weren't allowed. Czesiek didn't want to stay without me. He was too little to be on his own with strange people; he was just over two years old. I tried again a few weeks later but Czesiek's reaction was the same as before. He was happy to stay with me.

In the same building, on the ground floor, were two girls about the same age as myself. They had toddler siblings about the same age as my brother. Although we were from different countries, we managed to communicate with each other. We met in the morning after breakfast and went into the fields to play a little distance from the building. It was a lovely view looking onto the forest and the mountains. I never got tired of the scenery. Sometimes young mothers came to the fields, spreading a rug on the green grass and playing with their babies. They sat close sometimes, speaking a few words and showing us how to make wreaths from clover flowers to put on our heads. The women said it was what they did when they were young girls watching over their animals at home in the old country.

There was no school for children in this camp, possibly because there were too many different languages, and possibly because people didn't stay long. There were English classes a few hours a week in the afternoon for children, and in the evening for adults. I went to English classes with my dad after he came back from work. He worked in the forest, cutting down trees. There was plenty of work cutting timber to build new houses and to rebuild the ones that were damaged in the war.

The English we were taught was formal English, of little value to us, we realised later. When we came to Australia we were at a loss. The language spoken by Australian people was different. I understood what women said, but men had their own way of talking. We were not taught Australian Ocker!

In this camp, we were also shown films about Australian people and their homes. One of the films showed a lady getting out of her new car, which was parked in front of the average sized house with a front porch. The lady got her bag of groceries from the boot of the car and stepped on a small rock. She broke the heel of her shoe. Everyone laughed at that part of the movie. The lady limped along the path as she carried the grocery bag to the house. She fumbled for the keys in her handbag, opened the door and walked into the kitchen. She put the groceries on the table and opened the door of the refrigerator to put in the perishable food, then she put the groceries in the cupboard.

The lady looked so happy humming to herself. Then we saw her cooking on the modern stove. She set the dining table, preparing for her husband to come home from work. The husband walked in the door. After giving his wife a kiss, he walked into a cosy lounge room and turned on the radio. He walked into the lovely bathroom and washed his hands, and then the film showed every room in the house. It was very nice. The lady brought out the dinner and they sat together eating the meal at the table set aside from the kitchen.

Another film showed a family in Australia at Christmas. Everyone was dressed in their Sunday best. There was a grandfather clock at the entrance hallway and in the corner of the lounge room a large Christmas tree. Underneath the tree were presents. The house was big and expensive, with period furniture in the lounge and dining rooms. The little girl in the film must have had too much to eat because the doctor was called. He arrived in a big black car with his black bag in his hand. He entered through the front door and walked into the large lounge room where the little girl was lying on the lounge. The doctor felt her pulse and checked her throat. He patted the little girl's head. The day was very hot. The ladies were using their fans and the men were dabbing their foreheads with handkerchiefs. I imagine the doctor said the little girl was fine but I did not understand the English.

There were more films. Some were about the way of life of Aborigines in the desert, dancing a rain dance or something or other. Another film showed drovers moving sheep.

Saturday was a break for us girls. We picked wildflowers in the fields to put on the altar for Sunday Mass. I loved Sundays. They were special days for me. After lunch, Father and Mother and Czesiek and I, and friends from previous camps with their children, walked through the fields to the forest.

Dad knew the forest well. He took us to a lovely spot on a hill near a running stream. The water was so clean running over the pebbles. It was summer. We took off our sandals and refreshed our feet in the cool ankle deep water while the adults enjoyed themselves catching up on the events of the week. A man brought his sheep down to the stream for a drink. He had a hat on his head, and wore a long coat. He carried a long stick. I asked Mother, "Who was the man with the sheep?"

"He is a shepherd," said Mother. "He is the man who looks after the sheep."

"Is this man Jesus?" I inquired.

"Why do you ask me that?" Replied Mother.

"Last week on Sunday," I said, "the priest was talking about Jesus the shepherd and how one sheep was lost and Jesus left the others and went looking for the sheep that was lost. How glad Jesus was when the lost sheep was found."

"Yes I know that story," said Mother. "But this man is not Jesus."

"Does this shepherd have a wife and children?" I asked.

"I am sure that he has a family," said Mother.

"The priest didn't say at Mass if Jesus had a wife and children," I said.

"Next time you see the priest, why don't you ask him?" Replied Mother

I thought more about it, and said, "This man does not look like Jesus."

"No, the picture you see in the Church was painted a long time before we were born.

People in the time of Jesus wore different clothes, not like we do today. Life changes all the time," said Mother.

These were brief moments of conversation I had with my mother when she was feeling well. At other times she would say, "Go to your father. He will tell you what you want to know."

We picked wild cherries off the trees that grew in the forest. The cherries were small but sweet to eat. We gathered small chestnuts off the ground and had fun smashing the shells open and eating the nuts while our parents relaxed in the warm afternoon sun. Not until the sun had set behind the mountains did we make a move to go back to face another week of camp life.

For us girls, the days through the week were much the same. We took care of our siblings and watched people gathering certain kinds of leaves that grew around the camp grounds. Other people gathered some species of ants and sold them to the herbal chemists for pocket money. Wildflecken produced medicines from these things. My parents were great believers in herbal medicines. It's what they grew up with, and it was the herbalist's medication that improved my health. I am the living proof that these natural medications work.

These were happy months. It was a lovely time of the year. Everything was going well. Meta and I had fun together learning each other's language, a few words each day.

After rain, my family and I would go to the forest with Meta and her father to gather mushrooms for making soup. We had to be careful to pick the ones that were not poisonous. Some of the eating mushrooms were pink underneath and brown on top. Some of the pink had turned to light brown as the mushrooms aged and grew bigger. We left them alone in case they were poisonous. Some grew as big as a saucer. Pine trees produced lovely toadstools. Some were tall, with a kind of a tall hat with a fat stalk. Others had red tops spotted with white; they are often seen in storybooks. The mushrooms were a change from the food cooked in the camp kitchen.

Meta's father had a big electric coil that could be used to boil the water in big pots and tin bath tubs for washing. People used the socket from the ceiling light, pulling out the globe and adding extensions to connect the cords. Extension cords ran to every corner of the room in that building and the entire camp. With people using hot plates for cooking and heating water for children's baths, the fuses blew, so there were often blackouts in the barracks. The electrician in the camp was flat out fixing fuses. It was hours before electricity was reconnected. Sometimes we had to go to bed early without electricity because there was not much one could do without light.

It seemed to be only a short time that Meta and I played together. In just a few months the news came that we were moving to a camp in Bremer Haven, and that was where we would stay until a ship was available for our journey to Australia. In preparation for the journey, we needed new clothes. Mother said, "We can't arrive in Australia like beggars." All our clothing was worn out and too small.

Double-breasted navy blue suits with light blue pin stripes were tailored for Mother and Dad, and a sailor suit was made for Czesiek. Dad's old brown suit was cut down to make a suit for me. New shoes were bought for all of us. My feet were very grateful; there was more room for my toes to move. There were new hats for Mother and Dad, and a blue bonnet for me. With all the family dressed in new clothes, it looked like we had stepped out from a scene in a movie.

While living at Wildflecken, Mother heard that Renia, one of the twins from Ludwigsburg, had died. She didn't say any more than that.

We were to sail in two days. A young woman in our dormitory had a bath and at the last minute decided to go out into the cold winter air with wet hair to buy a Christmas present for the man waiting for her in Australia. The next morning the woman woke up sick with a sore throat. The doctor was called to examine the woman. He diagnosed diphtheria. The doctor had to report it to the health authorities and all the people in the dormitory were quarantined.

That put a spanner in the works. We were all moved out from the camp, and our voyage on the ship postponed to another date. What a disappointment! My family were moved, in a private car, to a two-storey mansion. Just my family in this lovely big house with lovely gardens!

We were not allowed to leave this house. All dry food, and bread and milk, were delivered to the front door. Mother cooked our meals for us. The health welfare people came every day to see if everything was in order and that no one in the family was sick. We were treated like royalty. I'm sure Mother and Father didn't mind. It was the honeymoon they never had. After all those years in concentration, labour and refugee camps, it was a delight to be alone in a house for a few weeks. There was no expensive furniture in this house, only beds upstairs in the bedrooms and a table and chairs in the kitchen. The bathroom was the biggest attraction. It was beautiful, with a big bath and plenty of hot water.

Czesiek and I played in a little house in the garden and on the swing. We could only stay out for a little while each day as winter was coming and the days were getting colder. Czesiek and I had the big empty lounge and dining room for playing ball games, and skipping. In the early afternoon we went upstairs and hopped in the warm bath together. We were not in any hurry to get out. We must have used gallons of hot water. I kept the hot water running. The bath would never overflow because it had an outlet one-third of the way up to let the cool water out. We were in the bath until our fingers shrivelled like prunes. We stayed in the heated house for the rest of the day.

That was the best time we ever had. After three weeks, a military officer and a group of official people from the IRO and the United Nations Refugee Association (UNRA) health department came to the house late in the afternoon to make sure that everyone in the family was in good health. After the health officers had left, the military officer stayed back to translate the conversation into Polish language so that Mother and Father could understand what the health officers had been saying.

He said, "The quarantine has been lifted. The doctor said you are all in good health. Be ready to move by morning. You and your family will be picked up sometime tomorrow to be taken back to a camp and wait for the next ship. Good-bye, and have a good journey to Australia. I hope you won't have any more problems."

Father and Mother were not pleased to have to go back to camp. "I hope we won't have to wait too long for the ship," said Mother.

"If we are lucky, maybe a week, or two weeks at the most," said Father. "I don't think it will be too much longer."

While we were having the last evening meal in the house, Father said, "It has been a wonderful three weeks living in this house. Sadly, we must go back to camp once more."

It must have been a purgatory for people like my parents. For the last ten years they had not known where or when they would be going next, or how long they would be staying there.

The next morning we were ready and waiting, with some regret, to be leaving this mansion. Before Father answered the knock on the door he said, "Maybe with the help from God we will have a house to live in when we go to our new land in Australia." When Father opened the door, a soldier with sergeant stripes on his uniform sleeve stood in the doorway. He asked "Mister Dron'"

Father answered in Polish, "Yes, that's me."

"The plans have been changed," said the sergeant. "I am to drive you and your family directly to the harbour. The ship is being loaded to leave sometime today. Are you ready to go sir? I left the car doors opened for you to get in as quickly as possible."

Father yelled with excitement. "Did you hear that Anna? We are going directly to the ship!"

Dad turned to where we were sitting and said, "No more camp for us, children!"

Mother let out a sigh of relief, and said, "I will believe that when I am on the ship and halfway to Australia. Knowing our luck, we might get on the wrong ship!"

"Yes, we are ready to go sergeant!" said Father.

The sergeant said, "Take the suitcases with you. The truck will come soon to pick up the trunks."

Father was a little hesitant leaving the trunks behind. "Don't worry,' said the sergeant. 'Everything is arranged."

It was like a dream, walking out of the lovely house into the waiting car. Mother sat in the back seat with Czesiek on her knees. I sat on the other side of her and Father sat in front. It was November and the morning was bleak. Father was uneasy, watching the road for the army truck. "You can relax,' said the sergeant. 'Here is the truck on its way to pick up your luggage."

Mother looked out of the car window, enjoying the journey on the way to the Harbour, and said, "For the first time in my life I feel I am someone important – if only for a short time. To be driven by a chauffeur! It's a lovely way to travel, wouldn't you say Pawel?"

"You are always important to me, Anna. Maybe in the future I will be your chauffeur," said Father.

"We live in dreams," said Mother.

"Maybe it's not so bad dreaming for something in life," said Father.

My parents were humble people, always praying for me to get well and stay healthy. All they would pray for was health and happiness. For other things in life one must put in a good day's work, and save money wisely for a house or something important. One must never get greedy for everything one wants, only for things one needs. That was what my parents believed and I grew up with these principles.

On the way to the harbour we passed an airfield. I saw a plane close up for the first time. "Look,' I said to Father, 'Look how big the aeroplanes are."

"Yes,' said Father. 'They are the same planes you have seen flying in the sky like little toys."

"There is no chance of seeing them in the sky in this weather," said Mother.

I was astonished to see how big the aeroplanes were on the ground. Some of them were huge. I saw men unloading big crates from these huge planes.

The sergeant interrupted, saying "It's not much longer now. We'll be the first to arrive at the harbour. I wanted to get you there early to get you on board the ship before the trucks with passengers arrive. Soon there will be chaos on the harbour. The trucks will be coming from all directions most of the day."

He went on. "Some children refuse to walk the gang plank to the ship, holding up the passengers. Small children get lost in the crowd. The ship's crew are experienced at this kind of work. The children will all be taken on board and cared for until they are reunited with their parents."

"You have done this kind of work before?" asked Father.

"Yes, I have been on this job from the time the ships started to carry the people to their new country. I was appointed for this job because I can understand several languages. There are many of us soldiers in the US Army that speak different languages. It puts people at ease when the soldiers speak to them in their mother tongue."

"Where do you come from?" asked Father.

"I live in Chicago. My parents originally came from Poland." He said.

"We were considering starting our new life in America,' said Father, 'but the books were closed for immigration to America by the time we were ready to leave Germany."

The sergeant replied, "I've been told that Australia is a good country to start a new life."

As we came into the harbour, there were so many big ships, much bigger than the house we had just left. It was daunting to me. I had never seen big ships or a big body of water like the sea. The ships were much bigger than the boats I had seen on the river.

"There she is,' said the sergeant, 'the ship *Skaugum*. That is the ship you will be on soon. I am asking you to stay in the car please while I go see the captain, to see if he will let you on board right away. Get your papers ready for the officer of the ship to check them and see that everything is OK."

"Yes I have them in my coat pocket," said Father.

"OK, I'll be back soon," said the sergeant.

The sergeant left us in the car. I am sure Mother didn't mind sitting in the car a little longer. I watched the big ships waiting for passengers, all of them like the ship *Skaugum* that would carry us across the seas and oceans to our new home. I saw the sailors working on deck of the *Skaugum*, preparing her for the long voyage.

The sergeant came back and said, "Everything is arranged with the captain. You can go on board straight away."

Before we got out from the car the sergeant opened the boot and got the suitcases out. He said to Father, "I wish you and your family good health and good luck on your journey to your new home in Australia."

Mother and Father were touched by his words and the way he had everything organized. Father said, "Thank you very much for taking care and showing your kindness towards us."

"I'm willing to oblige in any way I can. Again I say to you goodbye and good luck."

Mother said to Father, "These young men fought in the war and went through hell, and yet they have the courtesy and good manners to treat us with respect and kindness."

Perhaps Mother said this because some people had been a pain and difficult to deal with. Being transported from one end of Germany to the other made people tired and angry. The soldiers took some words of abuse at times, yet they tolerated it with patience.

After World War II, the Australian government was faced with the problem of a small population in a vast country. The government adopted the slogan 'Populate or Perish', and opened the door to immigration. Government policy was that nine out of ten immigrant families would come from English speaking countries to make their homes in Australia. But this was not realistic. The only ships available to transport migrants were contracted to IRO, and had to bring displaced people from European countries. So the Australian Minister for Immigration, Arthur Caldwell, tried to choose single young people from Baltic countries like Estonia and Lithuania, who were of good character and able to work hard.

Dad and the other men laughed at this idea. They said that the IRO didn't have time to choose what country people came from. There were too many people to be housed and taken care of; the IRO just wanted to ship them out. The ships were filled with families from every country in Europe, families that were already processed for immigration. It was a big job in itself for the authorities to take care of the sick people who had to stay in Europe until they were well and fit enough to work hard. My family had to stay in Germany until I was in good health. By the time my health had improved, some countries had already closed their doors to immigration.

This was the first post-war immigration to Australia on a large scale. Mr Caldwell and his government were not prepared for such a big influx of families from the other side of the world. The ships coming to Australia carried thousands of immigrants, single people and families. Sometimes three ships in one week arrived in Australia, one after the other.

THE SHIP SKAUGUM

We were ready to board the ship. The gangplank was made of slats, and I saw the gaps between the slats. It was a long way between the ship and wharf. It was a long way down to fall off the plank into the water. Fear overcame me, the kind of fear that strikes me at night when I am sleeping and dreaming of falling a long way down. My legs wouldn't move. I cried out, "Dad, I can't walk, I can't move!"

Father could see that I was terrified. "Don't worry,' he said. 'You stay with your mother. I will take the suitcases up and come back for you."

When he came back, he said, "Get on my back and put your hands around my neck. I will hold on to you."

I wasn't too sure about that but I had no choice. I trusted Father and did what he said. He carried me across the plank and I held onto him for grim death. Mother followed, carrying Czesiek in her arms. We were only a few steps from the ship when a funny noise came from Dad's mouth. He started to buckle at the knees. His face was turning blue. As soon as Dad put his foot on the ship he dropped me off his back like a bag of hot coals. He bent over with his hands on his knees.

Mother was worried. She thought that Father was having a heart attack. "Pawel! What's wrong Pawel?"

Dad waved his hand to indicate that he was alright. We waited for a few minutes. The colour came back to his face. When he got his breath back he straightened himself up and said, "I am glad that was a short plank. A few more steps and we would both be fished out from the sea! You sure have strength in those arms Terese. You held on to my throat so tight I couldn't breathe."

Mother was relieved that Father was alright, but commented quietly, "Terese is growing stronger every day.'

We made it on board the ship with not much fuss, only Father's neck was a little red. That was the last piggy-back ride for me!

The ship's steward showed us below deck to large dormitories in the ship's hold. "This is where the women and their small children sleep," he said. Rows of single bunks stood in the middle of the dormitory, and double rows of bunks lined the wall. The steward gave instructions: "Mother and child have a single bunk in the middle. The bigger and single girls sleep in the bunks along the wall. There are no quarters for families or married couples on this ship. Each bunk is numbered. Brown paper bags are on each bunk. These are to be used when one gets sick through the night, and take them with you during the day. We don't have buckets for all the passengers – use the bags and keep the sheets clean."

The steward handed the bunk numbers to Mother, saying "These are the bunk numbers for you and your children. You can put your suitcase under the bunk." The steward noticed the suitcase beside Father, and said, "That's a good suitcase. I don't see suitcases like that on the ship."

"This suitcase is genuine crocodile," said Father.

"It must have cost you a packet," said the steward.

"Yes – a carton of cigarettes and a handful of marks!"

"Yes, I see it's a fine suitcase. There is one thing you won't have to worry about sir. No one can walk off this ship in a hurry with a fine suitcase of that size and not be seen."

Without any more comment on the suitcase, Father slid the big black genuine crocodile-skin suitcase under Mother's bunk. That's where our clothes were kept during the journey. We were given strict instructions by the steward not to swap beds. No-one was to stay in the dormitory during the day. Everyone had to be on deck. If any person or child was sick, the ship had a sick bay and a doctor to take care of the sick. We were again reminded to take the brown bags with us in case we got sick up on deck.

On the way to the men's dormitory, the steward showed us the bathroom and the laundry, telling us that salt water was used for washing and showers. He then led us to the steps that led to the mess hall. "You stay,' he said to Mother. 'I will take your husband to his dormitory. You can help yourself to a cup of tea or coffee when your husband comes back.

'The mess hall room is open all day for tea and coffee, and there is fruit left on the table for passengers to help themselves through the day. Breakfast is from seven to nine, lunch is from twelve to two, and tea is from five pm. The dining room is closed at seven pm."

In a short time, Father was back and the dining room was opened. We walked in and had a drink of tea with biscuits. Mother found a spot on deck sheltered from the cold wind to sit and watch the convoy of trucks arriving with the passengers. Trucks with luggage followed behind. It was just like the sergeant had said: trucks arriving with people one after the other, all at one time from different camps. Most of the children were small and could not walk the gang plank. Some children got lost in the crowd. It happened just like the sergeant said it would.

The captain's officer announced to the passengers in several languages to not worry, the lost children would be taken care of by the ship's crew. There were Red Cross ladies helping children to cross the gang plank. Small children were given a piggy-back ride across the plank by the ship's crew. The children were entertained on the ship until parents came on board and fetched their little darlings. I mean that in a nice way: the little children were frightened but well behaved.

Father watched the men loading the ship, looking out for our luggage. He didn't have to wait long. Our trunks arrived on the first truck, followed by a truckload of passengers we recognised. Our dark cherry red trunks, with our name and AUSTRALIA written in white, stood out from the rest being loaded into the ship's storage. It took a load off Dad's mind, knowing that our luggage was on board safely. Everything on the wharf was going like clockwork.

Excitement rose as people came on board, meeting friends they had made in the camps but had lost contact with when moving from one camp to another. Father watched people walking up the gangplank, looking out to see if some of our friends might be travelling with us. He recognised two families; we had been very close with one of them at one stage. He went to greet them as they came on the ship. The passengers were coming on board all day long, until it was tea time. It was well into the night by the time everything was loaded.

The ship left Bremer Haven late at night on the 6th of November, 1950. Most of the passengers were asleep as the ship cruised on the North Sea towards the English Channel. It was the next morning when we were trying to get out of bed that we felt the effect of the sea. The steward knocked before opening the door. He said we must all get out of the bed and dressed. "No one is to stay in bunks lying about. You must all go to the dining-room for breakfast or make your way up onto the deck."

Mother, Czesiek and I, like most people in the dormitory, had trouble getting up and putting our feet to the floor. We felt dizzy. The constant swaying of the ship upset our balance. Slowly we got dressed and found our way to the stairs. Father was already waiting to carry Czesiek up to the dining room. Mother and I, feeling light-headed, had to hold onto the rail and walk slowly up the stairs; fast movement was not wise. What made us feel worse was that people walked in front of us, not using their brown bags, and vomiting on the stairs. That made us sick.

Breakfast was out of the question for Mother, Czesiek and me. We managed somehow to get on deck and find a place to sit away from the worst of the bitter cold and the sea spray. Wrapped in blankets, we sat on deck like three drunken sardines, not able to move during the day, not able to say a word to one another. Father was the one taking care of us, bringing hot tea. Just the word "food" turned our stomachs; sweet, warm, weak tea was all we could manage to drink for the first three days.

It was difficult to go below deck after sitting on deck. Winter on the North Sea was cold, but that was Mother's choosing. It was the only place we could get away from seeing people sick. It was difficult to sleep in the dormitory. It was stuffy and smelly with no windows to open for fresh air. We would have stayed out on the deck all night if it was summer. Getting up in the mornings was not a pleasant experience. Most of the passengers in the dormitory had used their paper bags during the night. Mother and I were not excluded; we used the brown bags, throwing up the tea. Sitting out on deck was cold, and Mother worried about my lungs.

Father reassured her. "Terese is fine,' he said. 'She is wrapped well in her sable coat."

"I don't know how I am going to manage the journey,' said Mother. 'The smell of the sea is unbearable to me."

"I will ask the doctor if he may have something to help you," said Father.

He came back with a lovely smelling hanky. Mother held it close to her face, and it relieved her of the sea smell. "You could go in the games room,' suggested Father. 'You can't be sitting out all day in the cold."

Some of the children were running around, playing games on deck. I could not move. I asked Mother, "Why am I sick? Why can't I run and play like the other children?"

"I don't know,' she said. 'Maybe in a few days we will all be better."

After three days our bodies settled down. We were getting hungry. We made our way to the dining room for breakfast and I managed to eat a bowl of porridge with plenty of milk. There was always plenty of fruit left on the table: oranges, apples and bananas. We were to help ourselves to as much as we wanted to eat between meals. But there was no fear of overeating; most people could only eat small meals.

One night the ship went through a storm. We had trouble sleeping and our bodies were tossed from one side of the bunk to the other. There were a lot of brown bags used that night. Next morning the dining room was almost empty. Hardly anyone turned up for breakfast. Boiled eggs were on the menu. The dining room was kept open for half an hour longer for the latecomers. A forty-four gallon drum was brought out from the kitchen half-full of boiled eggs. The cook's assistant told everyone on deck that we could help ourselves to the eggs.

The children playing on deck ate some. At morning tea time the rest of the eggs were tossed overboard.

Male passengers, including Father, had cleaning duties to perform on the ship. They were paid in packets of cigarettes. In those days, most men smoked, and they were glad of a packet or two. The captain of the ship had cut down on the cleaning crew to make more room for single male passengers.

We spent weeks on the ship passing the coastlines of many countries. The days on deck got warmer as the ship sailed into the Mediterranean Sea. An officer of the ship announced that passengers should wind their watches and clocks forward. This happened several times during the voyage, depending on what part of ocean the ship was travelling through. I was with my parents on deck when the ship was cruising past a country. I could see mountains in the distance. Father said the ship was passing Africa. I wished the ship was closer to the coast so I could see the monkeys eating bananas and swinging from tree to tree, and the elephants. How big and strong they were in the pictures I saw in the comic books we had at school, learning about African animals.

At about eight o'clock one evening, the ship stopped at Port Said to refill with fuel, water and provisions. To a ten year girl, it was strange to see buildings with flat roofs, and the silhouette of the palm trees. The sky was deep velvet blue. The stars and the crest of the moon made a beautiful picture.

In the morning, the *Skaugum* entered the Suez Canal. Father gave me a short lesson on history and geography, telling me that the land was cut away by big machines driven by men. They worked very hard for many years to dig the canal, separating this small part of land from Arabia and letting the water from the Mediterranean Sea join the Red Sea to make a shorter and safer voyage to the Indian Ocean.

This was my first experience of seeing a live camel walking along the edge of the bank. The only camel I had seen before was a picture on a packet of cigarettes. This was the place were two ships were destined to meet: the ship of the sea cruising in the Suez Canal and the "ship of the desert" walking alongside the iron giant. The donkey was another animal I hadn't seen before, walking with his master, carrying a big load hanging over each side.

I said to Dad, "There are no trees, and the people dress in strange clothes."

"That is because we are travelling in a different country, Egypt on one side of the ship and Arabia on the other side. People dress in clothes that are cool and suitable in hot countries like these," said Father.

The moment Father said "Egypt", and when I saw the way people were dressed, a strange feeling came over me and a picture formed in my mind: Joseph leading the donkey that Mary was riding, carrying her baby Jesus. Father Bonkowski had told us the story of King Herod in his wrath giving the order to his soldiers to kill every child up to the age of two in Bethlehem. That was when the Angel appeared to Joseph in a dream, warning him of the danger and telling him to take baby Jesus to Egypt.

There were no tall buildings or big trees to obstruct the view from the ship. I could see long distances into these strange countries of Egypt and Arabia, so different to where we came from. It was very hot as the ship cruised through the canal. The children playing on deck stayed in the shade, saying how hot it was. It was the first time in our lives we had experienced that kind of heat.

The most memorable images of the voyage to me were the beautiful sunsets in that part of the world. Half of the blue sky turned into breathtaking colours of soft pink and then orange from the red hot sun before it set on the horizon. The sky then turned almost red. When the sun was over the horizon, the evening skies faded into soft yellow and then a midnight blue.

In the early hours of the morning, the ship entered the Red Sea. It was very hot in the dormitory and I was restless, unable to sleep. The time zone was constantly changing and our biological clock was disrupted. I got out of my bunk and went up on deck to sit in the cool air. As the sun rose, misty clouds appeared on the distant horizon, giving an illusion of mountains. The clouds closer to the ship made it even more convincing, forming a lovely picture. That was something worth getting up early for. As the sun rose higher the illusion of the mountains in the distance faded away and the sunlight caught in the ripples of water looked like twinkling stars dancing on the sea. The fluffy clouds were with us all day as the ship travelled through this part of the sea, changing into different shapes during the day.

Late in the afternoon the clouds grew bigger and eventually filled the low parts of the sky. They looked like swirls of whipped cream covering a vast area of sky. The sea was smooth, not a ripple in the water. It was like a mirror reflecting the most glorious sky. The setting sun turned the white clouds slightly pink, with brilliant white edgings. The sun appeared through a part of broken cloud and brilliant light spread over the vast sea. On the still water, the horizon line was almost eliminated and it was difficult to tell if the sun was setting or rising. It was as if the ship was floating on clouds of fairy floss.

I don't know how long the ship travelled on the Red Sea. The sky was never the same. The patterns in the clouds changed as we travelled through the day. Sometimes the clouds formed like islands and it appeared as if a river ran through them. It was like looking at an atlas in the sky. I remember one day when the sky was blue and cloudless. As the sun set, light streaks of pink appeared across the sky, turning the blue into a pale mauve and purple and, finally, midnight blue. The banana moon and the stars appeared. On some cloudy nights, the clouds moved fast and gave the illusion that the moon was travelling across the sky with us as we sailed through the water.

Recently I was watching a documentary film on Egypt. The sunset was the same as I remember all those years ago. The rising and setting of the sun is one of the things in this universe that will never change, although the sun is not always seen, some days hidden by rain clouds. The brilliance of the sun is always somewhere in the sky. As much as I love pictures of trees and gardens on the walls of my house, I would gladly exchange them for a picture of the beautiful sunset on the Red Sea.

As I was writing this part of the book, I received a simple Christmas card from my close friend, Sister St Paul, who had been my primary school teacher in Australia. The picture on the card was the same image I saw in my mind when we were travelling on the Suez Canal: Joseph leading the donkey, and Mary riding it, holding her child Jesus in her arms.

The ship docked at Aden. It was to stay in port all day to fill up with fresh water, food and fuel. The captain announced to the passengers that we must not leave the ship. He didn't give a reason. That was a pity. I wanted to go ashore and walk through the street bazaar, but that was not to be. Later in the day there was a rumour circulating on board the ship of a confrontation brewing between Egypt and Arabia. That was the reason the passengers had to stay on the ship.

Peddlers from the Aden bazaars came on board the ship and set up a stall on the deck for the day, displaying and selling watches, jewellery, wall carpets, lovely ladies' slippers decorated with sequins, dress material (possibly silk), and holy pictures and rosary beads of all sizes. Some of the rosaries were so small that the case and the rosary could fit in the palm of the hand. I had never seen such lovely things. My wish at the time was that I could buy the small rosary beads but I had to walk away from what my heart desired. A kind of hurtful feeling came over me. I felt disappointed not to be able to buy just the small rosary beads; that would have made me happy.

The ship left Aden very late in the afternoon. The dolphins in the sea played their part in entertaining the passengers, swimming along with the ship as if they were escorting us into the Indian Ocean. There would be no more stops, as the ship was travelling the shortest route to Australia. Only on a ship do you gain some idea of how vast the ocean is.

The children on the ship were entertained every day with movies. Before the film started we were taught to sing songs in English. I still remember the songs: "My Bonnie Lies over the Ocean", "Are You Sleeping Brother John?", "Waltzing Matilda" and the anthem "God Save Our King". The movies were comedies starring Charlie Chaplin, Abbott and Costello, Laurel and Hardy, the Marx Brothers and the Three Stooges. We loved the movies. The Keystone Cops were most favoured. We were in fits of laughter watching those funny movies every day. The children were well taken care of.

For the adults there was a swimming pool and entertainment in the evenings. Some of the young people danced on the deck to music played by the men on piano-accordion, harmonica, violin and balalaika. Our journey on the ship was never dull. English lessons were held for a few hours each day, five days a week, for the people who were interested to learn.

About a week or so on the Indian Ocean, the deck chairs and everything on deck was put away. The captain and the ship's crew were preparing for a big storm. I was playing with two boys and didn't notice the deck being cleared and everyone gone. The boys and I were having fun. The front of the ship was nose down and up again, the big waves spilling over the top of ship and all that water running through the deck and back into the sea. We held onto the railing, not realising the danger. Just one slip and the three of us could have gone overboard with the waves. No one would have known what had happened to us. By the time we would have been missed, the ship would be miles away and we would have drowned.

It was fortunate for us that one of the officers saw us on deck before the storm was at its worst. His face turned grey coming down the stairs. He grabbed the arms of the two boys and told me to hang on to one of the boys' hands really tight. We were soaked to the skin. With a lot of swearing under his breath, the officer took us into the games room. The steward wrapped us in blankets and our parents were notified to come and pick us up. We changed our clothes and we came back to the games room to watch movies.

The sea was calm the next morning, but there was excitement on the ship. The crew were decorating the area around the pool for a celebration because we were to cross the equator some time that day. The sailors were dressed in costumes with their faces painted to resemble a sea creature. A party was held to welcome the arrival of King Neptune. He left the undersea kingdom, riding his chariot through the waves pulled by a team of seahorses. King Neptune sat in the pool on his temporary throne for the ceremony of initiation as the ship crossed the equator. The king of the sea demanded sacrifices to be made to him. The sea creatures targeted young people wearing bathing costumes for sacrifice. The young people had to be polite and obey. It was not wise to upset the powerful king as he was the god of the sea and had the power to cause earthquakes. To upset him would be a big mistake...! I sat to one side watching, and wishing I could be of the age to join the young people playing in the pool having a wonderful time.

During our voyage in the Indian Ocean, our ship *Skaugum* passed another IRO Immigration Ship carrying passengers to Australia. We were too far away to get a glimpse of the other ship's name. In the dining hall that evening, the news was that the ship we had passed hours before was slowly sinking. Mother was distressed by the news. She said, "I am frightened for those people on the ship we passed. Surely they must be rescued."

Dad assured Mother that no one would drown. He told her that a ship was on its way to save the passengers from the crippled ship. The next day, it was rumoured that after our voyage was over, *Skaugum* was to go back to pick up the passengers from that ship, believed to be the *Anna Salen*, and bring them to Australia. I am glad to say that I heard no news of any big drama on our voyage.

Only one accident happened on our ship. A woman was hanging out washing on deck on a Sunday and fell on something sharp. She ripped the top of her leg thigh open and was rushed to the sick bay. Her deep cut was stitched. In a week she was back in the dormitory. There was no sympathy for the woman; she was shunned by some of the women. They said she had brought this punishment on herself for washing on Sunday. In those days people finished work on Saturday evening for the weekend and no work was done until Monday. Sunday was taken seriously as a day of rest for going to church, spending time together with the family or for visiting relatives. Stories from the Bible were told to the children. My mother wouldn't even pick up scissors to cut a thread on Sunday. It was a day of rest and respected as that.

At breakfast on Saturday, the 9th of December, the captain announced that the ship would dock at Melbourne sometime that day. I was with my parents on deck when the ship cruised past Kangaroo Island on the way to Melbourne. As soon as *Skaugum* came close to the coastline every passenger was on deck to take a first glimpse at Australia. We were curious to see the country that we, the New Australian people, were going to settle in and call home. Some of the passengers were expecting to see Aborigines' humpies on the shore. Other passengers were expecting the Aborigines to be dressed in their native clothes and to be at the wharf dancing with spears in their hands to greet us in the same way they greeted Captain Cook.

It was a surprise then, as we came closer to Melbourne, to see commercial buildings in the city, much the same as in Europe. The ship docked at Port Melbourne in the afternoon. It was hot. The captain said that passengers would have to remain on board the ship until Monday morning because the Office for Immigration and Customs was closed on Saturday afternoon and didn't re-open until Monday morning. The passengers were disappointed that we had to stay another day on this overcrowded ship.

Recently, I was talking to a chap who happened to be travelling on the same voyage as me coming to Australia. I asked him if he could tell me anything more about what may have happened on the ship. He told me that he remembered a young man jumping from the ship into the harbour when the ship docked at Melbourne that afternoon, but he didn't know the outcome.

On Monday morning, the captain said goodbye to all the passengers and wished us good fortune in our new land. The Australian people were very pleasant towards us as we went through customs. This may have been because of the way we responded to them by saying "Good morning' and 'Thank you" in English. We were directed to shiny new buses that were waiting to take us to our destination. I had never travelled in a bus before, which is possibly why my eyes were attracted to them.

BONEGILLA TO COWRA

I will always remember the first day travelling on dusty roads in this strange land. My eyes focussed on the land and the scruffy bush. The leaves looked dirty. Everything looked dry. The trees were different from the trees in Europe. I didn't see a patch of green on the dry ground, and there were no houses or towns in that part of the country. The temperature in the bus was unbearably hot. Every person on the bus was wet from perspiration. We had no water to drink on this long journey until the bus stopped for lunch at a military camp. I was behind Dad as he stepped off the bus. When I put my feet on the ground the hot wind blew up my dress. I felt the heat from the ground as if I had stepped over a fire. I looked around as we walked to the mess hall. The ground was dry and some patches of grass were dead. I had never felt heat like this before.

I shook Dad's arm and asked him, "Dad, did we die and go to Hell?"

My question took Father by surprise. Before he could gather his thoughts to answer me, Mother said, "No, we have not died yet, but not far from it."

"No,' said Father. 'We are very much alive. We have arrived in the summer months. This country, it is closer to the sun. The heat is much stronger than it is in Europe."

"It's hot like Hell," I grumbled.

"It won't be hot like this all the time,' said Dad. 'It will cool when it rains."

"Does it rain in Australia? Everything looks dry like there is no rain in this country," I asked.

"We have to learn to live with this heat. We can't go back. It's not always hot like this. It will get cooler in the winter."

"Maybe it won't be so hot next summer," said Mother.

Our first lunch in Australia was cooked and served by the Australian soldiers. The tables were laid with meat and salad sandwiches, cakes and oranges on trays, coffee and tea for adults, and milk for children. I noticed that the bread was square and the sandwiches were cut from corner to corner. Back in Germany, the bread was round like a damper and Mother would cut the sandwiches into half circles. These square sandwiches looked appealing, and eating them was even better. After lunch, every child was given a banana to take with them.

Back on the bus my attention was drawn again to the environment so different from Europe. We had never seen or felt anything like this before. It was as if we had arrived on a different planet. The heat and the long distance travel were tiring for Czesiek and me. We leaned our heads on our parents and fell asleep until we reached our destination.

The bus drove through the gates to Bonegilla Camp. I saw rows and rows of huts.

"Santa Maria!" Mother cried out with horror. She put her hands to her face. She couldn't believe what she was seeing. "Is this what we are to live in? Huts?!"

The bus driver drove to the end of the camp where the huts, our temporary home, were ready for us. The bus stopped. As we got off the bus, the driver gave us a number for our hut.

Father opened the hut door. It was as if he had opened an oven door. Mother was still in shock. Her eyes filled with tears. "This is not much better than a hen's pen! We are going to fry in this tin hut!"

The long hut was divided into several small rooms by partition walls clad on one side. Each "room" was for one family. There was a door and a small window, but no insect screens. There was no bathroom or running water, and no fan. One electric light hung from the roof. Mother and Father thought they had left this behind in Germany. But they had chosen Australia as their new home, and we had to be grateful that at least we were provided with a roof over our heads.

I looked at Father. Disappointment showed on his face. There were only three beds in our "room", each one made up with dark grey blankets. That meant Father had to sleep somewhere else. The first day in Australia, and again families were separated. The separation on the ship was understood but this was something else.

"How can this be?!' cried Mother. 'We came to live in the land of milk and honey where the streets were paved with gold! That was the picture we were shown in the movies. What went wrong Pawel? What kind of future is this for us? How long will we have to live like this?"

Father had no answers. He saw how upsetting this was for Mother. I imagine he felt the same way. He was lost for words.

'How long will we have to live in these primitive conditions?" asked Mother again.

What was Father to say? I don't suppose he knew any more than Mother did, but, trying to reassure her, he said, "I will get a job soon. Maybe we will move into a house."

"A house!' said Mother. 'From what I have seen of this country so far, there aren't many houses about."

"Anna, I can only tell you we won't be saying in this camp for long," said Father

I had no questions to ask. My home was with my parents.

On the first morning, I stepped out from the hut just as the sun was rising. I sat on the step trying to familiarize myself with this strange country. The morning was hot like the day before. As the dawn turned into day, the air was filled with a fresh smell from the trees that grew along the fence of Australian homes neighbouring the camp. It was a change from the smell of ocean. I watched the beautiful coloured birds flying about from one tree to another.

I stepped out from the hut greeted by the morning sun

my nostrils filled by the fresh smell from tall trees

reaching on towards the sky

with drooping leaves of soft green and grey

gentle breeze moving the tree branches to a sway

pretty birds flying about free from tree to tree

the black and white birds yodelling

the big blue winged birds laughing

the pink and grey birds screeching

the sound of the birds is new to me

the smell gets stronger as that day is getting longer

the trees are different in a country hot and dry

different from the countries of Europe far away

Mother was dressed and ready for breakfast. We walked a short distance to the mess hall. The hall was decorated for Christmas with coloured streamers and paper lanterns. It looked impressive and inviting. I would like to have said the same about the breakfast. There was flour in what one would have called scrambled eggs; then again, the eggs may have been powdered. The rolled oats were like glue. We had toast and an orange. Mother and I didn't like bitter jam. For lunch the menu was old mutton stew. For us, the smell of mutton was nauseating and it was unpleasant to eat. Mutton fat stuck to one's gums and teeth. Sweet mashed potato and mashed pumpkin were the kinds of food we were not accustomed to eating. And boiled cabbage – well that was something else.

We had to learn to eat Australian food. We were hungry, and forced ourselves to eat the mutton stew. When Dad got work, he had to pay for this insult to our taste buds and stomachs. (When the men got work, they paid for food and accommodation at the camp.) My parents were not impressed with the meals in camp. It was something we would feed the dogs. Thank goodness there was bread and butter on the table, and an orange or apple for each person.

The amenities were in a shack separate from the huts, but with little privacy. This camp was built for soldiers, not families. Every time I used the primitive amenities, my eyes were focussed on the ground for lizards, snakes and crocodiles, and I watched out for spiders on the latrine seats. I certainly didn't come all the way across the ocean to die from the bite of a snake or a little red back spider. I thank the stars above that I did not encounter this.

The camp wasn't the only disappointment my parents faced. Father received news from customs that the eiderdowns Mother had brought from Germany had been confiscated because they were made of feathers. The crockery she had wrapped in the eiderdowns broke when the eiderdowns were taken out of the trunks. Mother wept. The eiderdowns were very expensive because it is time consuming work preparing the down feathers. It takes many hours to strip the feathers, and months to accumulate enough feathers to make one eiderdown. Mother had spent the money, promising herself that her family would have warm and comfortable beds to sleep in after the freezing nights we had suffered during the war. If she had known this would happen she would have kept the money and saved for a house.

We only saw Dad in the evenings. During the day he picked up odd jobs while he waited for a permanent position. Every evening, Mother and Father walked outside, past the end of the huts, to say goodnight. One evening, when Mother was on her way back, she was attracted by a creature in a tree near our hut. It was Mother's first encounter with an Australian animal. She came back a little excited, saying "Terese, I saw a cat in the tree! The cats are different in this country, not like cats in Europe! This cat is the same size as a normal cat. It has big eyes and little hands and a hook on the tail."

The next evening, on the way back from the mess hall, Mother pointed out the tree to Czesiek and me. The tree was no bigger than a tall shrub. Mother brought bread and jam to feed the new little new friend. "Look Czesiek!' she said. 'Look at this strange cat taking bread from my hand!"

Czesiek wasn't that impressed with this strange cat. He had never seen a cat before anyway. We learned that "the cat" was a possum.

The heat in the hut was unbearable. On most nights Mother left the door open, hoping a breeze would come and cool the walls and the roof, but the light attracted insects. As we were getting ready for bed, a big praying mantis flew into the room. I saw its coloured wings for a brief moment before Mother threw a sheet over Czesiek and me to protect us from being bitten by this insect. When it landed on the floor, Mother swept it out the door. I haven't seen a praying mantis since that night in the hut. Now I think back, the Australian soldiers who had lived in those huts, the men and women who sacrificed their young lives, deserved better.

A Christmas party was organised for the new Australians in the mess hall. The tables were set up with fruit, sweet biscuits and soft drinks. It looked so good. This was possibly the first Christmas party for some children. We had fun pulling the bon-bons: a little surprise, a paper hat and a small toy popping out. I remember eating the fairy cakes and waiting for the big moment.

Santa arrived on a big red fire engine, bringing with him a bag of toys and a bag of sweets. The children ran out to greet him. I couldn't decide which the bigger attraction was: Santa dressed in red with his floppy pointed cap and black gum boots, or the vintage red fire engine with brass fittings that caught every eye in the camp. It certainly drew the big boys' attention. They couldn't resist climbing on the vehicle. Eventually the driver took the older boys and girls for a short ride in the camp grounds.

Christmas in Australia was different. On Christmas morning we walked some distance in the heat to the community hall at the other end of the camp to a Christmas mass service. The hall was decorated with balloons and coloured paper streamers and on the stage stood an Australian Christmas tree. This hall was used for parties and the dancing on Christmas Eve. The same hall was used for church services on Sunday mornings. The mass was said by a Polish Priest. It was strange attending Christmas mass in a hall. In Europe there were many old churches in the villages and cities. Whatever camp we had stayed in, we had always walked through the snow to attend mass in a church.

I would like to have said I was looking forward to a good Christmas dinner, but, knowing what the food was like, I didn't hope for much on Christmas Day. We had a choice of roast old hogget or rabbit, and baked sweet potato, baked pumpkin and green beans. That was a change from cabbage. The baked vegetables looked good, but they were baked in mutton fat, and the beans were stringy. I chose baked rabbit and the spoiled baked vegetables. I left most of my dinner on the plate and ate the Christmas pudding. That was a change from every day bread and jam, or the usual Sunday special, rice pudding.

I loved going to church with my family and uniting with the people to pray and to sing hymns. The church service lifted our spirits for the purpose of living from one week to another and helped us cope with unpleasant things in life that may arise. A Polish priest said Mass on Sundays for all the people from different countries, and many people joined in, even the Italians. People left Europe to leave their tragedies behind and the priest welcomed the people into this new country. He stayed back after the service to talk with people about how he could help with everyday problems people were experiencing.

The people reached out for help. Some people had left their families and good friends behind in Europe. Separating from them to start a new life in a far away country was painful. People were still trying to deal with the loss of families wiped out in the war. They turned to the priest, who listened to their sad stories with sympathy and understanding. The people looked to the priest to give them comfort. He would try to consult every one of these people to ease their troubled minds.

Living in Bonegilla camp, we made the best of a bad situation. Mother soon learned that the Australian neighbours grew vegetables and would sell them to the people in camp. She took the opportunity to meet the neighbours and bought salad vegetables from them. I walked over with Mother and waited with Czesiek at the back gate while Mother bought tomatoes, onions and little apple size cucumbers. That was something different. I had only seen the long green cucumbers.

Mother became one of the neighbours' best customers, buying salad vegetables and eggs. She made sandwiches and salads when the food in the mess hall was unpleasant to eat (and that was most of the time.) Father would often eat with us. He bought Mother a kerosene primus stove to boil the eggs, and sometimes Mother cooked Maggi chicken soup on this small stove. The only foods I ate from the mess hall were oranges, bread with plum jam, and sometimes rice pudding.

On Sundays, after the church service, Father bought a half loaf of sliced bread and Australian empire sausage at the camp canteen, and we walked over to the Hume Dam for a picnic lunch. Sometimes we would meet people from the ship *Skaugum* and pass the day with them. Czesiek and I paddled our feet in the water to get some relief from the heat. Most of the people living in the camp spent their Sundays on the Hume Dam. It was an outing for families with empty pockets. On the way back to the huts we stopped at the canteen and Father bought each one of us an ice-cream.

Father took me to see the movies that were held in the camp community hall in the evenings. Before we went inside the hall, Dad gave me money to buy myself an ice-cream while he lit a cigarette outside the shop. I stood in the queue, waiting to be served. A man standing behind me started to talk to me and offered to buy me an ice-cream. I said to him that I had money of my own. He then said, "I will buy you a chocolate. Would you like that?"

"No, thank you," I said politely. I felt uneasy and hoped that he would get lost. Maybe he was just being friendly. I told him that my father was waiting for me outside the shop.

The movie that Father and I saw that night was a lovely concert movie. A pianist was playing beautiful music on a grand piano, accompanied by an orchestra on a floor floating on water. The floor broke away from the shore as the pianist played, rapt in his lovely music, and unaware of the floor drifting out to sea. That is all I remember of the movie. I fell in love with the beautiful music and my heart filled with joy. I left the hall with my Dad a happy little girl.

I said nothing to Father of the incident in the shop. I completely forgot about it. With music in my mind, nothing else mattered that evening. I told Mother the next day and she advised me not to go out on my own and to keep away from drunken men. Mother told me that when she was a young girl she saw a young woman stabbed by a drunken man.

The time had come for men to leave their families and join the workforce away from the camp. The men were informed by letter and placed wherever there was a position to be filled. On the 13th of January, Father received a letter from the Commonwealth Employment Service:

> *Arrangements have been made to place you, Mr Dron, in the employment of the New South Wales Railways Chief Mechanical Engineer at Enfield, NSW, as a labourer. You should commence work on arrival. The hours and shifts will be 40 hrs 5 days per week. Your wages will be minimum 9 pounds 2 shillings per week less tax. Board and lodging as per arrangement. You will leave Bonegilla on the 15th of January 1951 and the travel arrangements made for you are as follows: Leave Albury by train at 3:20 pm. On arrival at Sydney Central Station you will be met by a representative of your employer and given an allowance for two meals. You will remember that the Certificate of Exemption granted to you under the Immigration Act 1901-1949 requires you for a period of up to two years to engage in such employment as the Commonwealth Employment Service on behalf of the Minister for Immigration approves.*

A change of employment could be arranged only if there were very special reasons to justify it. Nothing was said in the letter about how far Sydney was from Bonegilla. There were no arrangements made for us to be together as a family. Mother was left alone in the camp with us two children. Mother didn't know if she would see Father again. She had no idea how big the states were, or how many there were. When the men left the camp for their work destinations, no-one knew when children would see their Dad, or when a wife would see her husband.

That night, it was difficult for Mother and I to sleep in the hot huts, left alone and facing the fact that Father was not with us. There were many families in the same position. I heard children outside playing and I went out to join them. It was a clear night filled with stars. For something to do, we counted them. There was something different in the sky that night. Behind a thin crest of moon were two stars. The three objects were in line, and all the same distance from one another. In the years since that night, I have watched the sky to see if this will appear again. I once saw one star behind the crest of the moon, but not the two stars.

The women were sad, left behind with their children and heavy hearts. They held back their tears so as not to upset the children. To pass the time the women grouped together for company and supported one another. During the day they found themselves a spot in the shade of the trees to work on their knitting, crochet and embroidery. They learned craft from one another, making things and hoping to put them in their homes some time soon.

Sometimes Mother joined in, sitting with the women to discuss things of everyday life, such as where their husbands had been sent to work, and their plans to leave the camp. I was usually with Czesiek, not far from Mother. One time, I heard the women talking about their husbands' wages. They said there was no way they could save money staying in the camp. Most of their earnings were eaten up by camp fees, and their husbands' board and lodging. There was little left to save. I heard the women say they were grateful that the Australian government issued endowment money of five shillings for the first child, and two pounds for three children. That was spent on food for the children, as the children were not able to eat the food from the mess kitchen.

Mother looked forward to going to the neighbours' home gardens to buy vegetables. It was an outing for her, and she had a chance to associate with the Australian people. She managed to say a few words like "Good morning" or "Good afternoon" and "How do you do?" She waited for the answer she had learned in the English classes held each afternoon: "Very well, thank you." But the answer was mostly "Fine thanks," "Good thanks" or "Fair to middling." That was not the answer she was expecting. This kind of talk was baffling to us newcomers.

Just three weeks after the men left Bonegilla, a young woman lost her husband. He was working for the forestry department, and was killed by a falling tree. Mother knew the young woman. She had come to Australia on the *Skaugum*, and she lived in the partitioned room at the end of our hut. Like most of the women, Mother was very upset. The young woman was devastated. She was unable to speak English and had no family she could turn to for support. Living in a camp, it was difficult to keep friends. People stayed for a short time and were then moved to other camps. The little girl kept asking her mother, "When is Daddy coming to take us away?"

How is a mother to tell her little girl that she will not see her father again? How is a little girl to cope with losing her father? The mother must be strong for her little girl when they are left on their own to start life in a new country. This woman turned to the priest for support.

The holidays were over. On the evening before I was to start school, I fell ill with a high temperature, shivering, vomiting and diarrhoea. Mother was frightened and called for the doctor to come to the hut. The doctor examined my throat, and checked my blood pressure and temperature. He said that I would be alright after a few days. He wrote a prescription for something to settle my stomach, and said that I should drink plenty of water and lemonade, and that I should stay in bed for a few days. This was the time Mother needed Dad's help. She worried when her children were sick. It was difficult for Mother to be on her own when the only communication was by mail. I recovered from the illness and was soon backing on my feet. I started my first lessons in an Australian school two weeks after the other children.

I stood at the school bus stop with children I didn't know. I felt completely alone. The hot sun burned my skin. I looked around to see if there was a tree close by that I could stand under. Just before the bus arrived, a girl came up to me and took hold of my hand. Speaking in Polish, she introduced herself and said, "My name is Danusza."

She was a little older than I was. She had been in the camp much longer than me and had started school at the end of the previous year. She knew some words in English and I was so relieved to have someone to help me. We boarded the bus together and travelled the short distance to Bonegilla Public School. Danusza and I walked into the school grounds together. I sat on the seat under the tree while Danusza went to see her school friends. It was strange to see children coming to school on horseback and leaving their horses in the school grounds until they finished school for the day.

The bell rang and the children formed a line. Danusza walked with me to the front of the assembly and introduced me to the schoolmaster. That was helpful to me because I didn't understand English. I could only say "good morning" and "thank you" and I understood a few words like "sit down" and "come here". The school started with a ceremony of raising the flag while the children sang "God Save the King".

We marched into the school. The building was small and divided into three classrooms. Although I had just turned eleven, I was placed in third class. They wouldn't place me any lower than that. The teacher distributed some books. Every child had to read one paragraph aloud. The girl sitting next to me read her paragraph and passed the book to me. She pointed to the place I was to read, and said, "Read."

How could I read a book? I only spoke three words in English! I shrugged my shoulders and moved my head from side to side, indicating that I could not read. The girl smiled and made a sign for me to pass the book on. In the lunch break, she kindly took my hand and led me to the shade of a tree to sit with her and her friend. They chatted something to me but I didn't understand a word. As I opened the spaghetti sandwich that the camp kitchen had provided for our school lunch, the look on my face indicated that I was not going to eat it. The girls gathered that I didn't like my sandwich so they shared their peanut butter sandwich with me

On that very day at lunchtime, I was surprised to see Meta, my Lithuanian friend from Wildflecken. I remembered waving goodbye to Meta when she and her family were on the army truck leaving Wildflecken. We were glad to see each other again but we couldn't talk for long as we did not sit together at lunch time.

The schoolmaster encouraged new Australians to sit and play with the Australian children. Playing together we could learn English so much faster. I came back from school that day with some knowledge of English words that I learned and understood the meaning of "read the book", "sit under the tree" and "wait here for the bus". Mother was pleased with the slight progress I had made. "That is good for the first day at school'" she said.

I told Mother about seeing Meta at school. Meta's family lived at the other end of the camp, near the canteen shop and the community hall. The camp was big and held a large number of people. Meta and I would have never have met if not for school.

Later in the week after school, Meta took me to see her family. They were pleased to see me again. Meta's mother invited Mother, Czesiek and I to go to the movies with them. Czesiek was only a toddler. He couldn't walk the distance and it was late for him to stay up, so Mother gave me permission to go with Meta. Mother insisted that her family escort me back to our hut. The movie we saw that evening was *A Tale of Two Cities*. It was frightening and I didn't go to any more movies.

I had been going to school for almost a week, sitting with my new friends under a tree and eating my lunch when something happened to my eye. It swelled almost instantly. The schoolmaster was informed and he called the ambulance. Children gathered around wondering what had happened to me. In no time at all the ambulance arrived at school. The ambulance officer spoke and I presumed he was asking me what was wrong. All I could do was point to my eye.

He looked at it and pulled out the insect, showing it to me while he put a bandage on the eye. He then said something to me I didn't understand. I presumed he was saying he was taking me back to Mother. I answered in the English I knew: "Thank you very much." The officer smiled at me and guided me to the ambulance. He opened the door of the front seat for me. I was then driven back to camp.

It must have been difficult for the schoolmaster and the Australian children at Bonegilla School to be constantly teaching the new Australian children. Every time a ship came to Melbourne a new lot of children came to school not knowing a word of English. In the camps in Germany, I sometimes went to English lessons with Dad. To greet a person at any time the words were to be "Good morning", "Good day", "Good evening", and "How do you do?" The reply was to be 'Very well thank you." When I spoke in this manner to the Australian people they looked, and wondered what I was saying. It sounded double-Dutch to us too. When we showed the Australian people that we were trying to speak English, they were only too glad to help.

When we purchased something at the shop, the words to use were "May I please buy...?" I was standing in the post office queue waiting to buy a stamp when the chap in front of me said, "Tuppeny please." The woman gave him a stamp. I was confused. I said to the woman, "May I please buy stamp." She passed the stamp to me and asked for "tuppence". I looked at the woman. She then asked for two pennies.

"Sausage" was another one. There was some confusion at the camp canteen when I asked for sausage to make a sandwich. I was given a small raw sausage. "No, no," I said, "not that." I pointed to the big roll of empire sausage, or Devon, that was in the showcase window.

"That's two bob," said the lady. What kind of language were they speaking? I didn't understand it.

Sometime in late February 1951, Mother was informed that we were to leave Bonegilla and move to a camp at Cowra in New South Wales. I presumed that was closer to Sydney where Father was working. With our bags packed early in the morning, we left Bonegilla. I don't remember the day of the week. I lost contact with Meta. We never crossed paths again.

We were driven by bus to Albury station. There were many people waiting for trains. Father was waiting to meet us on the station platform and we were so happy to see him. He had come all the way from Sydney on his rostered days off. He travelled all night to be with us and to accompany Mother on the journey to Cowra.

On board the train I rushed for a seat next to the window. I was eager to see something of the Australian country. Staying in Bonegilla we didn't venture out from the camp to see the outside world. When we were moved from Ludwigsburg to Wildflecken, and other camps we stayed at, for some reason it had always been important to me to know how far it was to the next town or city, and to know its name. I think I felt that as long as we were travelling, our life was moving forward, and I wanted to know how far.

As the train left Albury station I looked out of the window into the wilderness, seeing nothing, not even one tree. Some time passed before I saw some sheep grazing on the brittle grass stubble. More sheep were scattered over the land. From a distance the sheep looked like little white balls in this hot flat country. Occasionally, maybe twice, I saw a house and a tree in the distance. Travelling by rail in Germany, the train journey covered long distances and in that time I saw many towns, cities and farms. Travelling through forests and mountain tunnels, the train would come to the edge of meadows where cows grazed on green pasture. That was a beautiful scene. It was so different travelling through the vast area of Australian land. I saw nothing of trees or green pastures, only the blue sky on the horizon. Some miles before Cowra I saw a farmer ploughing the field. The earth was red, and Mother's comment was that the red earth represented gold country.

Trees and houses indicated that the train was coming to a town. We pulled into Cowra station in the late afternoon. A bus was waiting to take us to the camp only a short distance from town. The bus drove through the gate to the migrant camp. The reception office and the commandant's house were a welcoming sight. A colourful garden with lush green grass was well maintained. It was a small oasis, a stark contrast to the barren land we had travelled through. For a brief moment, we thought that we were going to live in a house like that. When the bus stopped at the reception office, a supervisor came on the bus with a cheery welcome. He distributed the keys with a tag number of a hut and block. The huts stood in rows, in alphabetical order.

While the supervisor was giving out the keys, Mother turned her head to Father and said, "It would be nice to live in a lovely house like that."

A woman sitting in the seat in front overheard the comment and couldn't resist adding, "Yes, we would all like to live in a house like that, not be put in hut cubicles, living like rats in a hot box, and husbands living hundreds of miles away from families."

Dad knew that Mother felt the same as many women. He leaned towards Mother and spoke softly. "We will have a house to live in, and a garden and green grass all around the house. Just be a little patient."

"What else can I do, only be patient and wait," said Mother.

Cowra camp accommodation was much the same as Bonegilla. The only difference was that this camp was built on open slopes. There were no trees, and no birds. The hot sun blazed on the hut all day. There was one shady place outside for us to sit and catch a breeze. This place was like a desert: not a blade of grass, only dirt baking in the sun.

Dad stayed with us overnight. Czesiek and I shared the one bed that night. Mother and Father were not aware that the family would be living apart in this country. The heat alone was distressing enough. Splitting families was something Mother and Father never expected. Mother, Czesiek and I were lonely in this strange country. It was a long way for Father to travel on his days off to be with us. Mother missed her husband, and Czesiek and I missed Father very much. Mother and I cried for days when Father left.

We arrived at Cowra four weeks before Easter. On the first Sunday, we walked to church along a farm track. Vines grew on one side of the track, covering the ground. Some big odd balls were growing on these vines. On the opposite side, the vines were different: the things growing on these vines were shaped like the coach that took Cinderella to the ball, only they were much smaller than the coach I saw in the picture book on the ship. Maybe those things grow big or maybe Cinderella was little, I thought. It had been a fairy tale book; maybe people in stories are little people. I asked Mother if she knew what these things were. She named them in Polish, and said it was something her grandfather fed the cattle on his farm. Sometime later I learned to eat the odd balls that were melons and pumpkins.

When the church service was over, the people stayed back for a talk. Mother had spoken to some of the people and asked how they filled in their time in this camp. She was told that local vegetable farmers needed workers for picking beans. During the week, they worked in the field until noon. The next morning, Mother was waiting with the women at the gate. By lunchtime Mother came back sick with a headache. She took medication and went to bed early.

The next morning she was back at work. This was the everyday routine while we stayed in Cowra. Mother always pushed herself to the limit. I was not well enough to start school when we arrived, so I stayed inside the hut, babysitting Czesiek. It was as hot inside the hut as it was outside. There was no cool place I could lie down. I didn't like living in this miserable camp. By the time I felt better, it was only one week to school holidays, so Mother decided that I would start school after Easter. This meant that Mother could work one more week in the field. The little bit of income helped towards the Easter festive season.

On the Thursday before Easter, Mother ventured out to town for the first time without Father. Mother, Czesiek and I went shopping in the small town of Cowra to buy a basket, some eggs and a cake to prepare the basket for our traditional Polish Easter. In the street, we met people from the ship and from Bonegilla. Mother talked with them. I remember some of the conversation. Most of the people were homesick for their country in Europe, and wondered if they had made the right decision coming to this strange country at end of the world. Would they be happier if they went back to their country, dictated by communism? These people knew better. That is why they came to a free country to make their home. Those people were just homesick. I, too, missed the rolling green hills and mountains, and the pine trees of Europe. The bare open space was hard for one to adapt to and accept.

I enjoyed my day shopping with Mother. People serving in the shops were helpful. Nothing was too much trouble. They took things down off the shelf so we could see them up close. My feeling was that the people of Cowra were a close community. The small town people are close to one another and ready to help each other. I sensed welcome in the town of Cowra.

On Easter Saturday we took the baskets of food to the church to be blessed. Arriving back at the hut, we were surprised to see Father sitting on the step waiting for us. He was to stay overnight. We were so happy to have him with us for Easter Sunday mass. It was a special day for us, and to have Father share the Easter breakfast for our first Easter in Australia made it more special. After the late breakfast he had to leave. It was a long journey back to Sydney for him to be back at work on Monday morning.

I started school in Cowra camp. The school building was a hut in the camp grounds, built up from the ground like most huts. I stood by myself at the hut, feeling like a fish out of water, and waiting for the other children to arrive. The school teacher saw me standing on my own. She came to me and said, "My name is Mrs Cowen. I am the school teacher. Come with me into the classroom."

I stood at the door waiting for the children to be seated. Mrs Cowen opened the enrolment book and asked me, "What is your name?" She wrote it in the book. Mrs Cowen was a pleasant lady of good nature and stature. She was a woman in her forties, well dressed, and a little on the large size. Her hair was cut short back and sides, just like a man, and it was blue. I was mesmerised by Mrs Cowen's blue hair. Was she a saint? Or an angel?

"Terese." Mrs Cowen broke my thoughts. "Terese, you are to sit here." She tapped her hand on the desk where I was to sit during the lessons.

After school was finished for the day, I told Mother that I had met a lady with blue hair.

"Blue hair? Are you sure it's blue, not green?" That was Mother's humour.

"No Mama, not green like grass. It's blue like the sky," I said.

"Are you feeling alright?' said Mother. 'You didn't bump your head at school?"

"No Mama, there is nothing wrong with my head."

"This is very strange. I have never seen anyone with blue hair," said Mother.

One morning I was running late for school. As I went to put my foot on the step of the school hut, I saw a reptile under the building. Its mouth was open. I stopped and opened my mouth to scream, but I made no sound. What was I to do? Standing at the bottom of the steps without moving a muscle and not able to make a sound, I waited for the creature to go away. I stood still, keeping my eyes on this reptile, studying it most carefully. What could this could be? Was it a snake? It had a long tail. No, I didn't think snakes had legs. The reptile had not moved. Was it a small crocodile? I was thinking, "I can't stand at the bottom of the steps all day. The sun is burning my face and neck. I will be sunburnt if I don't make a move soon. How fast can this creature run?"

Its eyes were glued to me, its head raised up ready to strike. Time was getting away and I didn't dare take my eyes of the reptile. I couldn't stand much longer. My legs were getting numb. I built up my courage and took the risk, running quickly up the steps and into the classroom. Mrs Cowen didn't approve of the way I burst into the room. I tried to tell her about the creature under the school hut, but I wasn't able to make her understand what I was saying. She quietly guided me to my desk. Later in life I learned that this reptile was a bearded dragon.

After three weeks in Mrs Cowen's class my English must have improved. I can't say what subject we were studying, but I remember Mrs Cowen saying to me, "That is much better, Terese, much better."

I felt overwhelmed to be praised by Mrs Cowen. I always worked hard at everything I did, whether it was looking after my brother or helping Mother. I never said "no" and never back-chatted my Mother.

In the short stay at Cowra we saw a big fire in the distance. In the evening the sky was red. It was very frightening. It seemed as if the whole world was on fire and coming to the end.

We were lonely and depressed living in Cowra camp. The environment was harsh; with no trees, the one-room huts were hot. Mother missed her husband, and Czesiek and I missed our Dad. Mother's friends from the ship were gone, scattered to different states. Czesiek's godmother went to Adelaide. It was difficult to speak to the new people from different European countries. We could not communicate with them. People in the camp were on the move and didn't stay long to get to know people.

In the short time I attended school at Bonegilla and Cowra, understanding only a little English, I remembered the lessons about Australia in the gold rush days, and the bushrangers. I didn't understand everything Mrs Cowen said, but I liked listening on the subject of Australian history and on the subject of Cowra. It was a town on the Lachlan River, between the slopes of the dividing range and central western plains. The industries were sheep, cattle, vegetable farms and the Edgell's cannery, famous for its asparagus. Some of the people from the camp settled in Cowra.

GRETA TO BERESFIELD

Our next move was to Greta, a camp in the Hunter Valley not too far from the town of Maitland. We were to travel by train from Cowra to Sydney, then change trains at Central Station to catch a train north.

As our train left Cowra, I sat by the window, looking out on the vast open space to see if I could spot men digging for gold, or maybe a bushranger holding up a stage coach. I had missed the point that these things had happened in the last century, nearly a hundred years earlier. Dates meant nothing to me at the time. I saw sheep in the distance and sometimes I saw a clump of small trees, twisted and crooked. They looked to me as if they were tortured and growing in pain. Under one clump of these painful trees, I saw a group of huge birds, much bigger than European storks, and not colourful like the parrots I saw at Bonegilla. These birds took shelter from the hot sun under the tortured trees.

Some hours had passed and the train travelled a little slower. The scene changed. There were more trees, taller and bigger, as the train travelled through the Great Dividing Range. I saw beautiful houses and gardens. I was thinking that I could be very happy living in a house like these homes with their lovely tall trees. Mother must have been thinking the same thing. She said to me, "This is a beautiful place, Terese. We must be coming into Sydney. We will be seeing Father when we arrive at Sydney. In the letter he said if he is not on the platform to meet us when the train arrives, we must find the big clock in the main building and wait for him." Mother didn't talk much while we were travelling. She was probably thinking or saying prayers. Mother always had a rosary in her hands when she travelled.

I can't remember the train stopping at the stations on the way to Sydney, but I remember seeing industries as we moved on. The houses were not as big or attractive as the ones we saw in the mountains, but I would be happy living in one of these houses with a little garden each side of the path from the gate to the house. It looked pleasant to an eleven year girl looking from the train window.

The train came into Sydney. There was more movement and the streets were busy with traffic. In a short time, the train pulled into the station. I could see Father running on the platform alongside the carriage we were sitting in. He must have seen us through the window. "Look Mama! Tatusz (Dad) is here!"

Tears filled Mother's eyes. "That's good,' she said. 'I don't have to worry about looking for the big clock."

Dad hopped on the train to carry the suitcase. As we walked to the main building I was confused by the sign on the platform. "Dad, is this Sydney station?"

"Yes," said Father.

"But the sign on the board is not Sydney." Although I didn't know how to read English, I saw that the writing on the sign was not Sydney.

"Yes, this is Central Station,' said Father. "Another name for Sydney".

Mother was surprised to see the written name of Kosciusko on some train carriages. She pointed it out to Father, saying "That is a Polish name on the train." She did not know of the Polish explorer in the early years of Australia.

We walked to the big clock. A visit to the rest room was a must for us after the long journey. The toilets on the station were different to the ones we used in Germany. Sydney station didn't look that much different from the stations in Germany, but the interior of the buildings in Germany were much more ornate. Walking into a big city railway station in Europe was like walking into a palace. Just like stations in Europe, there was a dining room where people could eat. There were shops selling flowers and newspapers, and a shop that sold sandwiches, hot chips and Australian pies. While Mother, Czesiek and I were in the rest room, Father bought coffee for Mother and orange drinks for us.

We had to wait for a while before the train to Newcastle was ready for us to board. Dad said, "I had no breakfast this morning. I am going to buy a pie. Would you like a hot pie, hot potato chips or a sandwich?"

I saw children sitting next to me eating hot potato chips that looked interesting and smelled good. I said, "I would like to have what the boy next to me is having." Mother said she would have the same.

"Alright, hot chips it is," said Father.

He came back with a packet wrapped in newspaper, ripping off one end so we could pull out the chips one at a time. "I like them," I said to Mother. Czesiek took chips out of Mother's pack and some from my pack. It was too many for a toddler to have a pack for himself. He liked eating the chips. This was our first "take away" food.

Father came with us on the train to Greta camp. We sat in the carriage. The train whistle blew and the train left the station.

"We are leaving the big city,' said Father. 'It will be a long journey to Hamilton Station."

"Hamilton!' said Mother. 'But we are going to Greta!"

"Yes, but we must get off the train at Hamilton station to change onto train that will take us to Greta," replied Father.

That was the end of the conversation between Mother and Father for the rest of the trip. Father was deaf in one ear; it was no use talking to him on the noisy train.

I looked out the window, watching the city slip away. The train picked up speed and the scene outside the window changed. We travelled through some rough rocky country. My eyes were on the world out there in the bush. The trees were different from one to another. There were tall trees, and among them were shrubs and smaller twisted trees growing from cracks in the rocks. I was thinking that must be the bush Mother had talked about back in Germany when we were deciding what country we would choose as our home.

I wondered how many creatures would be out there in those rocks, and if they were bigger or smaller than the one I saw under the school hut. Would they attack people? There would be a lot of snakes and spiders and different creatures in the bush. In the distance I could see a lot of mountains. Then everything went dark!

"We are going through a tunnel,' said Father. 'There are more to come, and the train goes across the water on a long bridge."

The train wound around the mountains, blowing its whistle every so often, and coming to the water's edge after it crossed a long bridge. We were coming into Gosford. Dad said to Mother, "A man comes on the train selling oranges. Would you like me to buy some?"

"Oranges!' I said. 'I love oranges!"

Mother nodded her head, saying "Oranges would be nice for the children to eat."

Just as Father had said, a man came onto the train selling small buckets of oranges. Dad bought the oranges and said to me, "Terese, you will have to carry the oranges."

"Carry them? I will eat some on the way!" I said.

Father left the carriage to light a cigarette while the train stopped for a short time. Then the train travelled through more bushland. This was a long day for us to be spending on the trains, and I began to feel ill. I had felt sick since getting on the train, but after Gosford, my head started to ache and my mouth tasted salty.

"Dad,' I said, 'I am not feeling well. I am going to throw up."

"Lay your head back and try to think of something pleasant," he said.

I was getting worse. I felt like my head was going to explode. "I must use the toilet!"

"I will come with you,' said Mother. 'Try to hang on!"

With Mother's help, I made it just in time. "Oh this is terrible!' I groaned. 'Why must I be sick?"

Mother wiped my face with a wet cloth. We came back and sat in the seat. At the next stop, Father bought an ice-cream for Czesiek and me. "This might help," said Father.

I didn't feel I could eat the ice-cream but it was cool on my tongue. I felt a little better. I was glad to get off the train at Hamilton. We had to wait for a little while for the next train and I felt so weak it was difficult for me to walk. Dad walked across to the hotel and came back with a small bottle of lemonade for each of us. I burped up the gas in my stomach and that made me feel little better. I don't remember coming to Greta. I was feeling very sick. I don't remember how we arrived at Greta camp.

At Greta camp we still lived in a hut, and shared with another family: a young woman with two sweet little girls. One girl was the same age as Czesiek and the other girl was a little younger. The family's name was Lesien. The mother's name was Anna, the same as my mother's name. The little girls were Aletia and Krystina. They were good people to share the hut with. There was an extra room in this hut, and we certainly needed it. We used it as a utility room to keep our trunks. It was also used as a bathroom for us children, and the mothers used it for cooking on occasion. There were beds for our Dads when they came to stay overnight. It was slightly better living than the other two camps, and the food was a little different. We had the choice of rabbit or stew with European potatoes, or, for a change, rice with the stew.

Father came to see us whenever he could. It was still a long way from Sydney to Greta, about five hours travelling each way. Dad didn't come as often as we would have liked to see him. Anna and Mother got on well sharing the room. Their outlook on life was much alike. They kept to themselves and stayed away from gossiping women.

There was always trouble in camp over children; it was typical of overcrowded camps. One day, Czesiek and I were playing with a ball. A boy passed by and couldn't resist kicking our ball over the hut to the other side where children were playing. This caused a problem. A boy on the other side caught the ball and claimed it as his own. I ran over and asked the boy to give it back to me. He lied and said it was his. I tried to take my ball off him. Then his mother intervened, slapping my face, and taking the ball off me. I ran and told Mother of the incident. She didn't hesitate to go to the other side of the hut, no questions asked.

Mother slapped the woman. A fight started between them. Women gathered around yelling out "A fight! A fight!" They urged Mother on, yelling, "Give the German a good punch for me while you got her!" Mother pulled the woman's hair and got her down on the ground, slapping her face and yelling at her, "You German bitch! You dare to hit my child because your bastard of a son is a liar!" She kept yelling at the woman, giving her another punch: "This one is from me! And this punch is for my girl! No German is going to get away hurting my children again!" Mother gave the German woman a good hiding, and did not let the woman stand up to fight back.

The police were not informed. The women in the camp didn't want to see the fight stopped by outsiders like the police. This fight was to be settled by the women themselves. The German woman did not press charges. It was tough for us living in camp, but it was much tougher for a German woman married to a Polish man. The women in this camp were not going to tolerate a German causing trouble. The German women kept away from the rest of the women in camp.

Another time I was the cause of trouble in the camp. All the girls and women shared the same shower. There were no partitions, just a row of shower heads hanging from the railing of the roof. Most women living in the camp were young and slim, but a few were old and big. Most times I had a shower with my mother, but on this occasion I was on my own. I had my head down. It was rather embarrassing for me taking a shower with grown women. I was busy washing myself and my hair, and, as I lifted my head to rinse my long hair, the eyes of the big old woman standing next to me met mine for a moment. She made a big scene, yelling at me and insinuating that I was a pervert: "Stop perving on me! Haven't you seen a woman taking a shower before?!" She embarrassed me in front of all the women.

A cake of soap flew past me from the other end of the shower hut, hitting the old woman. A voice came from the other end: "Wash your mouth out and keep your eyes off the girl!"

That started a row. There was soap flying from one end of the shower hut to the other. Two German women grabbed their towels and ran out into the open and into their own huts, leaving their clothes behind. Either they had experienced this kind of behaviour before, or word had got around not to touch Anna's children. Rumours spread like fire in camps. I said to Mother, "That is the last time I will step foot into the shower hut."

Mother suggested that I use the bath hut in the middle of the compound, between S and T block. It had one tin bath surrounded by a sheet of corrugated iron, with gaps of a foot and a half from the ground and a foot and a half from the roof. Three young boys saw me go into the hut. They climbed onto the rocks that were close to the bath hut and they watched me through the gap between the iron and the roof, peering and laughing. I stayed in the bath until a woman came past and saw the boys. She gave them a lecture and the boys bolted back to their huts.

That was the last straw for me. I told Mother that was the last bath I was having, there would be no more baths for me while I was staying in this camp. From that time on I had my bath in the utility room, using our small bathtub. This meant carting buckets of water from the shower hut to our hut, and, after the bath, carting the water back out. That was the price of having a bath in privacy.

Mother and I didn't like living in camps where there were constant rows over children. Some women could not mind their own business and caused trouble by gossiping. It was unpleasant and depressing to live in this kind of environment. To get away from the troubles and blues, Mother went to work on the farms, picking vegetables in the school holidays while I looked after Czesiek. (I wasn't to start school at Greta camp until after the May holiday.)

I had taken an interest in music to beat the blues, learning to sing songs from the radio in camp. It was put over the PA system every day. The first song I learned to sing was "Goodnight Irene". The other songs were "The Mockingbird Song" and "On Top of Old Smokey". Those songs were on the hit parade in the early fifties.

We were not long in the camp when I was taken ill and had to be taken to the camp hospital. The doctor said I was to stay in for a week and I was put on a strict diet. The doctor told Mother it was my liver that was making me sick. The German woman who slapped my face was working in hospital as a nurse in the ward. This time she had to treat me with respect and I must say she was nice to me.

It must have been September. The weather was lovely. The radio in the hospital was playing beautiful instrumental music and lovely songs. Listening to the artists singing, I drifted off into another place of peace. The music I remember are Jan Pearce singing "The Bluebird of Happiness", Ronnie Runnel singing and whistling "In the Monastery Garden", Joan Hammond, a soprano, singing opera, and Jan Kipura, a tenor.

The week had come for me to leave the hospital. The sister said I had to wait until the afternoon when Mother was coming to visit, but I didn't leave the hospital that day. The sister told Mother that the doctor wanted me to stay two more days. Mother agreed with the doctor's suggestion and left me for two more days.

It was the weekend. Again, I was looking forward to the afternoon when Mother would come. Father came with her that weekend. After a time sitting with me, Father said that the doctor was going to keep me in for yet another week. I didn't take that news too lightly. I was promised that I was only staying in hospital for one week. I was going with my parents that day!

When Father moved to get up, I grabbed the lapels on his coat and wouldn't let go. Still hanging on to my father, I screamed and kicked. Everything in my way became flying missiles: the water jug and glass tumbler were kicked across the room. I made up my mind they would not leave without me. The sister came running and saw the ward in a state. I was too much trouble for the sister. She told Dad to take me and leave quickly. She said to make sure that I stayed away from school until the doctor gave me clearance.

With care and medication I recovered slowly, missing lessons yet again. Staying in the hut all day was depressing. I continued listening to music and songs on the radio, and tried to sing along with the artist. The song that was easy for me to learn was "I See the Moon, the Moon Sees Me". That lovely song was repeated so it was easy for me to learn.

Mother went to work again. Czesiek stayed with me, and Mrs Lesien was at hand if needed. I commenced school when I was over the illness. I was still struggling to speak in English. My teacher's name was Miss Sealy. She was a beautiful young woman, no more than about twenty, neatly dressed, and a very good teacher. I learned a lot in the few months I was in Miss Sealy's class. I did well. I was top in third class at sums and Miss Sealy was very pleased with my progress. I liked her very much. She was nice and she was interested in children's work. I wished she was teaching me all the way through school. Miss Sealy made the school work easy and fun. She inspired me to work hard at my school work.

School was going to end for the year with a concert. Mother made the first trip to Greta town to buy clothing and shoes for Czesiek and me. The two ladies at the store were nice and made us welcome as we walked in, asking if there was something in particular that Mother wanted. The ladies were only too pleased to help, showing kindness to us new Australian people. One lady attended to Mother and the other lady was with me. I saw the shoes in the window that appealed to me. She brought the box, taking the shoes out and showing them to me, and asked if they were the shoes I wanted.

The lady saw the delight on my face and smiled at me. She put the brown leather shoes on my feet. The shoes were lovely, with a peep toe and a small wedge heel and sling back. I stood up and walked about in the shop, looking for a dress. There was only one dress that was my size and that was the one Mother bought for me. Shopping in a small town, I felt we got that personal assistance from the two ladies. I think Mother was rather pleased with herself taking the confident step to go shopping without Father at her side.

Father managed to come to see us during Christmas week with a present for Czesiek and me. I finally got a doll, as I had wanted before we left Germany. It was a Shirley Temple doll with blonde curls, dressed in a pink dress and white socks and plastic shoes. I was allowed to play with the doll during the Christmas week, and then it was to sit on my bed. Father said I was too old to play with dolls, and that I should concentrate more on school work and helping Mother. Czesiek's present was a big ball. I took him to the park every day so he had the enjoyment of kicking the ball. He had always been my priority since our brother, his twin, had died.

My school teacher in the New Year was Mr Dunn, a handsome young man, neatly dressed, but his way of teaching was different to Miss Sealy. I didn't understand Mr Dunn's way of teaching. I lost the interest in learning because I didn't understand. I remember the one story Mr Dunn told us many times about a man and his donkey bringing the wounded back from the front line at a place called Gallipoli. I remember the soldier's name was John Simpson.

Father sprang a surprise, coming to visit us for the day. This time he brought good news, telling Mother that he had been transferred from Sydney to work at Broadmeadow Railway Yard and that we would be leaving camp life for good. Dad said he was going to rent tents from the Railway for us to live in.

"Tents!' said Mother with disappointment. 'The films in Germany showed us Australian people had lovely big houses to live in with beautiful gardens and surroundings, a far cry from the conditions we are having to live in!"

Dad went silent for a moment and didn't know if he should continue to talk. Mother urged him on, saying "I am listening Pawel. You were saying?"

Father said "You will have more rooms in the tents – a bedroom for us and one for Terese and Czesiek to share. We will also have a utility room to use as a laundry and bathroom."

Mother shrieked. "Tents! Oh my, living in tents on bare ground!" She was afraid that snakes, spiders and other creepy crawlies could come into the tent and we wouldn't be aware of these pests, especially at night while we were sleeping.

"No, no,' said Dad, 'the tents are big and made of a heavy canvas, fitted over a square wooden frame with timber floor."

Mother was still not convinced. "It's going to be cold in winter living in tents."

"Don't worry Anna, I have made inquiries. The tents can make a comfortable home to live in."

He reassured Mother by telling her that he would nail blankets on to the wooden frame from the inside. This would add extra warmth to the rooms in the winter months and living in the tents would be no colder than living in huts. "The tents are insulated all year round, covered with a heavy canvas roof," he added.

Mother was beginning to show interest, asking "Where am I going to cook?"

"I will build a kitchen with timber walls adjoining the tents, and put in a fuel stove to cook and heat water on. I am really looking forward to having a good home cooked meal – I have missed your cooking all these years living in camps! I ordered two water tanks that will be placed close to the railway line."

"No running water or electricity!' Mother cried. 'This is going from bad to worse! You didn't happen to find a cave for us to live in, coming from the station through the bush?"

"Ha ha, very funny Anna. That was a witty remark," said Father.

"I don't know how I am going to manage living out in the bush," said Mother.

"Didn't I tell you? We will be living together. I will be coming home to you from work every day. It's only forty minutes by train from Beresfield to work." Father said that water would be delivered by train once a week. "Terese and I will carry the water from the tank to the kitchen for you." He went on to say that milk and bread would be delivered to the door five days a week. The green-grocer, the butcher and ice-man would come twice a week, and there was a shop at the end of the street. "And the rent is cheap. We can save money for a house, Anna."

There was silence for a moment.

"Did I tell you Anna, coming to camp today, I happened to see a strange animal. It looked like a cow sitting on its long back legs, with short kind of hands at the front and its head looked like that of a dog. This animal stopped me in my tracks. I didn't know if it was going to attack me. I looked around for a stick to protect myself with. As soon as it saw me, it hopped away into the bush."

I interrupted the conversation, saying, "Dad, what you saw was a kangaroo."

"Did you see this kangaroo Terese?" asked Father.

"No, we are taught at school. I have seen pictures of the Australian animals, birds and snakes. I think I saw a snake in the garbage can yesterday. I lifted the lid to put the rubbish in, and a feeling came over me not to touch it but quickly put the lid back down."

I was curious to know what it was that I saw in that garbage. Walking back to the hut I had tried to work it out. It was the colour of human flesh, and it was covered in what looked like small scales. "It wasn't a fish,' I said, 'and it came to me that it was a snake with its head buried in the rubbish. That's what it was – a snake."

"Good girl,' said Dad. 'Follow your senses. That will help you when you have decisions to make."

"Yes,' said Mother. 'I have a decision of my own to make. I don't know how I am going to manage living in the tents."

"Take all the time you need Anna, but it's not so bad. The tents make a good home. We are going to live together as a family. You won't be alone any more. I'll be home after work every day, and there are three Polish families already living on the Railway property, so you won't be alone when I'm at work."

Mother listened, and agreed that having more room would be a vast improvement on the conditions we lived in at the camp. Of most importance to me was to have our Dad coming home every day.

Father was anxious to get us away from the camp life. The sight of rows and rows of huts resembled a concentration camp. Although the camp had given us some security in this new country, it was depressing. The constant upheaval of camp life was proving to be frightening for Mother. She didn't know when we would be able to settle for good in one place.

Father wasted no time. Within three weeks of starting work at Broadmeadow, he had rigged up the tents and built the kitchen ready for us to move to Beresfield. But a week before we were to move to our new canvas home, Mother fell sick with cramps in the stomach, and vomiting. She was in great pain and was taken to the camp hospital. I was left alone in the hut, to take care of Czesiek. Our friend Anna Lesien kept a watchful eye on us.

Father didn't know that Mother was sick. There was no telephone to make a direct call. I presumed the hospital would have informed Father, but there was a possibility that he didn't receive the message.

Czesiek was difficult and stubborn. I couldn't get him to do what I asked of him. I gave him a slap and a kick but he just sat on the floor refusing to move. Anna said, "Terese, he is missing his Mother. Leave him. I will talk to him later." After we had finished eating our tea, I answered a knock at the door. I was surprised and relieved to see Dad standing in the doorway. This was the third visit he had made since he started working at Broadmeadow. He saw that we were alone in the hut.

"Terese, where is your mother?" he asked.

"Mother is sick. The doctor called an ambulance. She was taken to the camp hospital."

"When did this happen?" asked Father.

"The night before last," I said.

"Are you and Czesiek alright?" he asked

"I am alright, but Czesiek is unsettled. He is missing Mother," I replied.

Although Czesiek was glad to see Dad, he was a little hesitant, as if he were not quite sure who the man was. We had hardly seen Dad since we arrived in Australia. He had been away for months, working miles away. Dad sat on the bed and picked Czesiek up and sat him on his knees. "I am going to visit your mother in hospital,' he said slowly to Czesiek. 'Do you understand what I am saying to you?"

Czesiek nodded his head.

"When I come back I will stay and look after you and Terese until your mother is well enough to look after you," Father told us.

Father didn't stay away too long. He returned from the hospital bringing news that we wanted to hear. "I saw your mother. She is feeling better. She said for you two not to worry. She will be released from the hospital in the morning, after the doctor has made his rounds. I will to go to the hospital to walk her back."

"Now, get Czesiek and yourself ready for bed. If Mother is well, I plan to take you all to town. We are going to look for furniture. I will be taking you away from this camp on Friday to live together in our new home."

I was happy and excited to be going out with Dad and Mother to see what the town looked like, and what kind of things I was going to see in the shop windows.

"Try to settle down and go to sleep,' said Father. 'Tomorrow will be a big day for us all."

The next day, Dad walked Mother back to the hut. Czesiek and I threw our arms around her and said "We missed you while you were away!"

She smiled at us and said "I have missed you too.' Then she said, 'I am sorry to disappoint you, my kittens, but I have a dreadful headache and couldn't possibly make a trip to town today."

Father said, "I don't want to leave you Anna but I must go and see my boss today."

"You go Pawel, and take Terese with you,' she said. 'I will be alright. Anna is in the next room if I need help."

Father was frustrated. "It's no good living like this!' he cried. 'When the children and you are sick I am not with you. I am the father – I should be looking after my wife and my family. Coming to this new country, life was to be better for us. Get a job, make money, and save for a house. I get a job, I pay for camp, pay for hostel, not much money left. I work overtime, I get a little extra. I have money in my pocket, I come to see my family, buy some food in the canteen, money all gone...!"

This talk upset mother. She began to cry. She got up and pulled a suitcase from under the bed. She opened it and took out an envelope. "Take this money with you and after you see your boss, go and buy the furniture we need. I saved this money working on the farm at Cowra, and some weeks washing pots in the camp kitchen."

Dad looked surprised. He had no idea that Mother had worked and managed to save a few pounds. She handed the envelope to Father. He took out the money and was surprised at the amount. "I will only take enough for the furniture. You take the rest," said Dad.

"I was saving the money to buy a house" said Mother.

Dad turned to me and said, "Terese, come with me. I am taking you to town, we are going shopping."

The train trip was an exciting event for me, giving me a chance to spend time with my father. We caught the train from Greta station. The carriage was almost full. We sat on separate seats. The train stopped at every station on the way to Newcastle. The first stop after Greta was Lochinvar and more passengers boarded the train. The carriage was full and some passengers had to stand. Father offered his seat to a woman standing. She declined and said that she would be getting off at the next stop. The train stopped at Maitland station where most of the people got off. There were a lot more empty seats in the carriage, so Father and I moved over to the other side.

I sat opposite Dad and took a good long look at him. I saw a faraway look in his eyes. His face was strained with worry. After a few more stops the train pulled into Beresfield station. Dad tapped me on the knee and said, "Look out the window. You will see the tents I put up for us." As the train moved under the bridge, he pointed out the tents. "See our new home. It's the one close to the railway line."

I looked at the tents and said, "Dad, the tents are so big. Are they all for us?"

"Yes, we will never have to share rooms with other people again," said Father.

While Father and I were talking, the train made a few more stops. We got off at Hamilton station and walked up Beaumont Street, then caught a bus to Broadmeadow where

Father worked. We walked into the office, and Dad introduced me to his boss. Then he said, "I must talk to you boss. My wife, she is sick. You know I work afternoon shift tomorrow, I like to change shift tomorrow from afternoon to dog-watch please boss."

"I'm sorry to hear about your wife being sick,' said the boss. 'I'll go out to the workshop and see what I can do."

We waited in the office for a few minutes. The boss came back and said, "One of your workmates will be off tomorrow and he will work your shift. He is taking his wife to Sydney next weekend and needs the extra day. You can work his shift next week."

Father was so pleased that his boss went out of his way and allowed him to change the shift. He thanked the boss, saying to him, "You people in this country are good people."

The boss looked a little embarrassed, and stood up from his desk and walked towards the door. "You will have to excuse me Paul; I must get back to work." He opened the door for us to walk out.

We walked to the next bus stop, which was not too far from a hotel. Father went inside the hotel. He brought out a glass of lemonade for me and a glass of beer for himself. When we had finished our drinks, we walked back to the main street in Hamilton.

We went into a small used furniture shop cluttered with bulky wardrobes and a few bits and pieces of household goods and camping equipment. Dad purchased the things we needed: a wardrobe, a dressing table, a double bed, a three-quarter bed and a single bed, a kitchen table with four chairs, a kitchen dresser to hold our crockery and cutlery, and, most importantly, the ice chest. Lucky for us there was one in the shop. The ice chests were in demand as fridges in those days were very expensive for an ordinary wage earner. Father organized for the furniture to be delivered to Beresfield on Thursday.

We walked out into the street. Father was pleased. "We should be in our new home on Friday," he said. The next shop we walked into was the delicatessen. Dad introduced me to the people behind the counter and some of the customers that he knew. The shop was very busy in the short time we were there. Dad bought black bread, cottage cheese and gherkins for Mother, ham for me and salami for himself. We walked back to Hamilton station to catch the train.

This time, we sat on the other side of the carriage so we could take another look at our new home on the way back to Greta. When the train pulled into Tarro station, Father said, "Soon you will see our new place." I took another look as the train passed our tents and stopped at Beresfield station. "This is where you will be getting off the next time you catch a train," he said. When the train passed Beresfield I said to Father that I was tired. I rested my head on his shoulder, imagining what it would be like living on our own, and fell asleep for rest of the journey.

Arriving at Greta station we caught the bus to the camp gate. We walked from Chocolate City across Anvil creek to the second camp where we lived: Silver City, a fancy name for rows and rows of miserable huts.

As we walked, I asked Father, "What were you thinking of when we were on the train going into town? You had a worried look on your face."

Father answered in English. When we were out, he often insisted that we speak Australian. "I think to myself: what a long and tough was journey for us from time you were born. Seeing you sitting face to face to me, in my mind I go back to time you are little baby. German soldiers come to my country, Poland, and make much trouble, taking people from towns and farms, taking them to Germany in train wagon for work. Most young people work in coal mines, industries, farms. Old people not so lucky..."

Dad didn't continue on that subject. He went on to say, "When war finished, you were very sick. I carried you from hospital to your mother. You were dying in my arms. I look at your skeleton body, covered by skin only, holding to life by – how Australian say – thin cobweb thread. When I see you like that, I feel pain in my heart for you. Was horrible, I hurt like thousand knives stabbing my heart. I not believe see you so thin and weak. I cry and pray so hard to God "Let Terese live". We lose so much in five years of war and could not lose our Terese. It would be too much for Anna and me for Terese to die. Terese is treasure we have left. I say to God, "Please don't take Terese from us." A miracle and blessing from God. You live to another day. Mother and I we pray more to God all the time. Six and half years. You are twelve years. I am happy we walking together. That is all I tell you."

"Why did the soldiers take Wladek and me away from Mama?" I asked.

"Adolf Hitler, he makes war on my country Poland,' said Father. 'You are born in Poland. German soldiers take us to Germany for work in factories, coal mines and working on farms. War is a bad thing. We talk of this no more."

Dad pulled a handkerchief out of his pocket and wiped tears from his eyes. "I am asking you not to talk things like this and not for you to ask question for your Mother. This is upsetting for her."

Our conversation finished as we came to the huts. Nothing more was said.

Mother was feeling a little better. Father handed the bag of food to her, saying, "You won't be eating food from the camp kitchen again." Mother prepared sandwiches for tea that evening; they were a welcome change from the kitchen food. As I ate my ham sandwich, Mother noted the expression on my face and asked, "Don't you like your sandwich?"

"I don't like caraway seeds in the bread – yuk!" was my reply.

"Terese, you are so fussy about your food," said Mother.

"I don't like caraway seeds. They spoil the taste of good food," I said.

After we had finished eating, Father took Czesiek out to the swings in the park so they could spend some time together, and so Czesiek could get to know his father.

Dad stayed in camp with us that night, and was up early the next morning to be at Beresfield for when the furniture arrived. He worked on assembling the beds and arranging the rest of the furniture. He was keen to have all the jobs completed before he left for work in the afternoon.

Before lunch on that day, which was a Thursday, I went to see the School Principal, Mr Cox, to let him know that I was leaving Greta Camp and moving to my new home at Beresfield. Mr Cox wished me good health and good luck in my new school.

Just after lunch, the afternoon became extremely windy. Czesiek and I were not able to play outside. The wind blew so hard it knocked Czesiek off his feet. I was also finding it difficult to stand up. I would take one step forward and two back, trying to help Czesiek to his feet. With the winds so strong we had to spend the rest of the day inside our hut. All night the wind lifted the iron roof of the hut, making a frightening noise.

The next morning the wind had eased. We were up early for our breakfast, eagerly looking forward to moving to our new home. Mother had cleaned up and packed the last of the utensils into the small bathtub ready for us to leave. All morning we waited anxiously for Father to arrive. When he didn't turn up by midday, Mother said, with disappointment in her voice, "Father is possibly working overtime."

Just after midday, the camp supervisor came to see Mother. He said, "Mrs Dron, I have a message for you from your husband. He is not able to be with you today and the move has been delayed until Monday. He said not to worry he will see you on Sunday. If not able to come on Sunday, he will be here Monday morning with the truck."

Father kept his promise, arriving on Sunday. The moment he stepped foot in the hut Mother said, "I was worried, not knowing what happened to you!" She was so happy to see Dad, and to see that he was alright. Naturally she wanted to know why the move had been delayed.

We all sat on the bed, listening to Dad explain: "I finished work Friday morning, after working an extra shift, and I was on my way to Greta. As the train was coming into Beresfield I looked out the window to see that everything was alright, after the strong wind blowing on Thursday. I was shocked to see my tents lying in a heap on the ground! The kitchen dresser was leaning on the table, and the wardrobe and dressing table were leaning on the beds. Everything was in the open. My immediate thoughts were of you. I thanked God that you and the children were all still at Greta.

I jumped out of my seat and got off the train at Beresfield, and rushed over to the tents to see that the furniture was not damaged. Once I had a look and saw that everything was alright I ran to the post office phone box and called the truck driver to let him know what had happened, and postponed the move until Monday.

A gang of fettler men were working on the railway line close to where our tents were lying. Mr Murray, the boss, came over and told me that our tents had blown on to the track stopping the coal and goods trains from running. He said that he and his men had started work at the crack of dawn to remove the tents from the tracks. Mr Murray and two of his men live in tents on the railway grounds. They are to be our neighbours. The fettler gang finished work early that day and helped me rig up our tents again. This time I made sure the tents were pegged down securely, using iron rail tracks. That was the next job I was going to do at the weekend but the wind beat me."

Father was on night shift again and left late that Sunday afternoon for work. The next day, we were prepared and ready to leave the camp for our new home.

Dad finished work on Monday morning and arrived in a small battered farm truck. The old jalopy was covered in mud. It looked as if it had battled through a flood; the guards were badly dented and tied to the body with fencing wire. There was no need for air conditioning because the windows were missing. A blue cattle dog sat in the back. Dad and a young man got out of the truck.

Our luggage, consisting of two wooden trunks, a small bathtub and the crocodile skin suitcase, was loaded onto the truck. The young man opened the door on the driver's side for us because it was the only door that would open. The seat was dirty and torn, and rusty springs poked through. Mother hesitated to get in.

"Don't worry missus,' said the young man. 'She'll be apples." He grabbed the dog's blanket from the back of the truck and threw it over the seat. Dog hair and hen feathers flew about in the cabin. The shock on Mother's face!

Mother asked me what the young man was saying about apples. I shrugged my shoulders and said I didn't know. Father yelled out, "Anna, get in!"

With great hesitation, Mother climbed in first and nursed Czesiek on her knees. I sat in the middle between Mother and the driver. Father sat in the back of the truck with the luggage, making sure that his crocodile skin suitcase didn't walk off the back of the truck. It was finally happening: we were leaving camp life, never to return.

The excitement of our trip began when we came to the first right hand turn taking us out of the camp. As we turned onto the road, the door of the truck flew open, and the driver leaned out to grab the door. Mother grabbed my arm, frightened that I would fall out with the driver.

"Not to worry, missus – she'll be apples," he said, and jumped out. He cut some fence wire from the mud guards.

"What's with these apples the young man is saying?" asked Mother. The young man hooked the wire from the door to the spring of the seat behind him, and said again, "She'll be apples!"

Each time the truck hit a hole in the road, the springs in the seat hit our bum. 'Ouch! Ouch!' That was one way to keep score of how many potholes there were. "One more turn,' said the driver, 'and we will be on the New England Highway."

Then the little blanket friends ventured out for a nibble on the most tender part of our bodies, gorging themselves on our warm blood. I wriggled about trying hard not to scratch. Mother bumped me in the ribs with her elbow, giving me the sign not to even think of scratching, especially in company of the young man. I noticed she was moving in her seat at times.

As we came into the main street of Maitland, I noticed the cars parked on each side of the street were like the cars in the Keystone cops movies we had seen on the ship. I had not seen cars like that in Germany. Most of the cars I had seen there were military trucks and staff cars. Travelling through High Street, I tried to glimpse in the shop windows, but in no time we were over the railway bridge at the end of town.

The truck slowed down as it pulled itself up the first hill at East Maitland. There was no problem going downhill. A bigger hill came up and once again the truck struggled, moaning and growling. Every time the driver changed gears, the truck rolled back. Mother and I were fearful, holding on to one another as the truck nearly stopped half way on the steep hill and rolled back. We were hoping that the truck wouldn't roll into the deep ditch.

On the next hill, I was half expecting the driver to ask me to take the steering wheel while he and Dad pushed the old jalopy to the top. With a lot of effort the truck somehow managed to pull itself up and over the hill. What a relief to make it. We arrived safely at Beresfield and Mother and I were glad the journey was over.

After the truck was unloaded Father took out his wallet and paid the driver 25 shillings. Dad put his hand inside his coat pocket and pulled out a key, to open the door of the kitchen he had built onto our new tent home. Mother was the first to walk through the door. The first thing she saw was the fuel stove. Her eyes lit up as she clasped her hands together and said, "Finally, after all the years of living in miserable camps, I have a stove of my own and a clean kitchen all to myself! I can hardly believe this is true!" To the right of the kitchen were the two bedrooms and to the left was a utility room. Mother's eyes were filled with tears of joy as she walked from canvas room to canvas room, her hands still clasped together, convincing herself that this was not a dream.

She turned to Father and said, "Pawel, you were right. There is plenty of room here. We can make these tents into a comfortable home."

OUR CANVAS PALACE

We were so engrossed in looking through our new house that we didn't notice the time getting away. Czesiek broke the moment by pulling on the hem of Mother's dress, saying, "Mummy, I want a drink."

"Oh my,' said Mother, 'I have no food! I saw a shop as we were coming this way…"

Dad piped up and said, "There is no need to worry. There is milk, butter and food in the ice chest. There is also black bread in the cupboard."

Mother had never seen an ice chest. Father stood next to the ice chest, opened the top door and said, "This is where the ice is put in to keep the milk, butter, and meat."

Mother looked and said, "There is no ice."

No sooner had she said this than a man came to the door with ice tongs in his hand and introduced himself as the ice man. "Will you be wanting ice today?" he asked.

"Yes," said Father.

"The cost of the ice is fifteen pence," said the man.

In a few minutes the ice man carried a big block of ice into the kitchen and gently dropped the ice into the chest. As Dad paid him, the ice man said, "Thank you. I deliver Mondays, Wednesdays and Fridays. I'll be seeing you next time on my rounds."

Mother turned to Dad and said, "I am saying this from the bottom of my heart: thank you Pawel. You have been wonderful making this happen."

Dad held out his arms and drew us in close together. "You don't know how long I have been waiting and longing for this moment,' he said. 'I can hardly believe that we are all together again."

"This is a good start to our new life,' said Mother. She lifted her eyes up and said, 'Thank you God."

I could sense that Mother was more than pleased with the effort that Father had made so we could live comfortably in our canvas palace. Mother looked around at the living arrangements. She turned to Father and said, "Did the furniture come from the time of Krol Sasa?" (By which she meant that it looked so old it must have come from the time of the 18th century Polish king, Augustus III).

The furniture that Father had bought was big and bulky. Mother preferred things to be small and neat. Dad had tried his best, but what did he know about décor? Now that I think back, Father did not have much to choose from. He purchased the only furniture available at the time. People from European countries who had settled in Hamilton and surrounding areas bought old houses and second hand furniture until they could afford something better.

Mother was also concerned that the tents were close to the railway tracks; how would we get to sleep with the noise of the trains running all night?

Dad replied, 'It will only take a few weeks and you won't notice the noise.'

Mother started to unpack the kitchen utensils and crockery while Father lit the fire in the stove to boil water for tea. The fire in the stove would not die out. This was the source of power for cooking meals and heating water for the bath and washing. It also heated the clothes iron, which was placed on the stove to heat.

The next afternoon we had a visit from Vincent Murray's daughter, Eileen. She was not at all shy. She came with a warm welcome, introducing herself to my parents and inviting me to meet her parents and four teenage brothers: Joe, Patrick, Timmy and Mickey. Eileen was the youngest in her family.

Dad said it was alright for me go with Eileen. Dad had met Eileen's father a few weeks earlier; he was the boss of the railway fettler gang that helped Dad rig up our tents after the terrible wind storm. After I had met her family, Eileen said, "Come with me and I'll show you around the town." We walked to the top of the street and Eileen said:

"This is Cameron's corner grocery shop

and across the street, the Post Office,

and next to the Post Office is the Buffalo Hall;

further to the top of Lawson Street,

the Public School and across the New England Highway,

the crematorium,

and a little further on

the Pannowitz Mixed Business Shop;

across from the shop is the Memorial Park

and further down the rubbish dump;

across the road Neptune Service Station

and way down the end of Beresfield, in Byron Street,

that is where the coal mine is;

coming back onto the end of Addison Road

there is the railway station;

across the railway line bridge is the Radio Station 2NC

on the road to Woodberry;

now you have been all around the town

and back to the street we live."

From what I had seen, Beresfield was a few houses nestled in the bush among the trees. Many houses were half built, just two rooms. Their bathtubs, laundry tubs and coppers were just outside near the back door to the kitchen. Only the rooves were finished. The walls were hessian or corrugated iron. This was the way people lived as there was not enough housing after the war. People bought land and lived in temporary dwellings, building their houses in stages while they saved enough cash to buy more material. To borrow from the bank was not an easy task. The bank would not lend money without security.

A few days later, Mrs Murray came to introduce herself to Mother. The conversation was limited, as Mother could speak only a few words of English. Mrs Murray said to Mother that she was taking Eileen to the movies at Newcastle, and she extended an invitation, asking me to come along. When Mother understood, she said yes. ("If one is invited,' said Mother in Polish, 'it is bad manners to refuse.")

So that afternoon we were off to the pictures. Mrs Murray, Eileen and I walked to the railway station, bought our train tickets and boarded the train. While we were in the train carriage, Eileen pointed out spots of interest to me. She was full of enthusiasm, trying to teach me English. As the train travelled through the Tarro swamps, and then pulled into Tarro Station, Eileen said, "This is the station where I get off to go to school, after the school holidays are over. This train will stop at every station all the way into Newcastle."

When we crossed the Iron Bark Creek, Eileen cried out, "Look! There are the Shortland Swamps. Look! Look at the wild ducks and the two black swans with the red beaks swimming in the water." As the train headed into Newcastle, Eileen was constantly talking.

At Waratah we passed a row of tents. "Tent City!' said Eileen, 'just like the ones we live in, only there are more of them!"

After Waratah we travelled past the gasworks. A little further, before the Hamilton crossing, there were people living in corrugated iron huts no bigger than two chicken sheds put together. "Shanty Town," said Eileen. I saw some horses in a paddock next to the shanties, and Eileen said that they were ready for the glue factory.

We got off the train at Civic Station, crossing Hunter Street to the Civic Picture Theatre. We had come to see *Alice in Wonderland*. We walked through the doors, entering a grand building. I felt as if *I* was in wonderland. It was like the palace I had seen in Germany. Sitting in this beautiful theatre made me feel like I was someone special.

Eileen was jumping about, pressing her mother for money to buy a packet of Fantails. Mrs Murray gave Eileen the money to buy one packet, to be shared between the three of us. Eileen opened the packet and passed them to me. I took one only and said, "No more, thank you."

I was too busy admiring the splendour of the interior lights shining like little stars through the ornate ceiling, and the lanterns mounted on the wall. Red velvet drapes covered the screen. There were statues standing in wall cavities, and balconies up high at each end. This theatre was full of regal charm. It had a majestic feel about it. Even the ladies' powder room was majestic. This theatre was maybe not as big as a palace, but it was as beautiful.

After the movie, Mrs Murray suggested that we have a milkshake. I had no idea what a milkshake was, but Eileen left us and ran ahead to reserve a table at the milk bar. When we sat down at the table a waitress came to take our order, like I had seen in movies.

Eileen asked, "What flavour do you want, Terese? Chocolate or strawberry?"

"I don't like chocolate,' I answered.

"Well, will you like strawberry," she asked.

"Yes, please," I said.

The waitress returned, carrying a tray with three big silver containers and three tall glasses. Eileen poured the milkshake from one of the silver containers into a glass, and then passed the container and glass of pink milk over to me. I took my first sip, asking Eileen in broken English, "Das is milk, yes?"

"It's a milkshake. It's milk, flavouring and a little ice-cream all shook up in the mixer," said Eileen.

"I like das drink,' I said. 'Milkshake, das is good drink."

"Chocolate is my favourite drink," said Eileen.

When we had finished our drinks, we walked towards the station. On the corner, next to the picture theatre, was Darrell's ladies' dress shop. I walked over to look at the dresses displayed on the models in the window. Before we crossed the street to the station, Mrs Murray said to Eileen, "Let's go in and show Terese inside the shop."

I was very impressed by how lovely and spacious the shop was, with all the dresses hanging neatly in a row around the shop wall. The sales lady greeted us very politely. She asked if there was something special that she could show us. Mrs Murray said to Eileen, "Have a look and see what dress you would like."

The sales lady had taken out two dresses and said they were the smallest size they had. She opened the fitting room for Eileen to try on the dresses. Eileen came out in each dress to show her Mother. The dresses were too big.

"I am sorry,' said the sales lady. 'That is all we have."

We walked out from the shop and I said to Eileen, "I not see dress shop."

"You never saw a dress shop before?!" asked Eileen.

'No," I answered.

"Your Mother didn't take you into town shopping?" asked Eileen.

"We live in camp. No shops for dresses in camps," I explained.

Eileen said nothing, just shrugged her shoulders as if she didn't understand.

On the return trip home, we sat on the other side of the carriage. One of my memories of the train trip back home was coming into Hamilton station. I had been there before, but this time I noticed that it was well maintained, with hedges and a small garden, just like the train stations in Germany. It was the only train station I had seen like this. I saw vegetable gardens in the backyards of Islington homes. Eileen said, "You will see things on the other side of the track going back."

She pointed out industries and lambs in paddocks waiting for slaughter, and sheepskins hanging on fences. When the train stopped at Sandgate station, Eileen pointed out the cemetery and said, "That is where we will be going when we die!"

Eileen again pointed out the wild ducks and birds in the swamps before the train crossed the Iron Creek and stopped at Hexham station. At this station, the two hedges were trimmed neatly in a shape of a small rowing boat in the middle of the platform. The train passed the Oak butter factory. "That is where the butter is made," said Eileen. Coming in to Tarro station we saw Mutton's dairy farm. There were a few dairy farms around the Tarro,

Woodberry and Beresfield area. The next stop was Beresfield, where we got off the train and walked the rest of the way home.

What an exciting day I had had with my new friend Eileen and her mother. I enjoyed the experience of seeing a city for the first time since we had come to Australia. I could only speak broken English, and I said to Mrs Murray, "I am having a good day with Eileen. Much thank you for looking me today."

On Saturday, Eileen came over to our place to ask my parents' permission to take me to Mass on Sunday at the Catholic Church in Tarro. Permission was granted. Mother and Father were happy that the Murray family had extended their friendship, and made us welcome. On Sunday after Mass, Eileen said, "Come with me. I will introduce you to the priest, Father Hanrahan. He comes from Ireland. You may find his speech a little strange. Father comes to school once a week for one hour to teach Scripture and Catechism."

Eileen introduced me to Father Hanrahan. He was pleased to meet me, and said he was looking forward to seeing me at Mass next Sunday.

As we walked back home, Eileen pointed out the houses where the school children who came to our church lived. It was difficult for me to pay attention. We were walking in the hot sun among a plague of grasshoppers and flies. I waved my arms in front of my face, learning the famous Australian salute, trying to keep the flies away from my eyes and mouth. People in their gardens waved back. I saw it as a kind of Australian greeting.

In the evenings, the Hexham grey mosquitoes came out. They were like small tiger moths, diving on me like bombs biting into my flesh, sucking my blood. The insect bites on my arms and legs broke out in sores, and Mother was hoping that with treatment they would heal before school started.

There was a decision to be made. To be practical, the Beresfield Public School was within walking distance, just a few streets up from where we lived, but my wish was to go with Eileen to Our Lady of Lourdes Catholic School at Tarro. Eileen promised Dad that she would look after me at school. Dad could see I needed help and Eileen was just the girl who would do that. I was given permission to attend the same school as Eileen.

On the Monday after the school holidays were over, Eileen was waiting for me at the gate. We walked to the railway station and met the other children going to the same school. Children from Thornton also got off the train at Tarro, and we all walked to school together. When we reached the school grounds, the children from Thornton ran to meet their friends.

The children looked at me in a strange way. I was wearing my best red dress with white daisy print. My hemline was just above the knee. I wore long white socks, and my shoes were lace-up, two tone red-and-whites with a one-inch thick pig skin sole. My hair was braided with a French roll on the top of my head. I certainly stood out.

A boy from Holland also aroused curiosity. He wore wooden clogs and took them off when he entered the class room. This was strange to the Australian children, but not to me. In some parts of Germany, clogs were often worn. I had a pair of clogs myself at one stage.

The children coming from the train always arrived at school before the teachers. The nuns came from East Maitland Convent, and on their way to school they provided transport for the children from Four Mile Creek. Eileen stood at the gate watching the highway for the Sisters' car. As soon as she saw the car she yelled out, "Here they come!"

Sister St Paul zoomed her green Singer car into the school grounds and parked. The children got out first. The boys came to assist carrying the Sisters' bags into the classroom. When the Sisters were settled, Eileen introduced me to Sister St Paul. She was the Sister in charge. Sister St Paul greeted me, saying, "Terese is a lovely name."

She asked me to follow her into the classroom, where she gave me a brief interview and registered my name in the book. Sister St Paul told me I was to be put in Third Class. Sister Gonzaga taught the First, Second and Third classes in the first room, while Sister St Paul was the teacher of Fourth, Fifth and Sixth classes in the second room. Sister Gonzaga was to be my teacher until the end of the year. At the age of twelve I should have been in Sixth Class, but since arriving in Australia I had attended school for only a little time in each camp. This was my fourth school. I had managed to attend school for six months altogether and had learned a small amount of English in that time.

The school bell rang and children began lining up to enter the classroom. Sister St Paul introduced me to Sister Gonzaga and the school children. Once the children were seated in the classroom, Sister Gonzaga looked for a place for me to sit. She said, "I don't know how I am going to cope teaching you Terese. Your English is limited and I do not know how much you can understand."

In broken English, I replied, "I sit, learn what I can do." Sister Gonzaga was patient with me. This was her first teaching job after completing Teachers' College and she had been given the responsibility of teaching three classes in one room. Ten of her thirty students were new Australians.

Mother had given me money to buy my lunch at the school tuck shop. It was only held on Mondays, when mothers on tuck shop duty provided the fillings for the sandwiches and made cakes. There was a long wait at the tuck shop in the lunch hour and Eileen suggested that we go across the road to the shop to buy a meat pie instead of waiting for sandwiches.

After we had bought the pies we came back to the school grounds and sat under a tree with a group of girls eating our lunch. Not being accustomed to Australian food, I found it difficult to eat this pie. I stood up looking around for a bin to throw the pie in, but Eileen swiped the pie out of my hand, saying, "If you can't eat it, I'll have it. You're not going to throw this away!"

Eileen took a bite of the pie and said how delicious it was. Again she sunk her teeth into the pie. At that very moment a magpie flew into the tree and yodelled. Suddenly Eileen yelled out, "Curse that bloody bird shitting on my pie!"

The way she had yelled out, and the expression on her face, made us laugh. A blob of bird poo had indeed landed on the pie. It was destined for the garbage bin after all!

That was the best laugh I had had since I left the ship. The incident made my day. I came home from my first day at school, excited to tell Mother what happened at lunchtime.

I started to tell her the story, but she cut in and said, "Do your chores first, and you can tell me the news later."

Although I was living with Mother, and knew that she loved me, there was a distance growing between us. At times I felt like I didn't exist. She was a good mother to me, but there were no embraces or kisses, no praise, and no time for conversation. The war had left its mark on my parents.

In the evening, while we were sitting and waiting for Mother to serve the meal, Dad asked me about my first day at school. I said, "Dad, it was so much easier having Eileen with me. It was a great help. I was not alone; it was good to have a friend with me."

I told him the story of the magpie and Eileen's pie. He laughed out loud like the girls at school. Mother said it was a waste of good food. She didn't always see the funny side of life, but then she hadn't been there to see how funny the expression on Eileen's face was. Dad loved the story.

Father was interested to hear what I had to say about the school. I told him that the classes were held in the church building. During the week the church was partitioned into two rooms. The first room was created by a heavy curtain drawn across the altar, and this was pulled back every day for early morning mass. The second class room was separated from the first by a wooden folding door with glass panels at the top. Every day, before class began, a prayer was said. When we opened our exercise books to write our work, we had to write AMDTG at the top of the left hand margin. This meant "All My Duty to God." At midday, "The Angelus" was said, and every class ended with a prayer.

The prayers I learned in my religious upbringing have remained with me throughout my life. From my early years at home and at school I learned to respect people, and it became a habit for me. I consciously try not to hurt or offend anyone in any way, whether holding a conversation, shopping at the supermarket, or driving a car. At the end of each day I recollect my deeds, and if I feel that I have done or said something unpleasant, I do my best to learn from that mistake and not repeat it. I treasure my life, and I try my best to respect people in the way I would like be respected. The teachings in my early life helped me to learn common sense and take control of my weaknesses. It is a very simple rule to live by: remember that you represent your family, your school or your place of work. You are the ambassador for the people of your town or your country. Anger can only bring misery and destruction.

The Sisters were very mindful of their vow of obedience and the restrictions that were put upon them. I don't know how the Sisters tolerated the summer heat, having to wear the starched wimple that covered both the head and neck, and the black veil. Their full-length habits consisted of a full black underskirt and over that a long black pleated tunic with long wide sleeves and an inner pocket to carry all their needs. When walking, and when their hands were not busy, the Sisters folded their arms and tucked their hands into the wide sleeves. At the waist they wore a black leather belt, to which was attached a set of heavy rosary beads and a crucifix.

The Sisters of Mercy were very good and hardworking, putting all their effort and devotion into teaching and raising money for the school and sports. They received no wages from the government. Our school money, two shillings a week, was the Sisters' earnings. After school hours, the Sisters earned money teaching music.

Our school was a happy school. The Sisters were dedicated to teaching, and this was reflected in the students who had a great affection for them. The girls at the school were good to me; accepting me in their play and making me feel part of the group. They helped me by correcting my English. The boys behaved well at school, except for one boy who made a nuisance of himself tormenting us girls. When standing in line, if we stood in front of him, he would pull on our long plaits and call us names that we didn't need to hear. In due time, the Sisters ended the torment when they caught the boy in the act. Sister St Paul addressed him about his behaviour, and reminded him to behave like a man.

Growing up between two cultures was difficult for me. I was living a sort of double life. At home I spoke to my parents in Polish, but to my brother I spoke in English to prepare him for Kindergarten. Although we came from a country of the same religious background where the laws were based on the principles of the Ten Commandments, our culture and customs set us apart from Australians. In my short life time I had never lived in a place we could call home, but now, living in a place of our own, my family continued living in the way of the old country. At school I was taught the Australian ways to become a good citizen to my new country, but at home I was expected to follow the custom of my parents.

As the eldest child in the family, it was my responsibility to help with the household chores, as my parents had done when they were young. Every day, when I came home from school, I collected water from the big tank to fill the kitchen container. I had to be on the lookout for snakes in the long grass that surrounded the tank, as snakes favoured long grass and available water, especially in the summer. Grocery shopping was another errand for me in the late afternoon. I didn't mind helping. It was a pleasure. Working together creates a sense of belonging to a family.

I also had to collect coal from the railway track to keep the stove fire alive until the next evening. I had to be on the track early, before the neighbours from across the street came, so I could pick up the coal close to our canvas home. There was always plenty of coal farther down the track towards Tarro, but no-one wanted to go that far; it was a long walk back. Sometimes a friendly train driver bringing water to fill the tanks dropped off big lumps of coal in front of each water tank. We were able to fill a bag for reserve. The track was usually picked clean by the end of the day.

To be safe, I tried to be off the track by the time the Queensland express came through on its way to Sydney. Although I had a good long view of the track in the distance, that express train travelled at a high speed.

One day I was standing in front of our place, waiting for a coal train to pass before I went on the track. As the train stopped at the red signal, a big lump of coal fell from the overloaded hopper, and split open. I picked up the large piece and was surprised to see the wave of rainbow colours in the coal. Many times I had collected small pieces of coal in my bucket, and not seen the beauty of this mineral. One very hot day, I was sitting outside, hoping to catch a breeze of cool air. A coal train was passing. For something to do I counted the hoppers. A ray of the sun caught on a fractured edge of coal. It glittered like a diamond.

The coal was transported from the Hunter Valley mines to the coal plant at Hexham, where the coal was crushed and washed, then loaded on the ship docked on the Hunter River only three miles from where we lived. These days, the coal trains pass my brother's office daily, each one pulling about 150 wagons of coal.

We only got to see Dad was when he was on day shift. Sitting at the table one evening, Father asked me what I had learned in school that week. I told Dad that Sister St Paul had selected a group of children for a choir. "We have been learning to sing hymns for a wedding,' I said. 'The bride and groom want the school children to sing at their wedding Mass."

"That's very good,' said Father. 'Singing, dancing and a good laugh is important for a good healthy life."

Before we left the table, Father said "Did I tell you that the men I work with, we are like a family. Sometimes we have problems. We talk things over at lunchtime. One of our boys, Nick, was having a problem sleeping the last two weeks. Nick came to work angry and complaining to us of this annoying bird. Nick's problem was, as soon as he got to settle down to sleep from night work, this big bird sitting in the tree near his bedroom window started to cackle out loud."

"I get out of bed, I chase the bird away," says Nick. This was happening every day.

"One of our workmates piped up and said, "Nick, everyone in this country is free to have a cackle."

A suggestion was made to Nick to sleep in the back room for a while. Nick took the advice and moved to the back room. Just as Nick was about to fall asleep, the bird came and sat on the clothes line, making noises to be fed. Then he found out that his wife was encouraging the bird to come every day. She was making a pet of the noisy bird by feeding him. This was too much for Nick. "She must go!" he decided.

"A few days went by. There were no more complaints from Nick. One of the men said to Nick, "We haven't heard you complain. Did you solve the problem with the bird? Is everything OK?"

"Yes," said Nick, "everything is okay dokey. She laughs at me no more."

"What have you done?" this man asked.

Nick says, "I shoot her."

"We were astonished". We said, "You shot your wife for laughing at you? Do you know what you have done?"

"'Yes," said Nick. "I put her in the soup pot and I'm having her for lunch."

"Before anyone could say a word, Nick said, "I brought extra food today to share with my friends. Anyone like a sandwich?"

"No thank you Nick," we said. "We could not look at him".

"OK," he says, "all the more for me."

I sat at the table, silent and gullible. I didn't know if I should laugh or cry. I looked at Mother and the expression on her face. Father waited, and then said, "What do you have to say?"

Mother was the one who made us laugh. She folded her arms and nodded her head. "I am thinking that is a good story you tell us Pawel,' she said. 'You always were good at telling stories."

We learned that Australian men were always pulling the legs of their new Australian mates.

Living on the railway property, our Australian neighbours became our friends: Mr and Mrs Bryce and their four boys, and Mr and Mrs Folpp. Mr Bryce and Mr Folpp worked with Mr Murray as the fettler gang for the railway. Mrs Anna Witkowski and her husband and children Helena, Tonia and Heniek lived on the other side of the railway track. Mrs Witkowski and Mother became good friends. Czesiek and I often crossed the railway track to play games with the Witkowski children. There was plenty of spacious ground to play ball games on their side of the track near the 2NC Radio station.

Father started working on a vegetable garden almost straightaway. The neighbours laughed at him, saying he was crazy. They couldn't understand how Dad was going to grow a garden on a narrow strip of sandstone. Father would go out on his bike on his days off and bring back bags of soil. He went across the railway track to collect manure, laying the soil and manure on the rock and using coal ash from the stove. Mixing the ash into the soil made it light and airy. Dad built a fence around the garden, planting vegetables and seeds, and used a watering can to carry water from the tanks to the garden. To everyone's amazement a garden was created. Dad was satisfied. Mother felt a little happier that Father had fulfilled their dream of having their own vegetable garden, no matter how small.

Months passed. Mother never did get used to the trains rumbling by at night. When Father was working night shift, I heard Mother crying softly in her bed. At daybreak she would creep through our canvas bedroom, careful not to disturb our sleep, and go into the kitchen. After lighting the fire in the fuel stove, Mother took the watering can and went into the garden to water the plants. If it was a cold and rainy day, she used the time to darn socks and mend clothes.

Mother was a very proud woman. She would not let us go out into the street with holes in our clothes. It was an embarrassment to be seen in the street with holes in the clothes. We were to look neat and tidy and clean at all times. Mother said, "We may be poor, but we don't have to let that be known."

To My Mother

I am your kitten,

the one you lost for a time

while bombs were falling

and soil was drenched in blood.

From behind the barbed wire

your heart yearned for your children.

The pain was a blunt dagger ripping it apart.

At a time we your little kittens needed you most

we too were frightened,

and longed to climb into your arms

to touch your warm heart and hear it beat,

to listen to your sweet voice sing a lullaby.

We were ripped away from your loving arms,

we were robbed of those precious moments

and tender loving years.

I watch your morning ritual,

watch you tugging at the threads of life.

Deep scars in your heart filled your eyes with sorrow

for the loss of our two little sparrows.

You follow the path of your garden

to gather some strength and joy,

to carry you through tomorrow.

I never heard Father talk about his problems. He was on shift work and often he would work overtime on his day off. Dad would never refuse extra work; it was the only way to save for a house. Dad must have been very tired. When I did see my father, he never complained about lack of sleep or hard work. He kept busy working in the garden.

He had another interest apart from his vegetable garden. On weekends when Dad was home, I would hear him whistling tunes while he made boxes to breed pigeons for the dinner table. That project didn't work. It was too much work for such a small reward and, in any case, we didn't really like the pigeon meat.

Father liked his job and he made friends with the men at work. They were helpful to him with the work and corrected him on speaking English. The men he worked with were good and honest mates. One day, his friends who had cars came to visit us to see how we were settling in, and to see the garden Dad often spoke of.

Some weeks later Father's work mates came to visit again, this time bringing their wives and children and some clothing for me, a warm and welcoming gesture. At the time of their arrival Mother was making doughnuts. The ladies gathered around Mother as she made the doughnuts. One of the ladies asked Mother what she used to cook the doughnuts.

I translated for Mother, and told the ladies that the doughnuts were cooked in lard. After Mother had finished cooking, she laid the table with tea and doughnuts. In the blink of an eye those doughnuts were all gone! I can't say the same for the tea. As the ladies politely sipped the weak coloured water we called tea, their eyes nearly popped out of their sockets. The ladies thanked Mother for an interesting day, and complimented her on the doughnuts.

Mother loved the Australian people. She found them to be friendly, with the exception of Sheila across the street. Sheila appeared to have problems like the old woman in the nursery rhyme. She had so many children she needed more fingers on each hand to count them all. Her children were all under the age of thirteen. When she called out for them, she sometimes forgot some of their names. Not to worry, Shelia had some help from her pet, Charlie the cockatoo. Charlie had no problems. He knew every child in the family. All Shelia had to do was to say to Charlie, "Call out for the bloody kids!" and Charlie would yell out the children's names. Every one of them came running home.

Mother felt sorry for Sheila and her big family. Sheila's husband's wages would barely cover the cost of rent, bills and food. There was not much money left over for anything else. Sometimes the little ones came to our place while we were sitting outside eating our sandwiches. The two little ones looked at us with eager eyes and Mother would make a cheese and tomato sandwich for them. Mother knew that sandwiches made by someone else always tasted good.

Sheila appeared to have problems with us, the new Australian people. If anything went wrong in her house, it was the New Australians who were to blame. She would stand on her front veranda yelling out something about "You bloody New Australians! Go back to where you came from!" We didn't take offence. Charlie the cockatoo joined in, repeating every word Sheila said and adding his own colourful words. Charlie performed acrobatic acts and tricks on the veranda ledge and yelled out "Go back to your country where you belong, you silly galahs!" We admired how clever this bird was. Coming from a European country this was new entertainment for us.

When we met Sheila at the railway station waiting for the train, she would speak to us in a civil manner and bid us good-day, along with a few casual words until the train came.

We could sense that it was difficult and frustrating for the Australian people. The Australians were given the task of working and learning to communicate with people from different European countries. The Australians had to teach English to their new work mates. The war had changed life in almost every country of the world.

Dad kept a tight rein on me, but he allowed me to keep company with Eileen. He knew I had much to catch up on for growing and fulfilling my life dreams. Eileen played an important part in my life. I spent as much time as I could with her. We got on well. I looked on her as a sister. Eileen had confidence in herself, the very thing I needed. I was timid and shy, and it was Eileen's friendship that brought me out of my shell. When I was with Eileen I felt I was someone special.

Mrs Murray would write a long list of groceries for Eileen to take to the green grocer at East Maitland. I accompanied Eileen on the short train trip to drop off the shopping list. The grocer would put the groceries on the train to Beresfield station the next day, and Mr Murray picked them up from the station on the Sheffield Trolley. (That was a trolley with a handle that pushes up and down to move railway workers along the track to carry out maintenance work.)

At the same time we had prescriptions filled at the chemist and brought the medication back with us, because there was no doctor or chemist in Beresfield. Eileen and I made the train trip every two weeks. Father could see that Eileen was good company and a friend to me. He allowed me to spend time at the Murrays' house because I was learning from them how Australian people lived.

On payday, when Dad finished the night shift, he would meet Mother at Hamilton station and walk to the delicatessen owned by one of our European countrymen. It was filled with food that European people were accustomed to eating. The Australian corner shops didn't keep that kind of food. Hamilton became a meeting place. On paydays, people from Poland and neighbouring countries would get together in the street and talk in their own language. The Australian people showed their disapproval of Europeans speaking their own language in public streets, but this was how the European people found comfort and relief. Most of them had lost families and children in the war. There were no clubs or churches of their own they could congregate in.

Through these meetings, Mother found out about a Polish doctor practising at Swansea and she wanted to go and see him. Mother wouldn't go anywhere without Father, so we all went to see the doctor at Swansea. We travelled two hours each way for a half-hour consultation. Twenty-four miles each way was a long way by public transport. We caught a train in the morning from Beresfield to Hamilton Station, and then walked up Tudor Street to catch a bus to Swansea. It was not a pleasant trip for me. The diesel fumes from the bus caused a migraine headache and made me feel sick to the point of throwing up. When we finally arrived at the surgery, it was full of patients. We waited for hours before getting in to see the doctor. Then we repeated the long trip home in the evening. The trip to Swansea was to be made every fortnight, but after the second trip, Czesiek and I stayed home while Father went with Mother to the doctor.

Any decision for Mother to leave the house for the day was not taken lightly. It meant that her work did not get done. All the washing of sheets, towels and clothing was done by hand, with the help of the washing board. Ironing was also difficult. This was time consuming work. There was no time for pleasure; that was something of a luxury. We had no cars to jump into and be on our way to a doctor's appointment or a hospital visit. We had to walk to the train station, catch a train, and walk to our destination.

Mother's headaches sometimes confined her to bed. She looked to me for help. At times like these, my responsibility was to take care of Czesiek. That included giving him a bath. I had to carry the hot water in a bucket from the stove to the bath. All this had to be finished before nightfall, as we had no electricity on the railway property. When Father was working afternoon shift, I had to light the Tilley lantern which was fuelled by kerosene and used in the kitchen, hanging from the top of the rafter. No other lamps or candles were used in the bedrooms. We had learned from the experience of my First Holy Communion that accidents can happen with flames.

On one of the occasions we all made the trip to Swansea, we had seen a woman named Mary walking on the railway bridge towards Beresfield. Mary lived on a farm at Millers Forest and would come into Beresfield regularly. Mary had an unusual personality, similar to someone with what we now know as dementia. When I first saw old Mary, I was frightened. She was hunchbacked and wore ragged clothes. Her grey hair was long and matted. Mary would often be seen walking around Beresfield carrying a stick in her hand and talking to herself. The local boys tormented her, calling her crazy and getting her so angry that she chased the boys with her stick. Mother felt sorry for the way the young boys annoyed Mary.

Mother was concerned about Mary, and said to Father, "She must have a family. Someone should take care of Mary. She shouldn't be wandering the streets by herself. I hope that when I get to that age, I don't end up like Mary."

It was as if Mother had a premonition; she was afraid she would suffer the same fate.

A PERMANENT HOME

Any spare time Father had was used looking for a permanent house. After searching for some months, he found one that would be suitable for us. We all went together on a Saturday to take a look through the Federation brick house at Hamilton. It was a grand house. The ceilings were high with ornate plaster work and lovely light fittings. The lower half of the walls was clad with grooved timber and there was a picture rail around the dining and lounge room walls. It had a fire place, an orange tree growing in the backyard, and a garage. The house was only a short walk to the Sacred Heart Church at Hamilton and close to the main street shops. Mother would have liked it to be ours, and Father was set on buying the house, but it was not to be.

Father was admitted to Maitland hospital for a hernia operation. Unfortunately, that was a setback to buying the house. Father was off work for six weeks and the money that was saved for the deposit had to be used for living expenses until Father was able to go back to work.

In the end, though, it was just as well Father didn't buy that house. Only a few years later it was demolished for a two lane roadway. It would have caused disappointment and anguish to my parents if they had to look for another place to live.

Money was tight. One afternoon after school, Mother sent me to the shop for groceries. On the way to the shop, my mind was on other things. It had started to sprinkle rain, and my knees hurt. That morning, on my way to school, I had fallen on a sharp stone, and cut one knee and bruised the other. My hands had also been grazed. Two ladies on the train had bandaged my knee with their hankies as best they could. When I arrived at school, Sister Gonzaga had bandaged my knee properly and treated my hands with antiseptic.

That afternoon, shopping was the last thing on my mind. I was trying to hurry to beat the rain, and when I arrived at the shop I found I had no money. Not thinking, I went back to tell Mother that I had lost the money. Mother was relying on me for help and I had let her down. She was very angry, and sent me out to find the money. She told me not to come home until I found it. By that time the rain was coming down heavily. I walked back to the shop. I decided to follow the flow of the water, which was running in the opposite direction to the shop. I walked around the corner of the street, and there was the pound note floating in the gutter! My search was over. I was lucky that no-one had been out walking in the rain and picked up the money. That pound note was worth most of the groceries for a week.

Mother was not at all happy with me coming home with injuries to my knees that day. In a stern voice she said, "You are always falling over and getting yourself in a mess. If you are not bleeding from the knees, it's your nose that bleeds. What is wrong with you?"

I was not like the other children. They were carefree, having fun, playing and laughing. Although I joined in and played as they did, for me it was an effort, something I had to do. I couldn't rid myself of the blues and enjoy life like the girls I played with. Sometimes I sat by myself, wondering why I couldn't be like them. It was difficult for me to explain to Mother that my legs ached and felt heavy. It was difficult for me to run. I always felt tired. I had no confidence in myself and never looked happy. I was serious about my schoolwork, and about helping at home.

The doctor sometimes made visits at school to give the children a general health check. I tried to tell the doctor the way I felt. She told me that it was only growing pains and that I would grow out of this stage in a few years. I couldn't blame the doctor for that diagnosis. I looked quite well and she didn't have the knowledge of my medical history. She was only at school to check on our general wellbeing.

Occasionally on a Saturday morning Dad and I went to buy food from the delicatessen in Hamilton. We were walking over the railway crossing at Hamilton one Saturday when I noticed a beautiful handkerchief lying on the track. As I picked up the handkerchief, I heard a train whistle blowing. I looked up and saw a big iron monster almost on top of me. I felt someone grab my arm fiercely and pull me off the track. I looked up and saw it was Dad. I saw the horror in his eyes. His face had turned grey.

The day was extremely hot and the shock of the incident came over Father. He went weak in the knees and stumbled over to the station. He sat down. After he revived, we walked into The Station Hotel to cool down. Dad ordered a glass of beer and passed it over to me and before he got a chance to ask me whether I liked it, I had already drunk half a glass. He ordered himself a glass. By the time Dad had picked up his glass of beer, I had already finished mine. He asked me if I would like another drink. As I looked up at Dad, I could see that every man was looking at us.

Father had no idea that he was breaking the law by bringing me into the bar, and I am sure that the Australians were a little surprised at how quickly I downed my beer. Dad and I sat quietly at the table as he drank his second middy. Still recovering from shock and a little warm under the collar, we left the hotel and went on with shopping, then headed for home. In all my life I would say I have had no more than four glasses of beer since that incident at the Hamilton crossing.

My classes at school with Sister Gonzaga were coming to an end. I had made a vast improvement in school, speaking and reading English in twelve weeks. I could read the storybook of *The Three Little Pigs* that Miss Sealy had given me before we left Greta. Sister Gonzaga was pleased I had learned to read in such a short time. I found that reading came easily to me, but I cannot say the same for spelling. I was confused with words sounding the same but spelt in a different way. I could not understand how the words "door" and "sure" could sound the same but looked different, while "food" and "flood" sounded different, but looked the same. Although Sister found my composition interesting, she had difficulty in reading my work. She said to me, "I do not know how to mark your work, Terese."

"Mark mines the same as the others," I said.

"Your spelling might be correct in Polish..." said Sister.

Most of the new Australian children had more advantage in school work than I did. They were born after the war and had come to Australia when they were toddlers. They started learning English in kindergarten and First Class, as Czesiek would. When I was his age, I had been very ill after being a prisoner in that horror place. Before that, at a younger age, I had been left on my own in a room all day, only seeing Mother in the evenings to be fed and put to sleep. Learning speech and behaviour does not come naturally to an infant when left alone in the developing years. Children learn by watching, listening and imitating their parents. I missed those important years of learning.

I had started school in Ludwigsburg camp at the age of seven. I was very quiet and timid, and slow in learning. I was looked upon as an autistic child. Learning for me was difficult. I started lessons in the Polish language. I had the ability to listen, and was eager to learn, but I didn't know the alphabet and couldn't write. I learned from the teacher mainly by listening to what she was saying, and learning to write in Polish. Arriving in Australia, I had to learn a new language and the English alphabet. That was confusing for me. Maybe Sister Gonzaga realised that.

We had been living in our new adopted country for two years. It hadn't been easy. The living conditions and the climate were not what we had expected, especially the hot summer days. We hadn't imagined that summer days could be so hot, but we were grateful for what we had and we lived in hope of a better future.

As time passed, Mrs Murray came to see Mother frequently. She talked to Mother about the new house that her husband Vincent was building on the land where they were living in their tent home. Mrs Murray kept Mother up to date with progress reports on the house. She said that she wouldn't know herself living in a house with electricity, hot and cold running water and a fridge to keep the food for her family of boys. Mrs Murray said that she hoped the house would be finished before the hot weather arrived, ready for them to move in and be settled by Christmas. She said, 'I will be able to sit in the lounge room like a posh lady in front of the electric fan and cool off on hot days.'

The new Murray house was small: only two bedrooms, a kitchen and a lounge room. All the rooms were the same size. The boys' beds were on a veranda. The bathroom and the laundry were at the foot of the kitchen steps outside the house.

The Feast of St Nicholas on the 6th of December was an important day for us European children in the school. In Ludwigsburg, Father Bonkowski had told us a story about why the day is celebrated by giving presents to children. A family man was keeping money in a safe place and did not tell his wife where the money was hidden. But the man had an accident and lost his memory. The town bishop heard of the tragedy and pawned the ring he wore as a bishop. With the money he bought food and presents for the children so the family would have a good Christmas. The idea of giving presents to children caught on throughout the European countries, and presents were given to the children on the anniversary of St Nicholas' death on the 6th of December.

The children from the European countries brought their presents to school for 'show and tell'. The Australian children were puzzled when we told them that St Nicholas had dropped in for a visit in the early hours of the morning and left presents for us in a pillow slip. Sister St Paul came to the rescue, explaining that customs in Europe were different from that of British and Australian people.

Christmas 1952 would be my family's first Christmas celebration in our own home. Father finished night work on Christmas Eve, and was off work for the next two days. We were glad to have Father home with us over Christmas. It gave him the chance to participate in the preparation for Christmas Day, going out on his pushbike in search of a Christmas tree.

While Father was out in the bush looking for a tree, Mother was upholding one of the traditions from the old country: cleaning the house. An ancient belief has it that evil dwells in all things left dirty on that day (hence, perhaps, the saying "Cleanliness is next to Godliness"). Not that Mother had much to clean; the tradition was more about cooking. It was time consuming work making Polish dumplings and cooking lots of biscuits to hang on the Christmas tree, enough to last through the Christmas days. Father came back with a bush tree, not what Mother was expecting, but it was the closest Dad could find, and it was suitable for hanging Christmas ornaments.

It was good that Father was the first to walk in over the threshold during the festive season. A tradition from the old country was for a male to walk through the threshold first. It was a symbolic gesture for a male to let in the light of the world, bringing peace and joy into the house.

I was anxious to help decorate our Christmas tree. It was an exciting moment, especially for my brother and me. This was the first time in our lives that we had taken part in helping to decorate the Christmas tree with beautiful ornaments that Mother had brought with her from Germany, and that were left unbroken going through customs. To keep with the Polish tradition, we also hung biscuits on the tree for the children who would drop by our house and help themselves to biscuits and sweets from the tree over the festive season.

We had so much fun decorating the tree. We sang carols, and Dad played tricks on Mother, clowning around to make us laugh. After we finished decorating the tree, Czesiek and I were sent outside to watch for the first star to appear in the evening sky while Mother prepared the table for the *Wigilia* meal. It was a custom to put straw under the table cloth, and on the floor, but some traditions had to make way for modern times: there was no straw! Most important was the *Wigilia*. Not a fork or knife was picked up before the first star was seen in the sky, and meat was not eaten over the time of Advent until Christmas day.

Before the evening meal, prayers were said. A thin wafer procured from the priest was placed on the table. Before the meal, the wafer, or *oplatek*, is picked up by the head of the family, who breaks off a piece and passes the wafer on to the family and guests at the table. Christmas greetings and wishes of prosperity for the New Year are passed on to each person as the wafer is taken like a communion to honour the birth of Jesus. In our house it was Father who broke the first piece of the wafer and passed it on to Mother, then myself and Czesiek – just the four of us at the table. I could see the tears well up in Mother's eyes as she took the wafer, and I sensed the memories of the horrid years in our lives. Father sat with a distant look on his face, and for a moment we sat in complete silence. There would always be times like these, remembering the family members lost during the war. Father broke the silence by saying, 'We may eat.' We started our meal with *borscht*, followed by potato pancakes.

Our Christmas was a new experience for the Australians. Eileen came to our house on Christmas afternoon looking happy. She showed me the watch that she had been hoping to get for Christmas from her parents. As she came into the kitchen, the Christmas tree caught her attention. Eileen's face lit up as she said, "What a beautiful tree you have!"

Mother indicated that Eileen should help herself to the biscuits on the tree. Eileen asked if she could have two, as they looked so good.

"Why not? I make biscuits to eat," said Mother.

"Thank you, Mrs Anna!" Eileen said.

Eileen raced back home. Within a few minutes she was back with her mother. Mrs Murray said, "Oh this is very nice! What a lovely Christmas tree! Who would think to decorate a bush tree with beautiful delicate ornaments, and things to eat? Is this the custom of your country?"

"Ya,' said Mother. 'A long time back, in tree we put on apples, biscuits, lollies and candles. I not put candles. No good putting candles on in the tent. Biscuits, lollies, good for children to take and eat sometime through the day. This very good!"

"I like your custom,' said Mrs Murray. 'There are many things we can learn from the New Australians. When you are cooking doughnuts, Eileen can smell them from our house. She says to me, 'Anna is cooking doughnuts. I am going to see Terese."

"Mrs Anna makes lovely doughnuts!' said Eileen.

During the school holidays, I spent time with Eileen. She introduced me to the hobby of collecting pictures from the women's magazine after her mother had finished reading them. Eileen cut out pictures of her favourite film stars and pasted them in her scrap book. The film stars at the time were Anne Miller, the tap dancer; Elizabeth Taylor, the most beautiful woman in Hollywood; Rita Hayworth, the love goddess; and the singer, Doris Day. These film stars endorsed shampoo and soaps in the magazines. When Eileen had finished with the magazines, she passed them on to me and I made good use of the colourful pictures.

I took an interest in decorating our kitchen walls. These walls were made of fence palings because, as we were not going to live in the tents permanently, Father hadn't seen the point of spending money on good timber. In the processes of weather and the wood maturing, the palings had shrunk, leaving gaps in the wall. The magazines came in handy. I made paste by mixing flour with water and pasted a layer of pages on the wall. Each time I got another magazine, I added pages to the wall. I cut out the pictures of lovely gardens, plants, beautiful homes, bride dresses and wedding cakes, and pasted them on the writing between the magazine pictures. This kept the kitchen wall insulated from the cold, and made the kitchen bright and colourful. It gave me an interest and kept me busy during the holidays. At the same time, I was learning about the fashion in clothes, shoes and hats. The flowers and gardens in the magazine were beautiful, and I loved seeing photos of prominent people including the new Queen. I pasted up pictures of the Queen and Prince Philip. Our kitchen wall became a large montage.

Beresfield progressed slowly. A newsagency opened next to the Post Office. There was a rumour of a doctor and dentist visiting the town twice a week, and a chemist shop opening in the near future. As the school holidays came to an end, I was given money to go to the newsagency to buy pens and necessities to start the school year. I walked into the paper shop and my eyes opened wide. There were all kinds of books and magazines on the shelves. Big fairy tale books hung above the counter. The colourful children's story book *Puss in Boots* had drawn my attention. It was a large book with a picture of a cat wearing black boots. I was interested to read this story. The book also contained other stories. The temptation became too much for me. I asked the shopkeeper for the story book. I was sure Mother wouldn't mind me spending the two shillings on the book.

I walked home feeling very happy. I showed Mother the new book I had bought. She was extremely upset with me, and gave me a tongue lashing for spending money on a frivolous thing like a fairy tale book. I didn't understand why I was spoken to like this. Looking back, I can see that Mother was suffering a mental illness. Mother herself did not know what was wrong with her. All she knew was that she was sick and could not explain the illness to the doctor.

In the new year of 1953, Czesiek started school. He was placed in the transition class with Sister Goretti. His classroom was a converted lunch shed. It was difficult for people at school to say his name properly. Mrs Murray and Eileen suggested that we call him "Cecil", so he was enrolled under that name.

My teacher was Sister St Paul. The subjects she taught were more advanced than the work I had done in the previous year. The school work was interesting. I loved listening to what Sister was teaching, and I was good at remembering the things I learned during the day, except for numbers and dates. The subjects that interested me most were Social Studies, Geography, History and Religion. I especially loved the stories of Jesus when he lived on earth.

Like the rest of the class, I looked forward to the *Kookaburra* school magazine, issued by the Department of Education. I was glad when Sister considered me good enough to read a part in the play featured in the magazine. It felt so good to be included as part of the group in the class.

Every Tuesday, Father Hanrahan would visit our little school, teaching religion, morals and the obligations of being a good Catholic. He would ask questions from the Catechism. This was a small book given to the children to learn prayers, the Commandments and the Sacraments. We used this in preparation for our Confirmation. Father Hanrahan spoke about the soul living on forever after death. That idea disturbed me. I had trouble coping with every day present living. I didn't want to know about the life hereafter. I could not sleep for months. I kept wondering what my soul would do for eternal life. I had mixed feelings on the subject, as I did not want to die, and did not want to live forever. At that time in my life I couldn't cope with supernatural ideas. I already felt as if I was living out a kind of punishment in purgatory.

However, I could relate to Jesus because He was a man living on earth, not a spirit.

I remember Mother telling me, when I was little, about the Holy Family escaping to Egypt. The soldiers were on the lookout for the family. After a long journey, the Holy Family rested under a willow tree. As the soldiers were coming, the tree bowed its branches to the ground to protect the Holy Family. That is the story of the weeping willow tree.

Inspired by God's spirit, St Matthew tells the life of Jesus in his gospel. Most of the apostles of Christ had written some parts of Jesus' life on earth in their gospels. I believe it moreso, having travelled through that land when coming to Australia. Learning about Jesus' life, I was convinced of the good work Jesus did, and, at one stage, prepared myself to join the convent to serve Jesus and try to follow his footsteps.

Mother learned to speak English by listening to me talk with Cecil, and by talking with Mrs Murray. She would come over with Eileen to chat with Mother, and admire her vegetable garden. She started a conversation with Mother, asking, "How do you get the garden to grow so well?"

Mother pointed her finger to the garden. She picked up the watering can to demonstrate how she poured water on the plants, and said, "Funeral."

Mrs Murray showed some concern, and, with a puzzled look on her face, said to Eileen, "That must be some ritual they have for a funeral."

"They do live different to us," said Eileen.

Mrs Murray was concerned, and asked Mother, "Is Paul alright?"

"Ya, ya, Pawel at work," Mother said.

"Yes",' said Mrs Murray. To be a dinky-di Australian, the word you must say is "yes"."

There was silence for a moment. Then Mother said "Yes, thank you. I must learn to say "yes" Australian way. You are very good helping me speak Australian English."

"I am glad to be of help," said Mrs Murray.

Mother pointed to the garden again, trying to show Mrs Murray what she had wanted to know, all the while saying, "Funeral, here".

Mrs Murray asked, "Is Cecil sick?"

"No, Cecil he's OK," was the reply.

Mrs Murray again asked, "Did someone in the family die?"

Mother again pointed to the garden, saying, "Here, here – funeral."

In her frustration, Mrs Murray turned to Eileen and said, "Anna is saying something about a funeral. I said how lovely her garden was and she is talking about a funeral. I am beginning to think that Anna has a screw loose."

"You can't tell with these New Australians Mum. Do you mean that she has lost her marbles?' said Eileen.

I was standing listening to them talk and said, No screw loose in our house. My Dad, he fix."

"No, no, not the house,' said Eileen. 'It is a saying for someone who's gone funny in the head."

"My mother, she not have funny head, and she not lost marbles! My Mother, she not play marbles," I said.

Eileen and her mother had a laugh. Listening to all this talk, Mother didn't understand. She picked up the spade and dug a hole in the garden and placed some seeds in the ground, covering them with soil, and again saying the word "funeral".

Mrs Murray said to Eileen, "Ask Terese to ask her mother what she is trying to say."

I explained in the best way that I could: "Mother put seeds in the garden, put soil on top. Watering makes garden grow."

"Oh, I see!" said Mrs Murray. She turned to Eileen and said, "Anna is burying seeds and watering them! That is what she is trying to tell me."

Mrs Murray said to Mother, "Planting" is the word you want to say, not "funeral".'

Everything was sorted out in the end. Mrs Murray and Mother laughed about crossing their conversation. Mother was happy keeping company with Mrs Murray. She would learn a few more words of English after each visit, and Mother would never let Mrs Murray leave with empty hands when there were vegetables in the garden ready for picking.

I could tell Mother was feeling better when she hummed hymns softly to herself. At last there was happiness in the family. The burden of the war and the camp life had been lifted off my parents' shoulders, and they were able to live life feeling more at ease and carefree.

Everything was going well. I continued speaking English to Cecil. Mother's English continued to improve, allowing her to communicate with the Australian neighbours. She joined the Mothers' Club at school, and worked in the tuckshop once a month. She enjoyed the company of the ladies. It was an outing for her.

In the eighteen months of living in camps at Bonegilla, Cowra and Greta, it had not rained. When we first came to live in Beresfield, it seemed to rain constantly, moreso in winter. I can remember going to school in the rain and coming home wet, catching colds and staying home sick, missing out on my schoolwork. The weather was unpredictable. Strong winds made Mother uneasy. She was on edge; worrying that the tents would not stand up to the winds blowing like a small hurricane. Dust storms sprang up from the dirt roads. Mother pointed to them and said, "The Devil is dancing".

During the winter months, Mother had the stove fire going on full steam to make our canvas home a warm place for us when we came home from school, and for Father coming home from shift work in the rain. When the rain set in for days, Mother kept Cecil and me home from school. She didn't want us getting wet and staying in school all day with cold, wet feet. That kind of weather didn't agree with my health.

There were two floods in the two years we lived in the tent in Railway Street. Living in the tent we had no electricity, and, with no radio to listen to, news communication was slow. At that time the telephone was rarely available in homes; people used public telephone boxes in the streets. Beresfield had one telephone box at the Post Office, close to the train station. The other phone box was at the end of Beresfield, near the coal-mine.

So all I knew of these floods was that the swamp waters overflowed onto the railway tracks, stopping the trains, and there was no traffic on the highway. School was closed for a few days because our teachers from East Maitland convent were cut off by the floodwaters.

I was not aware of the disaster the flood had caused in Maitland and the surrounding farm areas. The only disadvantage for us living in the tents was that there was no coal on the railway track for me to collect when the coal trains stopped running.

At the time of this flood, my friend Helena, and her sister Tonya and I were playing on the railway track at the edge of the swamp, not far from our tent homes. We jumped on and off the track, picking up stones, and tossing them into the swamp to see which one of us could throw a stone the furthest, unaware of danger. As I turned to walk off the line, I saw a big red-bellied black snake making its way to the swamp. All the time I'd been jumping on and off the line and picking up stones, I hadn't seen the snake lying stretched out under the sleepers. My feet had been only three inches away from the snake. Luck was with me that day. I would have been in big trouble if I'd been bitten. There was no treatment of any kind in Beresfield – no doctor, chemist or ambulance – and we could not leave the island of Beresfield surrounded by floodwater. Seeing all this water, I couldn't imagine it had all come from the clouds in the sky. It covered miles of land, but disappeared in a few days. "Where did the water go?" I wondered.

Once a year, a small circus came to our town. This gave us something to look forward to. We were entertained by the small monkeys, poodle dogs and clowns. The clowns put on a good performance, spraying each other with water and spraying a little on the children in the audience. That was fun. The small poodle dogs were dressed in frilly dresses and walked on their hind legs, pushing a small pram into the arena and sometimes doing a back flip. All the children loved that. The monkeys were dressed as jockeys and rode the bigger dogs. This gave us a good laugh; we were happy for days after that. It relieved the boredom of everyday life in the bush.

The rest of the time, we found our own entertainment. Occasionally, school friends invited me to go bike riding. I had no bike of my own, so I borrowed my father's pushbike. It was just an ordinary pushbike, but it was big. My feet could hardly touch the pedals. One Sunday we went for a long distance ride, three-and-a-half hours on dirt roads, passing farms.

When we came back, I was extremely tired. The next day I couldn't get out of bed to get ready for school. I felt terribly sick, and had no energy to move. I stayed home from school for two days until I was able to walk to the station.

Mother took me to see a doctor at East Maitland. After examining me, the doctor suggested that it was my tonsils making me feel sick, and that the best option was to have my tonsils out. I had never complained of a sore throat, but Mother put her trust in the doctor. A week later, I was admitted to the Mater Misericordiae Hospital at Waratah to have my tonsils removed. The nursing staff were Sisters of Mercy. I was put into the women's ward. A dear old lady in the bed next to mine had the wanders. It was difficult to keep her in bed. She wandered about the ward with a rosary in her hand, saying prayers for me. I was frightened when she woke me up during the night to tell me she was dying. She gave me the rosary to say prayers for her.

The nursing Sisters were very pleasant to the patients. They assured me that there was nothing to worry about. After my operation, they said I was to drink plenty of water, and they brought me jelly, custard, junket and small amounts of ice-cream to eat at any time of the day.

I stayed in hospital for two days. On the third day I was discharged. I felt very ill when Dad came to take me home. I complained that I was ill and had a bad headache. I was weak and could hardly keep my head up. I told Father that I couldn't walk all the way to the railway station. Despite this, we left the hospital. Each step I took felt as though someone was hitting me about the head with a hammer. My body ached all over and my throat was dry and sore. I kept complaining to Dad that I could not walk, and my legs were not strong enough to carry me. We were only half way to the station. Father half dragged me along. It was the middle of winter, and my body was hot. The perspiration ran down my back. All I wanted to do was lie down by the side of the road. The ten-minute walk became an agonizing half hour.

Dad reassured me that it was only going to be just few more short steps, just a short walk to the train station. When we finally arrived at the station, I walked to the edge of the platform, away from people, and threw up. My throat felt like it was on fire. Dad then went into a panic and did not know what to do. There were ladies on the platform that came to help and clean me up the best that they could with their handkerchiefs. When we boarded the train, I thought "Thank heavens!" Finally I could lay my head down.

When we arrived at Beresfield, my legs folded under me. I could not walk. Dad carried me home on his back. The shortest way home was along the railway track. When we arrived home, Mother was very angry that the doctor had sent me home when I was so ill. She was terribly worried, and started to use some home remedies. She made chamomile tea, adding drops of lemon, honey and an aspirin. She put cold compresses on my neck and head to help ease the pain and bring down my temperature. I remained sick for another two weeks. Only after my tonsils were removed did I suffer frequently from sore throats and fatigue. It got worse. I didn't know at the time what was wrong with me, but I knew I was not feeling well. When I went back to school I learned that other girls had also had their tonsils removed. I don't know whether it was an epidemic, or a trend at the time.

Father resumed the search for a suitable house. As months went by nothing was found. The houses for sale in town were old, and Father was not interested in renovating. He felt it would be easier to build a house from the beginning, so he decided to build a new house. The search then was to find suitable land. On the weekends, Father took Mother, Cecil and me with him all the way to West Wallsend, Cardiff and Sandgate, giving Mother the choice of where she would like to settle. Mother and I were not good travellers; we came home sick after every trip.

Mother and Dad agreed that Beresfield was the place to look for land. Walking through the bush, they found some land that was suitable. Mother liked the street. It was a reasonably short walk to the railway station and to our grocery shop. A new joinery had just opened and a hardware shop was being built in the next street. That would be handy for Dad to buy tools and doors and windows for our house. Beresfield is between Maitland and Newcastle, only a short train trip each way. It was good for Dad travelling to work. He went ahead and purchased the land. There were other people building houses in Beresfield. Some were new Australians from the European countries.

On weekdays it was back to school for Cecil and me. I remember some of the fund-raising ideas the Sisters organized for the school. On one occasion, a guessing competition was held. Mother said, when giving me the competition money, that if I won the prize I was to donate it to the Sisters. The prize was a cup and saucer with sweets in the cup, and we had to guess how many sweets were in the cup. I was the lucky winner. The temptation was too much for me. I kept the prize to myself. I had been buying tickets for twelve months in various competitions, and this was the first time I had won a prize. I was not going to part with it. It meant so much to me to be a winner, and to bring a cup and saucer home for Mother.

When I took it home, I said, "Look Mum! I won a prize! I know you told me to donate it but I just couldn't."

Mother didn't say much. I think she knew that it meant so much to me.

Later in the same year there was another competition held for the biggest and smallest jug. The pupils brought in their jugs and their entry money. I had never seen so many jugs in one place. It was an exciting afternoon. Children waited for the big moment to see who had won for the biggest and the smallest jug. Everyone thought that my jug was the biggest of all the jugs on the table. When the judges came to making the decision, they disqualified my jug, as it was a coffee pot. However, the Sisters decided that I was to get the prize. Sister St Paul explained to the children that in Poland, a tea, coffee or milk pot made from porcelain was called a jug.

Sister St Paul felt she was preparing us for life by teaching us important things like dancing. She arranged for a lady dancer to come and teach us. We all stood in a circle. The woman began with a warm-up exercise, letting her limbs go loose, shaking herself and her arms. She said we must imagine we were a willow tree, with loose branches waking up from winter. Maybe the woman got the wrong message about what kind of dancing we were to be taught. Sister watched for a few minutes, then shook her head. The students were in fits of laughter. Sister said "Time!" and showed the woman to the door.

The next week, a woman came to teach us how to use cane to make a serving tray. The classroom was full of cane and buckets of water. The cane had to be pliable to work with, so first it had to be immersed in water. The wooden bases of the trays were already prepared for us so we could thread the cane through. We had two afternoon lessons learning to make the trays. We had to work quickly; the first part of the tray had to be finished on the first day. I was naturally heavy handed so I managed to pull the cane through very tight and that made it tight and neat. The next day the tray had to be finished with a nice braid edging on the top. Then we put a transfer in the middle and finished it off with varnish.

My tray looked good, and I was pleased with the work I had done. Mother asked me to donate it to the school as a prize. The Sisters accepted my tray, and filled it with bananas, oranges, peaches and grapes, and wrapped it up with clear cellophane and a big yellow bow tied in the middle. The tray of fruit looked good. I bought tickets in the guessing competition hoping to win back my tray, but luck was not with me that day.

The papers were finalised to say the land belonged to us. I hardly saw Dad from that time on. He was busy clearing the scrub on the land to get it ready for the construction of the house. The only tools Father had for clearing land were a broad axe that he brought with him from Germany, a handsaw to cut the small branches and foliage, and a pick and spade to dig up the roots. Things were done the hard way in those days. Some months later, Father bought a cross-saw to cut down the big trees. The work was hard and demanding, and Father asked our neighbour, Mr Bryce, to help him. Mr Bryce was also building his house, and he was willing to help for a little extra cash towards his family house.

Dad spent months clearing the land. Mother helped him while Cecil and I were at school. On weekends, when Father was working night or afternoon shift, we all went to our land to help pick up the branches and put them aside to dry out so they could be used for stove fuel. I didn't mind the work, as this was to be our home. It was on one of those weekends clearing the land that Father came across a small tree stump. He recognized it as the little tree he had cut for our first Christmas tree in our tent home. It had already grown new shoots. "This land was meant to be for us," said Mother.

It took weeks to prepare the block before construction could begin. Father and Mother dug the trench, and Father mixed the concrete for the foundations. Again, Father asked Mr Bryce to help with the brick work.

The Coronation Day of Queen Elizabeth II was to be in June. There was so much excitement. The magazines had the story and pictures of the Queen weeks before. One of our school projects was about the new Queen. Some of the girls spent two weeks making up a magazine on the life of our Queen, from her childhood to the coronation. When I saw other children making crowns, I did the same. I made a small crown to go on top of a golden coach. I collected gold wrapping from chocolates, and used cardboard, cotton wool, glass diamonds from a hat, and an imitation pearl from an earring. I was more than pleased with it, and felt that all my effort was worthwhile. I was happy that I had achieved one of the school projects. I was happy that I had understood what to do.

I loved the excitement of Coronation Day. I saw it on film in the picture theatre. The Palace housemaids, chefs and gardeners gathered inside the Grand Hall at Buckingham Place to see the Queen leave for Westminster Abbey. It was raining that morning, but nothing could spoil the parade of the Queen's Guards riding on horseback, escorting the Queen and Prince Philip through the streets of London. The Queen's subjects crowded the streets to see her travelling in the most ornate golden coach pulled by eight grey horses. The young Queen was dressed in a beautiful gown. I could hardly believe that the Queen dressed in ceremonial clothes in real life; I had only seen pictures like those in make-believe story books. The sound of the trumpets and the organ music in Westminster Abbey was the sound of Heaven to my ears. The dramatic music moved me. People held parties in the streets, singing 'God Save the Queen'. Congratulations and wishes for good health and a long reign were sent to the Palace from all over the world.

CHANGES

The good life for us was not to last. The trouble started with our Polish neighbour. Living in tents on railway grounds, the neighbour's children didn't have much room to play. They were growing up, and were bored. The boy especially found pleasure in throwing stones at me every time I passed his family tent on my way to the gate opening to the street. He also incited his sister to do the same. I was told to ignore their behaviour because in time they would stop. But the throwing continued for some time; the boy used big rocks and bruised my foot. Dad spoke to the boy's father, but the talking fell on deaf ears. Not wanting a confrontation with the neighbours, Father told me, "It won't be long and we will be in our own house."

The foundation brick work and piers were already finished and ready for the timber structure. Dad bought small amounts of timber at a time, and everything was paid for in cash. That was the beginning of more trouble with the Polish neighbour. He was also building his house in the next street, not too far from our house. Father ordered and purchased the timber to begin our house structure. The timber arrived on a Thursday, and nothing could be done with it until the weekend. Mr Bryce worked day shift during the week and only had weekends off to help Dad, who worked afternoon shift. His roster changed at the weekend.

Dad went to the house site on Friday to see if the timber had arrived. He found that half the timber had been stolen from our property. Our new neighbour, whose land backed onto ours, told Dad that he saw the Polish neighbour going past the back of his place carrying the timber. He knew the Polish neighbour from the railway. Pointing him out to Father, he said, "With friends like him, who needs enemies?"

Father approached the Polish neighbour and tried to reason with him, but to no avail. A feud started about the stolen timber. Father reported the matter to the police at East Maitland, taking me along to translate. While we were away that afternoon, the neighbour and his wife invaded our tent and assaulted my mother. The neighbour across the railway track could hear the feuding. She sent her husband over to stop the assault. If she hadn't insisted on her husband helping my mother, the result could have been death. When Dad and I came back from seeing the police, we saw that Mum had been beaten and that my brother was in shock. Cecil could not speak for a few days, and when he did finally speak, he stuttered.

We reported this to the police. The police insisted that Mother go to a doctor and get a certificate, then come into the Police Station to file a complaint. Mum was beaten so badly she could not walk to the train station. The closest doctor was at East Maitland.

With all this going on, Dad found it hard to cope. He had come to the end of his tether. With money in his pocket, he went to visit some casual new Australian friends to find relief from the trauma. They invited Dad in for a drink of Vodka and a game of cards. Dad came home drunk and penniless. He had gambled away all of his money. That night we lost our loving father.

He acquired the taste for drinking and gambling. It happened every payday for weeks. My father became dependent on alcohol. The meetings with Father at Hamilton on paydays were no more. Mother had always looked forward to that; on occasion she would come home with a new hat or a length of material to have a dress made. All this came to an end. Mother stopped travelling to Swansea for her visits to the doctor. She stopped going to church and her involvement in the Mothers' Club and tuck shop for school ended. She was too embarrassed about Father's drinking. She had lost her trust in Father, and lost confidence in herself.

The bad habit only got worse. The behaviour of gambling and drinking was too much for Mother. She and Dad quarrelled when he came home drunk, mainly on paydays. One night Father turned into a monster. It was similar to a Jekyll and Hyde experience. He began smashing everything in the kitchen and threatening to commit suicide. He walked out onto the railway track. The fighting terrified my little brother, who cried so hard he stopped breathing. His face turned blue. I hit him on the back to make him breathe again. Mum was very frightened. She sent me out to find my father and bring him home.

It was the middle of the night. I was on the railway track looking for Dad, hoping to find him before he was hit by a train. In the distance I could see a train coming, and I said to myself, "I must find Dad before the train comes closer." There was no moon out. It was very dark. I was crying and the tears in my eyes blurred my vision. I could see the light of the train getting closer. I had to get off the track. I was hoping and praying that my father was not on the track. As the train passed, I saw Dad's shadow and ran towards him, grabbing his sleeve. I tried to convince him to come home with me. He turned and pushed me with such force that I fell on the track and bumped my head on the railway line.

I must have been knocked out for a few minutes. When I came to I felt something cold pressed against my face. My head and arm were lying on the railway line, and I could see another train coming towards me. I was paralysed with fear. I couldn't move my head. I could hear myself saying "Get up, get up!" but I couldn't get my body to respond. I don't remember what happened next. I heard the whistle of the train and felt a strong gush of wind as the train passed by. I was still in one piece. I sat up. My head felt like a heavy brick. I got to my feet and fumbled my way home. I didn't think of my father; my only concern was to get home. When I arrived back, Dad was already at home. It was a relief for me to see him as I knew that I would have been sent out again to look for him.

None of us could sleep that night, except Father. He passed out.

When Dad woke up the next morning and walked into the kitchen, he saw the broken crockery and the glass of the kitchen door smashed on the floor. He looked somewhat puzzled and asked, "What happened? Who did this?"

Mother was still angry. "Don't you remember? You did all this!"

"I remember nothing of last night," said Father. He sat at the kitchen table holding his head between his hands for some time, trying to work out what had happened. He lifted his head and looked at me. My eyes were red and swollen. Cecil was still in bed, frightened and sick, unable to speak.

Neither of us could go to school that day. My mind was numb and clouded, my body shivering with shock. Just as I thought I was improving in my school work, these events set me back again. My self-confidence was shattered. My small amount of learning ability was at a standstill. I just could not concentrate on the school work. That was the time I missed my extended family: my grandparents, aunties and uncles, and my little brother Wladek. I missed him very much. At times like this, I had no-one to go to for comfort. Knowing how lonely and frightened I was at times, I was always there for my little brother Cecil. He was frightened by Dad's actions and Mother's anger.

From that time on, this happened every so often. Father lost many of his friends through his bad behaviour. Mother put more restrictions on me. The children from across the street stopped coming over to visit. Mrs Murray and Eileen visited less often. Everyone became frightened of my father's behaviour.

At school, preparation for the 1953 Christmas concert was well on the way. The Sisters had been working on it for some months. I needed a long dress for my part in the concert. Being at the school for one complete year, I had learned to speak most English words, so Mother felt confident enough to go shopping in Newcastle with me. Cecil stayed at home with Father. We caught the train to Wickham Station, and walked all the way up Hunter Street, going into every large department store looking for a dress for me. The shop windows were decorated. The spirit of Christmas was in every large store with a Christmas tree and carol singing in the background. Entering the large store was like a breath of fresh air. It was hot outside. We were still not used to walking around the streets in the heat.

There were no specialty shops for teenage girls that I can remember at the time. The larger stores like Marcus Clarke, Cox Brothers and Wynn's had children's sections on the first floor, and then began with XXSW in the women's section. Finding something for girls aged twelve or thirteen was almost impossible. There were shops in town selling dress material and patterns and sewing machines. Every year, my friend Jessie's mother made her a new dress to wear to The Show. Most mothers were good at sewing and made dresses at home for their girls. I remember Eileen and I ordering XXSW dresses from a Mark Foy's Sydney catalogue. The dresses were a little big for me at first, but in six months I had grown into them.

Scott's was the last large Department store in Newcastle, and my last chance of finding a dress for the play. We walked in and the first thing I noticed was that the staircase was moving up. Mother and I stood for a moment watching people getting onto the moving stairs and being carried up to the next floor. It looked easy: just one foot on the step and we were on the way to the first floor.

In the corner of the store was the children's section. We finally found two dresses in my size. One was plain pink, the other a plain washed out blue. They were both knee length and made from organza, a see-through material. The two dresses were not lined. I chose the pink dress. Mother bought pink material and some pink organza. She was not much good at sewing, but she managed to make a slip and add a valance to lengthen the dress.

Our next purchase was a new pair of shoes. As we came to the shoe shop, I stopped to have a look in the window before entering. I saw the shoes I liked: a pair of black patent leather shoes with an ankle strap. I set my heart on these shoes. Once in the shop, we sat down in the chair for a sales lady to assist us. A young lady came to ask how she could help, and I replied, 'I would like to try on the black patent leather shoes with the ankle strap.'

The young lady went into the storeroom and returned with three boxes of shoes. She fitted the shoe on my foot, but Mother said a firm 'No' to the ankle strap shoes. Mother had chosen the shoe for me: attractive black shoes with a strap across the middle and a small gold buckle on the side. We finished our shopping with one more purchase. Mother bought a shirt and tie to give Father for Christmas. After that, we walked to Newcastle Station to catch the train home.

After the Christmas concert, the bottom of the slip was cut and the valance was taken off so I could wear my dress to church on Sundays. Wearing my new shoes was a painful experience. The leather in the shoe was very hard and they were a tight fit. I always had trouble wearing in new shoes. Walking to church on Sundays I got blisters on my heels. Coming home from church, I was tempted to take my shoes off and walk home barefoot, but the ground was too hot to walk on. By the time the shoes were comfortable to wear, they were just about worn out!

Father worked the afternoon shift on Christmas Eve. At midnight, I attended mass with Eileen to celebrate the birth of Christ. The church was overcrowded with some people having to stand out on the church porch. It still seemed strange to be looking at a decorated bush tree standing in the corner of the kitchen in our canvas house on a hot Christmas morning. It was one of the many things we learned to accept. We still had our presents given to us from St Nicholas on the 6th of December. Cecil got a tricycle to ride, and I was given a box of beautiful hankies. Hankies were a popular gift in those days. They were usually embroidered on one corner and had lace all around the edge. Three in a box made a lovely gift.

Our Christmas dinner was soup with noodles, followed by braised steak and Polish dumplings served with sour cream. Dad loved dumplings. They were his favourite food. After we had eaten, Father was off to work. We had little visitors from across the road; they liked picking the biscuits and sweets off the tree.

New Year's Eve was a disaster at our house. Father was drunk.

During the Christmas break of 1953 –1954, every chance I had I spent time at Eileen's place. The Murray family had moved into their new home, and electricity had changed their slow existence. Radio brought the outside world in. On weekdays, Mrs Murray sat in her lounge chair and listened to the serials. In the evenings Mr Murray liked to listen to the news on ABC followed by the serial *Dad and Dave*. I was allowed to walk over to the Murray's house to listen to it. Eileen and I liked listening to the popular songs on the hit parade.

When Eileen's family lived in the tent home before the radio days, the boys had bought records and a packet of needles for the wind up gramophone. Every week they played their favourite records, changing the needle after each one. I could hear the music at our house. They played Patti Page, Slim Whitman, Smokey Dawson and Frankie Laine.

The boys also entertained themselves buying and reading comic books. Joe, Pat and Timmy liked *The Phantom* and *Dick Tracey*. Micky and Eileen liked to read *Archie*, and the *Blondie and Dagwood* comics. Eileen loaned them to me to read. Mother wasn't keen on me reading comics. She was hard on me, and expected too much of me. I liked reading comics. They were funny and I needed to laugh sometimes. Mother didn't realise that reading comics was an easy way for me to learn to spell simple words.

On Saturdays, the Murray house came alive. Each of the four boys had a radio of their own, and while one listened to the horse races, the others were listening to football games on a different station. But not everyone was happy. Shelia, the neighbour across the street, complained about the noise coming from the Murray's house. Her cockatoo, Charlie, took to squawking all the weekend. That didn't go down well with the neighbours.

The exciting news in 1954 was that the Queen was coming to visit Australia in February. Everyone worked hard preparing for the visit. The Queen's plane was to land at Williamtown Air Base near Newcastle. I learned later that the gardeners prepared the grounds and gardens for weeks, but that some of the flowers had died during the hot days. The gardeners planted plastic flowers at the last moment to fill in the space.

Painters put a fresh coat of paint on Newcastle Station and the council workers cleaned the streets and sealed roads for the Queen's car to travel comfortably. I remember Father working on his rostered days off preparing extra carriages for every train. Dad said that the railway authorities were drawing up rosters for the day of the Queen's visit, putting on extra trains to accommodate people coming from the country. The extra carriages made the trains so long that they had to make two stops on the same platform to cope with the crowds boarding the train. Every station was crowded with people waiting for the trains to Newcastle. The trains kept on coming all morning and the carriages filled quickly. People stood in the aisles and in the spaces at the end of each carriage.

The shop windows in Hunter Street were decorated with flags, portraits and souvenirs of the Queen and Prince Philip. School children were given the day off from school to see the Queen. There were faces in all the office windows on the first floor buildings in Newcastle and people sat on the awnings above shops to see the Queen on the route to the Town Hall. Every person working on the railway and in the police force was rostered on to work, and had to work overtime to cope with the crowds of people coming to see the Queen.

The Queen travelled in an open car, touring the streets of Newcastle. She was driven to the Town Hall for a reception and then driven to Newcastle Station. The Queen and Prince Philip left from Newcastle Station on a special train to their next destination. It was the biggest crowd of people that Newcastle had experienced. Fortunately, none of the awnings collapsed. From what I can remember of that day, everything ran smoothly, and the crowd behaviour was good.

Going back to school in 1954, I had a better understanding and was much better at speaking English, especially in the subjects that were interesting to me, like Social Studies. Listening to Sister and watching her teach, some of the information was starting to sink into my somewhat cloudy mind. I struggled with remembering dates and times. I would cry in class when we were learning about the convicts and the cruelty they suffered for being hungry and stealing a loaf of bread. My classmates looked at me strangely when I cried during these lessons. Sister spoke to the children in the class, explaining to them that I had an understanding of what suffering was through my own experience. Sister went on to explain that pain is not easily forgotten.

I was interested in how Australia developed from the time Captain Cook and the first convicts were sent over to this strange country. I liked to learn about the early Australian settlers, and about the men going over the Great Dividing Range to open the plains, and how difficult that was on horseback, with only axes and long saws. How hard they worked against all odds: the drought, bushfires, floods, oppression from the law, and the bush rangers. Those people worked by principles and morals, and hope in their hearts to make Australia a good country.

Speaking with and listening to Australian people, I learned that in the early days people lived by hard work and plain living. It was the same for the people who had migrated to Australia from different countries during the forties, fifties and sixties. We new Australians had left Europe and its politics behind to start a new life and to contribute to this country. We accepted the way of Australian living, its principles and its laws. When we arrived, we accepted the sovereign King of England and Australia, the defender of the faith, to be our King. We tried to integrate with our Australian workmates and neighbours and to learn from them. We were people from all European nations living as one in the country we had chosen as our home.

I was interested to learn about the first explorers crossing central Australia on horseback looking for an inland sea. I was especially interested in learning about Mount Kosciusko and the Polish explorer, Paul Strzelecki. He joined the army before completing school and travelled through many countries before coming to Sydney in 1839. His main Australian expedition involved following the Great Dividing Range south through the area now known as Gippsland. He named it after Governor Gipps of New South Wales. He explored the Snowy Mountains and was probably the first European to climb to the top of Mount Kosciuszko. He climbed it in 1840. I remembered that date because it was one hundred years before I was born. Strzelecki named the mountain after the Polish hero Tadeusz Kosciuszko.

Strzelecki was remembered in 1988 by the Maitland branch of the Polish Association of NSW. They erected a plaque at East Maitland Park. It asks that Paul Edmund Strzelecki, KCB, CMG, FRGS, be remembered "for his contribution to Australian exploration, discoveries and immigration."

From what I could see, Sister St Paul was a good teacher, but I couldn't always follow what was being taught. Sister St Paul would give us projects through the year on different subjects. I saw children writing things down and taking books home for homework, but I did not work on those projects. These subjects were difficult for me as I had no idea what I was to do. I was ignorant of some English words that were said in the class. The children brought the completed project back to school, showing the work they had done during the week at home. They had cut out pictures and pasted them in the book from magazines and from books their parents read. It was very interesting work, but I didn't work on any of the projects. I didn't understand what I was to do and I had no-one to help me. I tried to learn what Sister said by watching. When she drew a map and pointed out the rivers and the ranges, I could understand that.

Sister asked what plant was sugar made from. I was very confident to answer that question, as I remember learning this in the Polish school. I put my hand up, and Sister pointed to me. I stood up and said, "Sugar is made from white beetroot." Everyone in the classroom laughed. Sister told the children to stop laughing and to listen. Sister said, "In European countries white beetroot *is* used to make sugar. Can someone in the class tell Terese what sugar is made from in Australia?"

Every child in the class knew the answer. They had just finished the project on sugar. Everyone put up their hand. Sister pointed to a boy. He stood up and told the class the story of sugar.

Sitting at the table after tea that evening, I said to my family, "Today I learned the story of sugar in Australia. Sugar grows mainly in Queensland, like a tall grass called sugar cane. When the season comes, the grass is set on fire to get rid of snakes and rats before the men cut down the cane and send it to the factory to be processed into sugar." Cecil, now aged six, took an interest.

Weeks later, on a warm sunny morning, I was walking to the latrine. There were two steps to walk down past a big flat sandstone rock. I saw two small black snakes stretched out on that big rock. I thought they were dead and I walked past them. When I came back, the snakes had gone. I told Mother and Cecil to watch out for the snakes in the grass when they went down to the latrine. My little brother, remembering the story I had told weeks before, took it upon himself to be the Pied Piper and get rid of the snakes.

He went down the two steps near the latrine and lit the long grass. The grass exploded into a fierce fire. Everyone came running with buckets of water to save their tents. One spark on the canvas and our homes would be ashes in minutes. There were no hoses; we only had tank water. Luckily, there was no wind that day and the fettler gang were working on the line just in front of where the grass was burning. They helped to put the fire out with wet bags. My brother was not punished for his behaviour. The fright of the fire was punishment enough. He was only trying to save us from the snakes.

The Sisters taught us behaviour and manners to become good citizens. Some of the rules given to us by the Sisters were: when passing your way through a crowd, walk gently and say "excuse me"; when you see someone across the street, don't yell out, but give a wave, or nod your head to acknowledge them; don't talk too much, give the other person a chance to speak; learn to listen, don't be rude by breaking into a conversation with your opinion on the matter; if you see a woman struggling with a stroller, or a mother with children boarding a train or a bus, ask if you can help and give them assistance if needed. These rules are important to make life pleasant for everyone.

We were also taught to take responsibility. We were to polish our shoes every day, and to make sure that the shoe laces were in good order; if they were worn out, we were to replace them; we were to get our uniform together and set the clock for the morning. We also had school homework every night which kept us occupied and helped prepare us for the future work force. Teachers, parents and the community worked together to keep youngsters off the street, helping to ensure a better life for children.

At school we had sports, concerts, and singing practice to train our voices for singing at local talent quests. The Quest at Hexham was open to children as well as adults. Some children from our school, including myself, put in an entry to sing at the Glen Levit Community Hall at Hexham. My desire was to sing opera in my later years. I went on the train with Mother and Father that evening. The artists came from around the areas of Raymond Terrace, Mosquito Island, Mayfield and Ash Island.

Hexham was a beehive of activity before cars and the big flood. Hexham held dances, movies and spring balls. Young people came on the milk trucks, on horseback and in row boats. People loved coming to the events held at Hexham in those days.

I loved Friday afternoon school sports. We wore a sports uniform of a blue tunic tied at the waist by a gold cord with tassels on the end, a gold blouse, white short socks and spotless white sandshoes. Our school had two sports outings a year. One was at Beresfield Memorial Park, playing against the neighbouring public schools of Hexham, Beresfield, and Thornton. Our school had the least number of pupils to compete in the games: nineteen boys and thirteen girls. However, we had four strong athletic boys and four very good athletic girls. They were fast runners.

We did not win the sport trophy for our school, but we did well. The boys won the running race, the jumping and the relay race. The girls did well in running and the ball games. I was included in the ball games, not for my athletic ability, but because I helped make up a full team for our school to enter the ball games. Sister St Paul trained us in the skill of catching the ball: not to hold onto it but to return it quickly to the captain. That was our secret in winning the ball games. We were pleasantly surprised when it was announced that Our Lady of Lourdes School from Tarro had won the ball games for girls and boys. The Sisters were very pleased with our performance. We enjoyed the sports carnival day.

The parents and the Mothers' Club put time and effort into that picnic sports day. It was a very hot day. There were drinks, toffees, toffee apples, and homemade ice blocks with fruit in them. We were entertained with the help of radio. Some of the songs I remember being played on the radio were "How Much is that Dog in the window?", "The Shrimp Boys are Coming", and Frankie Laine's "Kids, Kids, What Can We Do with Kids Today". I had a wonderful time.

The other sports day we played was against St Joseph's Convent school at East Maitland. We travelled by train to Victoria Station at East Maitland. We were instructed to be on our best behaviour, not to forget our manners, and not to dishonour our school. Forty years later when I started classes to learn ballroom dancing, one of the ladies in the class recognised me from the time we were young, playing sport at school. She had been on the opposing team at St Joseph's School. I was amazed that she remembered me after all those years; I only played twice in the time I was at school. She told me she remembered me because I was different from the rest of the girls. Maybe it was my shyness, or my lack of English. It was certainly not for my lightning speed in the games. The only fast move I made was for the shade of the tree after every event!

The fathers working on shift work were our escorts on the sports days, but neither of our parents turned up for Cecil and me. When Cecil started school, I was there with him for important events like picnic sports day and the school concert. My parents didn't come to special school events; they were not like the Australian parents. Mother rarely went out without Father by her side. Being alone made her feel anxious, and she always needed our support to feel safe in the new country. The effects of war would be with Mother in many ways.

In that year, Mother had an operation on her nose. Dad took us to visit her at the Mater Hospital in Waratah. Mother could see that Dad was concerned. She assured him that there was nothing to worry about; she had been looked after well. Mother spoke well of the nursing Sisters, and said how pleasant the young nurses were to the patients. Mother was back at home within a week.

Somehow, under the strain and pressures, Dad and Mother still managed to work on the house. It was to have three bedrooms and a porch at the front and back. The only time Mum left home now was to help Dad build the new house. She helped to lift and hold up timber for Father while he was on the step ladder. Sometimes the work had to stop for a few weeks until more money was saved. In the spring, Father stopped working overtime to give himself more time on the house. He concentrated on putting on the iron roof, so he could sleep in the house and guard the rest of the building materials. After Father put on the roof, he worked on fitting the fuel stove in the kitchen.

Between Father's drinking and Mother's nagging, Cecil and I had some moments of happiness. We loved going to the house on the weekend and helping with the work. Before the walls were built, we sat on the floorboards and dangled our legs over the edge when eating lunch. There were always small jobs for us to do, like picking up the bits of timber and putting them in a pile for use in the stove.

On rostered days off, Father worked on the house from the break of day until dusk. Cecil and I went directly there after school. Father depended on us for help. One of us had to be with Dad to pass the tape measure or tools when he was on the ladder and while Mother was cooking tea. When the boards were nailed half way on the walls and the bathtub had been fitted, we had finally come up to modern civilisation, bathing in a full size bath. However, we still had to carry the water in and heat it on the stove. Mother hung a sheet between the bath and the kitchen for privacy. Cecil was first to have a bath. I followed, adding more hot water. When we finished bathing, I let Cecil pull the plug to let the water out. Cecil watched with excitement, watching the water going round and round and disappearing down the plug hole. We stayed at the house until Father began dropping tools. This was an indication that he was tired, and that it was time to go back to Railway Street. That was our daily routine.

In springtime, the longer days allowed Dad to work on the house a few hours more. His goal was to move into the house by the end of the year. After Dad finished putting up the weatherboards, and the windows, and front and back doors were fitted, the house was at lock-up stage. Mother spent more time on the site painting the weatherboards.

Mother was a resourceful woman. She used big 25 pound bags of flour to make her own pasta, doughnuts and Polish dumplings. (Dad would have had dumplings every day of the week.) Mother saved the soft cotton flour bags and made small cafe curtains to cover the bottom part of the windows. The front yard was clean. Mother and I cut the little bits of grass with dress maker scissors. From the outside, the house looked finished. Dad notified the Council that the house was ready for inspection.

Within a week, the Council inspector was at the house, making sure it was built according to specifications. The house was just a shell, not yet lined inside. Only the water and the taps were fitted. Dad was hoping that the building would be passed and that the Council would let us move in because the lease on the railway land was coming to an end.

Some weeks later, Dad received a letter from the Council. It was good news: permission was granted to move into the house on the understanding that Dad must keep working on the dwelling at a reasonable pace.

In October 1954, we left railway property and moved to our new house. It was two streets from the railway line, behind the post office. We unpacked and finished putting things in place before lunch because Father was working night shift and needed to get some sleep. Cecil had plenty of room to ride his tricycle and wander through the bush next to our house. For the first time, Cecil and I were to sleep in separate rooms. The rooms were partitioned with wardrobes, dressing tables and blankets from the tents. The bathroom was attached to the back of the house, and its doorway was to be from the back veranda. But at that stage, the wall between the kitchen and the bathroom was not finished. When we heated water for the bath on the fuel stove, we carried it to the bath by stepping through the half-finished wall. There was no electricity for a few weeks. Nothing in the house could be worked on until then.

Mother was so thrilled and excited, she couldn't sleep that night. Father had gone to work, so she talked to me until well after midnight. It was the first time she spoke to me as an adult. I was the only one at the time she could talk to. She told me it was a long and difficult journey we had travelled in the last fourteen years, always on the move, not knowing whether we would live or die, or where we would put our head down next.

"I sometimes thought I would not live to see the day I would be in my own home,' she said. 'Finally we are safe, never having to pack and move again. Yet so far away from my country where I was born. Terese, you don't know how I have longed for this day; to be in the house we have built with our own hands. This means so much to Dad and me, to have a house for our children in a good country."

"It's strange,' Mother continued. 'The past has just crossed my mind... Living on my grandfather's farm – I was only young. Gypsies often came to our part of the country, settling themselves down for a week. Two gypsy women came to our front door. They spoke politely, offering to read cards to reveal my future. One of the women took my hand to read my palm. Of course I was interested in what she had to say! I opened the door to the women. They came in and sat at the table. One read cards. She said, "You will marry in a few years and have children and live in a house of your own. Your husband and you will build together after some years of marriage, but it will not be on this soil. You will cross a big volume of water. One of your children will live a comfortable life in later years."

"While the two women were with me, the other gypsy women were in the back yard helping themselves to eggs and hens, hiding them under their full skirts in hidden pockets. They considered it payment for giving me a reading. My grandfather was a gentle soul. He didn't make a fuss. He said they only took food to get them through the day. He turned a blind eye to the theft. Small theft was overlooked in the part of the country where we lived.

But Grandfather was very angry when the gypsies came back to the farm some months later and stole two of his good horses at night. He never let them on his farm again. After two years had passed, the stolen horses came back to the farm in poor condition."

Mother continued talking, and I listened. I didn't want to interrupt her. She told me that her father had fought in the First World War against the Turks. He came back wounded with two bullets still in his body. He died not long after his wife died. She was only thirty six. "When we all came home from the funeral,' said Mother, 'her chair was rocking as if she was still sitting in it. It was too much for Father; he broke down and wept."

After Mother's parents died, her grandparents took care of the children. Mother didn't say which grandparents: the Hnat family on her mother's side, or the Woujnorwicz family on her father's side. Mother said that she and her twin sister were the youngest in the family. Her twin sister (I think her name was Zosza) may have died in that same year as their mother died. Mother didn't mention how many girls were in the family, but she did name the boys. I can't remember their names.

Mother said it was too much for her grandparents to care for all the children, so they sent Mother to live with nuns for three years. Her chore was to water the flower pots with the Sister in the convent. Mother didn't say if this convent was an orphanage, but she did say that her grandfather always brought food to the convent.

Mother couldn't sleep and continued talking. It was late, and I may have drifted off and missed some of what she said. She told me that her grandfather owned a self-sufficient farm. He had hens, pigs, cows, and horses for ploughing. Among them was a grey horse, used for pulling a cart. Mother often rode him bare-back. She said, 'When the grey horse wanted a drink, he didn't go to the boys. He came to me and nudged me all the way to the well. There was no tap water on the farms in those days. I had to draw the water from the well. He had the habit of biting me while I drew the bucket of water. When I was riding on his back across the creek, he often threw me off his back into the water.'

Mother didn't say if he was a mongrel of a horse, or a playful horse. She said, "I had enough of his moods and kicked him. Grandfather saw me mistreating the animal, and gave me a hiding. In my spite, I went down into the cellar where the preserves and food were stored, and took a bite from every salami sausage that Grandfather had just made to carry the family through the winter months."

I laughed when Mother said that. I could imagine my mother as a young girl, running to the cellar and sinking her teeth into the sausages. My dear mother, fighting back in her own way. I presume that being the youngest, and competing with boys, was not easy.

Mother and I finally went to bed and fell asleep.

When Father came home from work in the morning, he made porridge on our new fuel stove. It warmed the house. Mother often made porridge for our breakfast, and always put a pinch of salt into it. I said I didn't like salt in my porridge. Mother then told me the story of a devil living in a barn loft. He was fed porridge every morning, with no salt or sugar, and would go berserk while the family were all in church. The devil turned the barrels over and spilled porridge salt and sugar all together, and even managed to bring a cow up to the loft.

I laughed and said, "That is a very amusing story, Mother."

When he was in a good mood, Father also told little stories like this from the old country. One of the stories was about a chap in the village who bought a horse and read a book of instructions on how to take care of his new horse. The proud owner read that he was to feed his horse every eight days. The horse died on the seventh day. Was there a moral to this story? Maybe it was "Don't believe everything you read."

Father also told me a story about how to get rich quickly, and make easy money. Of course I was interested! "All you have to do,' said Father, 'is carry an egg under your arm until it hatches. The hatchling will bring you luck, and you can make money the easy way'"

"Yes, Dad,' I said. 'If things were that easy, every person in the district would do the same. There would be no working days for us, and we may have to be eating square shaped eggs until the hatchling died. It would be a short living for us rich people."

These stories sounded Jewish to me. Where my parents had lived in Poland, there were a lot of Jewish people. Mother told me that every Friday evening, she would light their candles. "They were so strict in their religion,' she said, 'they weren't even allowed to strike a match after the sun set. I lit their stove for them in the winter time."

On Monday morning I let Sister St Paul know that we had left the tent and moved into our new house. I gave Sister my new address, and she asked if the new house was closer to school. "No,' I said, 'only two streets further. Dad said that after Christmas I could ride his bike to school. He won't be needing it because he is going to look for a new job."

Dad started working overtime when it was available. There was money still owed to the Beresfield joinery for the front and back doors. That had to be paid before anything could be done inside the house. While saving money, there was still work to be done outside digging trenches for rain water pipes running from the house roof. On weekends, Mother and I still cut the little bits of grass with scissors to keep the front yard looking tidy until we could afford a push mower. The Council inspector dropped in occasionally to see the progress being made.

All spare time was spent working on the house, and Dad worked hard. There was no time for other things. The only time Cecil and I spent with Mother and Dad as a family was building the house on weekends and school holidays. There was always something for Cecil and me to do. Father said I could sort out the bricks, putting the small broken bricks in a pile where the garage was to be built. The broken bricks were filler for the floor. Nothing was thrown out; everything was used. The bigger bricks where stacked in a neat pile. Some were to be used for a walkway to the vegetable garden. Later, Dad mixed cement and poured it over the rest of the bricks to make the garage floor.

School times were the happiest hours of my day. On some Mondays, I was able to work in the tuckshop with the mothers. The Sisters realised that it was important to me to gain experience by working with older women. I kept this secret all to myself. I looked up to the Sisters for their kindness and adopted them as my aunts. I wasn't trying to seek attention from them; I just enjoyed the feeling of knowing that I had someone I could talk to, not about the problems at home, but just small talk about the colours I would choose for a new dress or shoes, about my likes and dislikes. I was sorry to hear that Sister St Paul was leaving our school. She was a good teacher, and I felt I was losing a friend. Sister was going to teach the natives in New Guinea.

When Sister St Paul left, my new teacher was Sister Bernard. She was much older, and I could tell the difference in her teaching. Sister St Paul was young and had taken part in sports activities with the children. Sister Bernard was more practical. The girls did needlework, which included making a skirt and blouse for ourselves stitched by hand. I made a peasant blouse for myself from the soft cotton flour bags. While the girls did needlework, the boys were outside playing sports with the parents who came to the school to help.

Sister Bernard showed her concern towards me. Knowing that my schoolwork was not what it should be, she knew that I would probably be unable to sit for the bursary exams at the end of the year. I had been at a disadvantage. There were no newspapers and no radio in our house. I didn't know the events of the day in the country. I didn't know what a Prime Minister was. Even though I did not complete any of my schoolwork, I still had a sense of fulfilment because of my interest in people and history. I had learned many things since starting school in late 1952.

To prepare for the bursary exams, I attended school on Saturday mornings at St Joseph's at East Maitland with the rest of the students in Sixth Class. I was hoping I might catch up with some work. In sitting for exams, however, I often did not understand the questions and my spelling was appalling. I had no confidence and was frightened that I would fail. I chose not to sit the bursary exam.

Christmas 1954 in our new home was very quiet. We did not have a Christmas tree, and there was no celebration of the *Wigilia* meal. Dad was working day shift, and had his own celebration. He came home from work late. He had been drinking.

Cecil and I still went out to look for the first evening star. When he saw the star, Cecil ran in to tell Mother. The tradition of St Nicholas had been changed in our house so as not to confuse Cecil. We now received our presents on Christmas morning like the Australian children. I opened my present. To my surprise, it was a silver watch. I was so happy with my present. To own a watch in these times was a luxury. It meant a lot to me.

New Year's Eve was another disaster for us. Father went to his drinking mate's place to play cards. After he had a few drinks, his personality changed. Mother sent me out to bring him home. I was sick of this. When I caught up to Dad, I stood up to him and told him how his behaviour was disturbing our family. He then turned around and pushed me across to the wall of the house. He yelled at me to leave him alone, that I was embarrassing him in front of his mates. I came home without Father. Mother was very angry. She turned on me for coming home without him. I was miserable and heart broken. I was being used as the punching bag for my parents.

I had always been obedient to both my parents. I had never given them any trouble. Everything I was asked to do, I did, no questions asked. I was obedient out of love for both Mother and Father. But the next morning I stood up to my mother, showing some anger towards her. I told her to stop nagging Father; that it made him angry and violent towards us. Mother became angry with me, and hit me. I didn't know why I deserved to be treated that way.

During the January school break, days were on the glum side for me. I helped Mother with the house in the morning, and there was little to look forward to for the rest of the day. Things had changed. Since moving away from the street where the Murrays lived, I hadn't seen Eileen much. Eileen was spending time with her boyfriend, going places with him on his motorbike.

Father was very strict with me, not understanding my needs as a growing teenage girl. I wanted to go to town to see the pictures on a Saturday afternoon, and sometimes on Sundays I wanted to go to the beach with girls the same age as me. I was invited by my school friends' mothers to come along with them, but the answer was always "No". Father didn't understand – or refused to understand – that I was growing up and needed some independence. He was my father and I had to live the ways of the old country.

He was not the Dad I knew. His drinking changed his personality; over time he became strange and very strict. It affected my younger brothers, Cecil, and then Peter, who would be born the following year, 1955. They didn't know Father as I had known him. Dad had been a man who loved life and music before he became so strict. I had the feeling that Dad didn't like his new job at BHP. He was not happy like he had been when he worked on the railway.

Meal times at the table were quiet when Father was home. I remember one mealtime when Cecil was sick with mumps. We were eating our meal, and Cecil licked my cutlery. He said he wanted to pass the sickness on to me. I think he only said that to break the silence at the table. (He must have been disappointed that I didn't get the mumps!) I was looking forward going to school to get away from the day to day tension in the house. I liked schoolwork. Having very little knowledge, there was so much for me to learn.

THE FLOOD

In the New Year of 1955, when I was fifteen, I was accepted to start school at St Mary's Dominican High School at Maitland. It was a strain on the family budget to purchase a new school uniform for me. Dad had started work at the BHP steel works in the open hearth section. It was hot hard work cleaning out the furnaces, but there were bonuses, and more overtime. It was important to earn extra money for living, and to finish the house, because Mother was expecting a baby.

I had to leave home one hour earlier to catch the train to Maitland. It was twelve miles from Beresfield, and I walked some distance from the station to the school grounds. The first term subjects I chose were French and Home Science. I coped well with Home Science, and French was a subject I thought I could manage. I settled in well in my new school and started to make new friends. Most of the girls lived in Maitland and East Maitland. In our lunch hour, we sat together getting to know each other. The girls talked about where they lived, and I liked to listen to them talk about their homes and properties and how they spent their weekends. It had never entered my mind that life for other girls of my age living in this country was different to my life. There were no stories I could tell; I had nothing to say at the time.

I remember the fascinating stories they told. One of the girls said she lived on a farm, and sometimes, when walking to school, she felt uneasy when she crossed a bridge on the farm in the fog. It was spooky, she said, especially when the cows were standing still. She said she was half way across the bridge when one of the cows bellowed, and she nearly jumped out of her skin with fright and ran all the way to the main road.

Another girl said she lived close to the East Maitland Gaol, and sometimes, on still and foggy nights, she heard screams from the ghosts of prisoners who served time back in the convict days. A shiver ran up my spine hearing of ghosts still hanging around the gaol after all those years. The girl living just opposite the Maitland Park told her story about the floods her family had to cope with every time the rains came down heavy for more than a few days. Everything had to be lifted off the floor. The swamps filled up and their house was flooded. She said the worst flood she could remember was the 1949 flood. It had spoiled her birthday. I don't remember the names of these girls, except for Pamela. She lived at Beresfield, and we travelled to school on the same train together.

After only two weeks at my new school, the rain set in. It was miserable trudging to school and then back home in almost daily rain. My feet were constantly wet. I came down with a sore throat and had to stay home. The rain was heavy for over a week. There was no sign of it letting up. From our kitchen window we could see the water rising, filling the swamps across the distance to Millers Forest, and almost reaching the Seaham Mountains.

Seeing those mountains from our kitchen window, I had sometimes imagined a village like Blue Hills being somewhere in them. Electricity had just been connected to our house, and the first appliance Dad bought was a radio. On the evenings when Dad wasn't home, we listened to the serial *Blue Hills*, where there was always something exciting happening.

The rain continued, and, for the first time, the radio in our house was left on all day. Like most people, Father listened to the radio hoping for good news about the weather. The forecast was for more rain. The low lying farm land at Woodberry, Tarro and Millers Forest was filling with rain water, and the back road through to the towns of Raymond Terrace and Seaham was cut off. The water in swamps and rivers was rising.

By the middle of the third week, sand bags at Maitland and Raymond Terrace had been laid on the river banks in the hope that the rivers would not rise above them. Business people and residents of Maitland and Raymond Terrace were depending on the stability of the levee banks to hold the water.

Father was working day shift that week. On Wednesday, he came home early from work and told Mother that BHP was preparing for a flood. He said that as he was coming home, he saw water from the swamps at Hexham and Tarro already covering the railway lines, and the river at Hexham had started to overflow. The workers in the flood prone areas had been told to go home to prepare their families for evacuation if the rain continued. The boss had asked the men who were not in the flood area if they would stay at work to fill the gap. There were going to be plenty of double shifts and overtime. Dad told Mother he was taking extra clothing and going back to work on the next train, and that he might not get back home for some days. Dad said that BHP would be providing hot meals, and were arranging for the men to sleep in train carriages at Port Waratah.

Father left for work on the next train. Mother and I listened for the latest news on the flood. Announcements were made every hour up to the time of the evening news. The news reader said that all the rivers in the Hunter Valley and the Upper Hunter were rising. He said that if the heavy rain continued over the next twenty four hours, people in the low lying areas of Maitland and the Hunter Valley would have to be ready to evacuate their homes.

Mother was anxious. She said to me, "You haven't seen a flood. You don't know what a body of water can do, rushing through farms and towns, destroying everything in its path, causing loss of livestock, sickness, and misery. The torrent of the river can be savage." She said that when she was a young girl living on her grandfather's farm by the river, a flood had taken the livestock. The cattle could not swim against the strong current.

Then she told me that she had lost her teenage brother in the flooded river. She said her grandfather was very much in grief over the loss of his grandchild. Mother said, "Grandfather broke down and said it was he himself who should have died, and that our parents should have lived." It was at odd times like this that I learned a little bit more about Mother's family.

The next day, Thursday, the rain continued over the Hunter Valley. We knew that Dad would not be coming home from work. The morning news was not good. The newsreader said the river was overflowing at Singleton. Roads were cut in many places. Floodwater moving at several feet per second had cut the New England Highway at Branxton, and at many towns all the way up to Murrurundi. The Pacific Highway was cut at Hexham and Raymond Terrace. With the two main highways cut, transport came to a standstill. Many people were stranded. Mother became concerned at the thought of Father staying away from home.

All day and into the evening we listened to the news. The Paterson and Williams Rivers were overflowing at Dungog. The waters were rising in the Hunter River at Maitland. Wallis Creek and the surrounding flood areas were becoming critical. People were given warnings to evacuate their homes. The Upper Hunter and the Hunter catchments had now received more than twice their average rainfall in the last four months. The weather forecasters described the deluge as unusual. We went on to hear that the Comerford Dam at Seahampton was full to capacity.

At 7am on Friday, a warning went out for the residents of Maitland and lower East Maitland to evacuate immediately. The water in the Comerford Dam had increased and was spilling over. By 8:15am the water was flowing freely and pouring into High Street Maitland. In some parts of Maitland the water was over five feet deep. Many people and families were reluctant to leave their homes, not realising the danger they were putting themselves in. A warning went out to all residents living in the Hexham, Millers Forest and lower parts of Raymond Terrace to evacuate their homes. Beresfield was only three miles from Millers Forest.

Between 11:30am and midday, the levee banks protecting Oakhampton broke. Others followed. Hundreds of people were trapped by an enormous wave of water, ten feet high, which hit the town when the first of the levees broke. People clung to whatever they could as they waited to be rescued. Someone said that a pregnant woman had floated on a mattress in the torrent of flood waters, and was carried all the way to Fishers Creek.

All the creeks and rivers in the Upper Hunter were now spilling over, and the floodwaters were coming down from Muswellbrook, Denman and Singleton, moving at several feet per second, flooding the lower part of Branxton through the town centre and cutting the New England Highway. From our kitchen window, we had watched the swamp across the railway line filling fast. Beresfield, Tarro and Woodberry were now an island surrounded by a huge lake.

The 1955 Maitland flood was recognised as one of the biggest natural disasters in New South Wales, and the worst flood in the history of Maitland and most of the Hunter Valley. In February 2005, the City of Maitland and the SES, with other organisations, commemorated the 50th anniversary of the flood with an exhibition of photographs, slides and newsreels showing the great flood, the task of cleaning up the debris left in the homes and shops, and the farmers' massive clean-up of dead animals.

People who experienced the 1955 flood were in demand to tell their stories. One man who experienced the flood, and who still lived in the Maitland area, was retired Sergeant Police Prosecutor, Edward Cahill. The Provost Club I belonged to invited Mr Cahill to be a guest speaker. He accepted the invitation to tell his story at the Provost meeting held at East Maitland Bowling Club in June, 2005. Many of the ladies at this meeting had not been living in Maitland or the Hunter Valley district at the time of the flood, and they were interested to hear the guest speaker. Mrs June Cook, the President, addressed the ladies, saying, "Welcome to the Provost Women's Club.' The ladies sat quietly, waiting. Mrs Cook said, 'I am pleased to introduce Mr Edward Cahill to our meeting."

Ted Cahill walked forward and thanked the ladies for inviting him. He told the audience that he was born and grew up in the Hunter Valley. He went to primary school at Kurri Kurri and finished secondary school at Maitland. He went to work in Sydney in 1934 and joined the police force in 1939. He came back to Kurri Kurri in 1952 as the District Police Prosecutor. He told us that he would attempt to answer some of the questions about the flood, such as why flood warnings were ignored, and why people involved in the 1949 flood were prone to make comparisons. This is what he told us:

"Each flood in the Hunter River was compared with floods as far back as 1893, when the first records were taken. As a matter of course, comparisons have been made, and so were made in 1955. Up to the afternoon of Thursday the 24th, this flood was following the same pattern as 1949. The Hunter Valley is surrounded by mountains from the Central Coast to the Liverpool Ranges. It had been raining constantly for over a week in all the catchment areas. The rain from the mountain ranges filled swamps and creeks, and all that water ran into the Goulburn River on the eastern side and the Pages River at Murrurundi in the upper Hunter. The heavy rainfall caused swamps, creeks and rivers to rise and flow into the Hunter River. The swollen river closed the flood gates at Pitnacree, and this caused the rise in the Dagworth and Wentworth swamps in the Maitland area.

Subsequently, the low lying areas of the city were flooded with the still rising waters of the swamps overtopping the Comerford Dam at Oakhampton Road. The water from the dam flowed down behind the Maitland Hospital, under the Long Bridge and onto the railway and swamps beyond. It had never rained in all the catchment areas at the one time, not in the time of keeping records. The 1955 was like no other. This flood caught people by surprise. When the riverbanks gave way, the raging torrent tore through the Hunter, causing devastation and heartache across a wide range of towns and farms in the valley as never before.

On Thursday I had been preparing for a case at the Kurri Kurri courthouse. I was told to go home or I would be cut off by the flood. I came back to Maitland and went to the police station courthouse, which was one and the same building, to help the local police. I was receiving telephone calls from Upper Hunter police stations and from Constable McMahon stationed at Singleton some 56 kilometres upstream. I got the reading of rising rivers on an hourly basis, and passed the information onto the Lord Mayor, Alexander McDonald, at Maitland Town Hall.

On Thursday afternoon, Constable McMahon said, "Ted, this will be the last river reading you'll be getting from this station. The river has reached 14 metres. I am standing in the station, in water waist deep." These were the last words spoken by Sergeant McMahon from the police station at Singleton.

I knew that the police station at Singleton had not been flooded in the last flood, or any that I could remember. I then realised this flood was going to be much bigger than anyone could have imagined. This was no surprise to me. I had been studying the weather pattern on the map and listening to the weather forecast on the radio. Studying the flow of the rivers I knew that this flood was not like the last.

Again I passed the information on to the Lord Mayor. The general attitude seemed to be that this flood wouldn't be worse than the last flood. The Lord Mayor issued flood warnings and suggested that people in low lying areas evacuate their homes. These warnings were ignored.

I went out in the rain, knocking on doors in Mount Pleasant Street, suggesting to people that they might consider evacuating. The reaction of the people was: "What would a young police prosecutor know about floods?" Most people had experienced flood before, and assumed they would deal with this one as it came.

The water was still rising with no current and no debris. Records that I had at the Maitland Police Station showed that on Thursday, at 5:50pm, the rising backwater in Bulwer Street was about one hundred yards from the intersection of High street.

On Friday morning there was an influx of shoppers and others coming to town, which I thought was unusual. At about eleven am on Friday, the river could no longer be contained. There were two major breaks in the levee banks. One was at Oakhampton Road and the other was just in front of the police station. When the river banks gave way, a wall of water hit the police station and the Belmore Bridge that crossed the Hunter River to Lorn and surrounding farmland. The only sign of the bridge then was the top railing showing from the flood water. That was when all comparisons with past floods ceased.

Constable Firth and I, together with police personnel, were on the first floor of the police station when the banks of the river broke. All communication was non-existent. Water, gas and telephone cables were washed out. The raging river flowed through the town. The people in Central Maitland were forced onto the shop awnings, waiting to be rescued. This was out of the question, as the raging torrent of the river rushed through the streets of Maitland, destroying shops and other property.

People sat on the rooves of their houses, in the rain. Other people ran to high ground. The torrent ripped cars off the street and smashed them against the buildings and shop windows. One of the constables lost his new car that was parked in front of the police building. The force of the water lifted some houses off their foundations in Mount Pleasant Street and carried them to the Long Bridge. Some people managed to cling to trees when the house was carried towards the Long Bridge. Some didn't have a chance; they went down with their house.

'There was four feet of water inside the court house police station. The debris constantly hit the wall, shaking the building. We opened the doors at each end of the building. The Army and RAAF men guided the debris, with the rats and snakes, through the court house to the other end. That took the pressure off the building.

'Debris from farms – vegetables, trees, and animals still alive in the torrent – passed through the flooding town. People marooned on high ground grabbed the vegetables floating by.

'I had no way of letting my wife know where I was. She had no idea what had happened to me. Constable Firth, Constable Bailey and I, together with the Army and RAAF personnel, spent the rest of the afternoon and night on the first floor at the Police Station.

'At about midday on Saturday, we were picked up by Army Duck and taken across to the high ground at Maitland Hospital where most of the flood refugees were taken. The hospital was completely stranded. There, the wave of water had smashed everything, cutting off the water supply, electricity and communication. I had to deal with the catastrophe.

'In the hospital grounds, I established a police station under a tree to shelter Constable Firth, Constable Bailey, and myself from the constant rain. Not having experience in that field I had to get my thoughts together as to what was the first thing I must do. Without communication, nothing could be done. I asked if there was a technician in the crowd.

'A man by the name of Rex Mitchell came forward and said "How can I help?" He said he was a radio technician in the RAAF.

'I asked him if he could manage to get something set up on the hospital roof so we could communicate with Head Office and with a radio station.

Rex said, "Yes, if I can get a battery."

'There weren't many cars on the road in those days. I saw an NRMA panel van and I said to Rex, "There must be a radio and battery in that van." I went looking for the driver, but he was nowhere to be seen. Rex tried to start the radio in the van, but the battery was flat. No battery, no communication.

'I knew the chap at the petrol service station, not far from the hospital. I was a customer of his. Rex and I went to see if we could get a battery. The owner agreed to provide us with a battery, and communication was set up on the hospital roof.

'My immediate task was to organise water and food. With the help of Constable Bailey and a few men, I organised for 1000-gallon water tanks to be transported from Kurri Kurri and erected on the sleepers along the hospital driveway. Water tankers from Newcastle trucked water from Lochinvar. A 20,000 gallon supply had been established by nightfall. Next, we organised the cooking at the Monte Pio Orphanage near the hospital. They had coke fires to cook food for patients and staff.

'The flood refugees were constantly coming to the hospital grounds. Their names and addresses were taken, and they were sent to Greta camp where beds and food were provided. Constable Firth recorded every person that came to the hospital grounds and what camp they were taken to. This was all recorded in the police book.

'People injured during the flood came into the hospital. There were no local doctors to deal with the growing casualty list. Doctor Ken Barton came from Sydney to help out. He brought with him a bag of medication and other things needed to treat patients. I set up a place up for him away from the hospital, similar to a casualty clearing station. All the walking patients were sent to Doctor Barton. He did a good job taking care of the outpatients, which was a relief for the hospital staff.

'The President from Coffs Harbour Growers' Association came and said there was a train stranded at Dungog station with a load of bananas from Queensland and Coffs Harbour plantations. "If you can use them," he said, "you are most welcome to them."

'I sent out the RAAF truck to Dungog for the bananas. We sent crates of bananas to the hospital, and some crates to the Monte Pio. It was a challenge for the cooks to find ways to use the bananas. They were on the menu every day. I was giving out bananas to every person I spoke to, and to everyone I shook hands with. Everyone in town was eating bananas. There was not much else to eat for the first few days. When people saw me coming with a crate of bananas, they turned and walked the other way.

'The manager of the local abattoir, Ted Benson, came forward and said, "I just came from the abattoir. The freezers are still cold." While we were talking, a message came from Sydney wanting to know about supplies in the abattoir. Ted said, "Tell them there are 49 beef bodies in the freezer. That's what they want to know. They were slaughtered the very day the flood hit."

'Rex operated the radio on the rooftop, relaying the messages. I yelled out to him, "Pass the message to Sydney that there are forty-nine bodies in the freezer."

'A young journalist hanging around looking for some news overheard me pass the message to Rex. The journalist only heard half of what was said between Ted and me. The headlines next morning in the Sydney newspapers said there were 49 people drowned in Maitland and kept in the abattoir freezer.

'Constable Firth, Constable Bailey and I spent ten long days working from our office in the hospital grounds. With so many people coming and going, the hospital was a bog hole. It was difficult and tiring working under the tree in those conditions.

'Some time after the flood one of the hospital patients met me in the street with a greeting and a compliment, saying what a good job the boys in the police force had done during the flood. "Yes," he said, "a very good job, and I must thank you for the bananas. We had fried bananas, grilled bananas, battered bananas. Thanks to you, I don't want to see another banana as long as I live!"

We ladies laughed at the end of Ted's story. The 1955 Maitland Flood was a catastrophe as big as Cyclone Tracy in Darwin in 1974. Sergeant Cahill, with Constable Firth and Constable

Bailey, and other resourceful men and women, got Maitland moving at the most critical time. Sergeant Cahill was recognised for a job well done during the flood.

At the time of the flood, a friend told me that a crocodile was caught in the Hunter River. There was nothing said about the crocodile at the Provost meeting. Sometime after the flood, I saw a crocodile mounted in a Maitland shop window. I presumed this was the crocodile that was caught in the flood. It was in the shop window for a good many years, and I pointed it out to my children when we were shopping at Maitland. The owners of the shop retired and the crocodile vanished.

Curiosity is my strong point, so I started to inquire about the crocodile that had become a landmark in Maitland. I asked people living in the Maitland district if they had any idea what had happened to the crocodile. Most people didn't remember seeing it. Somewhere in the back of my mind I had an idea that the crocodile had been moved from one shop to another. I phoned the people who had last owned the shop. The old lady said that her husband had passed away and, to my surprise, she told me that she didn't remember seeing a crocodile in her husband's shop window.

I finally went to see the friend who had told me the story of the crocodile. His sister told me I could not ask him questions on the subject as he was no longer with us. I was persistent and asked everyone I knew. A friend's husband had heard something about it sometime during the flood, but he hadn't seen it. I spoke to people at the dance, trying to find out how I could remember seeing the crocodile in the shop window. The wife of one of my friends vaguely remembered seeing the crocodile in the shop window when she was a young woman.

I spoke to my friend Peggy about it, and she said, 'I don't remember seeing or hearing any stories of a crocodile, but I can tell you a true story of a pregnant woman being carried away on a mattress when her house was lifted from the foundations in Mount Pleasant Street. She was carried away with the torrent of water towards the Long Bridge. The house was smashed by the torrent. The water carried the young woman on a mattress for about a mile. She was picked up at Fishers Creek by a rescue boat and taken to the hospital grounds.

"I know this story to be true,' said Peggy. 'The woman's husband was building our house when the floodwaters hit Maitland and he told us that his wife was lucky to have been saved by floating on the mattress. Ray and I offered our house to them until they found a place of their own. They declined the offer. They moved away from Maitland to another state."

My mission continued to find that crocodile. I decided to phone Mr Boyle, the historian of Maitland. He was not at home on the evening I phoned. His wife answered, saying that he was at a meeting. "Can I help you?" she asked.

"Maybe you can,' I said. 'I am looking for a crocodile that was in a shop window in Maitland some years back. I was told by a friend that it was caught in the 1955 flood."

"No,' said Mrs Boyle. 'We can't remember hearing of any crocodile in the flood."

While we were talking, Mrs Boyle told me the story of how she, her husband Harry and their children had spent the night sitting in a boat in the hayshed. They packed up all the food they could carry, and rowed the boat to the hayshed. The water rose above the haystacks.

"It was frightening,' she said. 'I can't swim." The water was coming up high in the shed, and there was so much noise. The debris was hitting the shed. Harry kept bumping the side of the boat with the oar every so often through the night. It was after we were rescued that I asked Harry why he was hitting the side of the boat all night. He said there were rats and snakes trying to get into the boat. I'm glad I didn't know that at the time."

The subject came up about their prize-winning cow. "She was also trying to get in the boat,' said Mrs Boyle. 'Harry had to push her away. She bellowed as she was carried away by the strong torrent of water. You won't believe this,' said Mrs Boyle, 'but the cow floated all the way to Raymond Terrace and climbed onto the awning of a hotel. She was recognised as the prize-winner by a farmer. He told Harry where she was and Harry brought our cow back home!"

I was still on the hunt for the story of the crocodile. Luck was on my side the day I met a Polish woman named Lottie, who had owned a dress shop in Maitland. As I got to know the woman better, I asked her if she knew anything about the crocodile. "Oh yes,' said Lottie.

'My husband caught the crocodile and killed the little beast and had it stuffed and mounted, and put it in our shop window."

That fitted the description. It was a small crocodile, maybe about three feet. I asked if she knew what had happened to the crocodile. The woman said, "It was a long time ago." She couldn't tell me where it went after they sold the shop. I could put my mind to rest now that I had found the end to the crocodile story. The stories of the crocodile and the woman floating on the mattress were stories of the flood that didn't reach the news.

When the waters of the flood finally receded, our priest asked the parishioners to help out with the cleaning of the church and the schools in Maitland. My friend Pamela and I caught the train to High Street Station and walked through the mud still on the footpaths. We were not sure what damage the flood had caused. The debris from the street and the shops was piled up to be cleared. The smell was terrible.

We somehow managed to enter the school grounds. The Sisters gave us the job of cleaning the holy pictures and things brought from the convent kitchen that we young school girls could manage to clean. Pamela and I were outside, cleaning the objects. Pamela was on the lookout for the death adder snakes. Everything she picked up she knocked with a stick to make sure that it wasn't a death adder. After some time, this was giving me the jitters. I said to Pamela, "Can't you tell what a snake looks like from the object you are picking up?"

Pamela said, "My grandmother told me that I should watch out for the death adder. She said the snake can camouflage itself to the environment."

There was some years' difference in our ages. I was fifteen; she was no more than twelve. "Well if I were you,' I said, 'I would stop tapping things with the stick. The snake will get angry and strike at you before you know it."

I don't know if my saying that frightened Pamela. There was nothing said until lunchtime. Pamela invited me to go with her to have lunch with her grandmother. We walked to the street where the gasworks once stood, and where Pamela's grandmother lived. The house smelled of flood. The walls and floorboards were still wet and muddy. We sat on wooden boxes. Lunch was peanut-butter sandwiches. When I saw the disaster the flood had caused, I thought it was the end of the world. I suppose the people of the flood just thought that they had to start life over again.

In July 1955, my youngest brother Peter was born, five months after the flood. Walking to the Maitland Hospital to see Mother and the new baby, I saw that the debris from the streets had not yet been cleared. Some of the shops were open for business in the main street. It started to rain. I stopped at a shop and bought an umbrella, but the rain stopped.

I came to the place where the house had been lifted and carried by the flood, and smashed against the Long Bridge. The bridge had also been damaged. I had to step from one slab of concrete onto another. Every slab was moving under my foot. I had just walked off the bridge when it started to rain again. I opened the umbrella, but it was of little use. It was full of holes. I couldn't go back to the shop to complain. My problem was nothing compared to the troubles of those people trying to start their business over again.

OUT IN THE WORLD

After the flood, Maitland was still in turmoil, so I was sent to St Aloysius School at Hamilton. Travelling on the train through Hexham swamps was unpleasant. The stench of drowned cattle in the paddocks was unbearable. Nothing could be done to remove the carcasses until the swamps dried up for tractors to move in.

I did not make progress in the new school. I tried my best but the lessons were difficult. I couldn't cope with the work. I spoke to Father, telling him that I was not doing well in school and that I had reached the age to look for work to support myself. Father agreed, saying that if I hadn't found a job in two weeks, I was to go back to school.

In the May school break, I went out every morning, walking the streets of Newcastle, knocking on every factory door and walking into every restaurant and café. Within a week I had found a job in the sewing industry. I started work at Johnson's Men's Clothing factory on the corner of King and Steel Streets, clipping threads off the finished garments.

I worked in the factory for three weeks without making a friend. We were not allowed to talk during work hours, and in the lunch break all the women on sewing machines sat together in groups with their work mates. The girls working next to me went out for lunch, and I was not invited to join them. Then a new girl started working next to me. Her name was Margaret. She and I sat together in the lunch break. Margaret had worked for two days in this factory.

"I don't like working in this place,' she said. 'The boss is always on your back. I'm going back to the Style Master factory to see if I can get my old job back. The conditions and wages are better there."

Then she said, "You are welcome to come if you like. You may get a job with me."

I trusted Margaret and said I would go along. In our lunch break we were on a bus to Cooks Hill. Margaret walked into the office and asked to speak to the boss. Mrs King walked into the office and stood at the front desk. Margaret asked if she could have her job back.

Mrs King agreed. "The rules are still the same,' she said. 'Remember: no talking in working hours, no smoking in the toilets. You can start work on Monday."

Margaret then introduced me to Mrs King and asked if there was a position open for me. Mrs King looked me over and said, "Yes, but you must get a health certificate and bring it with you next week the day you start. Working hours are from eight to four thirty. The rules apply the same to all girls working for me. The radio is on through the day to help you girls with your work."

I was pleased to get the job at Style Master so easily. It was a good start for me to be with Margaret in a new place of work. As we left, I said to Margaret, "This building is much bigger than the other place."

"There are a lot more young girls working in this factory,' she said. 'You are sure to make friends working in this place."

We went back to Johnson's and handed in our resignation, saying we were leaving work on Friday.

On Monday morning, Margaret waited for me across the street from the station. We walked through Civic Park up to the Darby Street factory. Margaret and I worked together on the clipping bench. The wage at Style Master was three pounds fifteen shillings a week.

I went to see Sister Mary Bernard, my last teacher at Tarro School. Sister was pleased to see me. I told her that school days were over for me, and that I was working at Style Master.

"I am pleased you came to let me know that you are working Terese,' she said. 'I hope you will stay away from girls who can lead you astray."

I assured Sister that I worked with nice ladies and good girls. Sister gave me her blessing and wished me a good life and happiness in the future. Sister Mary Bernard and I had a special bond. I would have liked her to be my grandmother. I could speak to her freely. Sister always had time to listen to me. I couldn't talk to my mother openly like that.

After we had worked three months at Style Master, Mrs King promoted both Margaret and I. Margaret went to the sewing bench where she made up canvass for the inside of coats to give the lapels of the coat a neat finish. I was promoted to the position of a supervisor floor walker in a building next to the main factory. There was only one bench with twenty sewing machines on it. The rest of the building was a lunch room and storage room for material.

The work on my bench was assembly line sewing of casual trousers. I had twelve girls working on my bench, some of them married women. Every morning, bundles of cut material were on my table. My job was to sort the bundles and to distribute the work to the girls to sew parts of the trousers together. The young girls sewed the smaller parts together, then I would take the made up parts to more experienced girls. They sewed in the pockets and the zipper at the front of the trousers.

A woman named Barbara sewed in the back pockets of the trousers. When the pockets were finished, I tied the back and front of the trousers together and took the bundle into the main factory to a woman working on a special machine sewing the back and front together. I then brought the bundle of trousers back to my table and tied the bands onto the trousers. I took them to Betty, and she sewed the bands on to finish the trousers. I took the finished bundle of trousers to the presses in the main factory. Phyllis and the other press workers put the finishing touch on men's trousers and suits. The clothes were then loaded on the truck and transported to Sydney stores.

It was good working with the girls. I was pleased there was no jealousy over Mrs King choosing me, the youngest girl, for the job. I was happy. Sometimes mistakes were made, and I would unpick the work for the girls. This saved them time, as they had to put in a tally. I was on the go all day. Time passed quickly. At the end of the day, it was my job to collect a tally from each girl, and hand the total over to Mrs King. I was also to report to Mrs King any accidents. My pay increased by ten shillings a week.

I had very little to wear in the way of work clothes. The married women on my bench asked me if I would be offended if they passed their clothes on to me. In those days, women passed on clothes to someone they respected. I felt privileged and grateful to the ladies for their gesture. I accepted the ladies' dresses, and they were pleased that I was giving a new lease of life to their clothes. It gave me the chance to save my money for a deposit on bedroom furniture. Mother couldn't buy such things for me because she needed money for the new baby.

Barbara brought in a gabardine winter coat for me, and a grey suit. It had a jacket fitted at the waist, and a sun pleated skirt. She had only worn it once. She had sat too close to a radiator and scorched the bottom of the skirt. Barbara, kind lady that she was, measured my length and cut off the bottom of skirt. In the lunch hour, I hemmed it up on the machine. The suit looked as if it had been made for me, although grey was not a colour I would have chosen. I learned the Australian saying: "Don't look a gift horse in the mouth; be grateful." A red velvet rose pinned onto the lapel of the jacket gave the grey a lift.

In those days, velvet roses were worn on suits, coats and hats. Also popular were hand-made sprays of sponge rubber flowers, sprinkled with glitter, and flowers made from stockings stretched over fine wire. No woman would walk out the door without a hat and gloves, stockings, smart shoes and a handbag to match. In vogue for a time were stockings with coloured heels and seams to match the shoes she was wearing. These heels and seams came in red, green and black. There were four millinery shops for ladies' hats in Newcastle.

Similarly, menswear stores had a special corner for hats. In those days, a man would not dare leave the house without a hat on his head. Young men didn't wear hats; they put Brylcream or Californian Poppy on their hair to stop it blowing in the wind. A man always wore a suit or a sports coat, with a clean handkerchief in his pocket, and kept his shoes polished. On the train or bus, if there were no seats vacant and a woman had to stand, a young man would stand up and offer his seat to the woman, unless he was disabled. Some returned soldiers wore a badge on the lapel of their coat, so everyone knew that they were not able to give up the seat.

Clothes and shoes were expensive in the fifties. I had trouble buying shoes, as Australian made shoes didn't fit my feet. I had to go to more expensive shoe stores and buy imported Italian shoes. The cost of those shoes was more than my weekly wage. "Noggie shoes for Noggie feet," said my friend Wilma.

She made me laugh. "It's true," I said.

"You know that was meant as a joke,' said Wilma. 'I meant no harm."

"No offence taken," I said.

We are still friends today.

There was a woman, however, who made negative remarks to me in the lunch hour. When a bottle of milk was left overnight, and the girls were going to throw it out, I said, "I will take the milk home for Mother to make cottage cheese from it." This woman said, "You shouldn't eat things like that. And that salami sausage laced with garlic – it comes out in the sweat pores of your skin, and your body smells of BO." As she told me this, she drew on her cigarette and blew out a puff of smoke. Australians at that time had no knowledge of making cottage cheese or yoghurt. It wasn't until the early 1960s, when I was working at the Oak factory, that the manager of that factory spent time overseas and learned how good and healthy this food was. He brought the ideas back to make these products at the Oak.

At the end of the working day, I walked up Hunter Street to Newcastle Station with Betty and Phyllis. They were stepsisters. It was a longer distance than walking to Civic Station, but we filled time by window shopping on the way. We got to know one another's likes and dislikes. After a few months, Betty and Phyllis invited me to spend the weekend at Cessnock with them. I was thrilled, and accepted their offer of friendship.

We finished work on Friday, and arrived at Cessnock Station at six o'clock. It was only a short walk to the girls' home. We walked in the door, and the parents of my friends made me feel most welcome. The table was set for five people. On a red and white checked tablecloth were bread and butter, a sugar bowl, salt and pepper, and a modern plastic tomato sauce dispenser shaped like a big red tomato with a green stalk on the top. It looked as if it had just been picked from the garden, and was more attractive than a big bottle of tomato sauce standing on the table. A prayer was said before the main meal. After having tea, the usual past-time was to relax in the lounge room listening to a favourite serial on the radio before bedtime.

On Saturday afternoon we got dressed in our best. I wore my grey suit, red high heel shoes and a handbag to match. We walked to the picture theatre in the main street to see the movie *Baby on the Ship*. Betty and Phyllis met with friends in the street and stopped to have a short conversation before walking into the picture theatre. The movie was the best comedy of the year. Every person in the theatre laughed all the way through the show that afternoon.

The sun was just setting as we walked out the door. It was too early to go home. Cessnock was a coalmining town. People were friendly, and enjoyed their leisure day meeting friends in the street and stopping to chat for a while, or going to movies and dancing. People in Cessnock did not rush in the streets like the people in Newcastle did. Perhaps people in the city were in a rush to catch trains and buses, travelling longer distances to get home.

We strolled through the street, window shopping. That was my favourite past-time, as it was for many people in the fifties. Window artists were hired to dress models and create a background scene of spring, summer, autumn or winter in the store window. A mannequin in the window was dressed for autumn in a circular skirt, a twin set and a tartan scarf around her neck. Some leaves were scattered at her feet. The artist had used pins and fishing line to make it look as if the wind was blowing the clothes. It looked so realistic. It wasn't only ladies dressed in the windows. Male mannequins were dressed in suits and hats with a few small branches of twigs lying on the ground.

Once a month the windows were changed. In August, mannequins were dressed in evening gowns, white gloves and dancing shoes, or dinner suits, for the spring ball. Betty and Phyllis were not interested in ball gowns or dancing. They liked reading books and working for the church. The girls were good, honest people. They welcomed me into their home as if I were someone special.

On Sunday morning, I was invited to go to church with the family. It was not a church of my religion, but that made no difference to me. I was taught that there is one God, and we are all his children. I was interested to know how other people worshipped God at Sunday services. After the church service, Betty and Phyllis asked if I would stay back with them. They were teaching Sunday school. I said I would stay. Sunday school was a lesson for me. Little children loved listening to the Bible stories, drawing pictures from the story they heard, and cutting pictures to paste in their Sunday book.

The girls' Aunty Miriam invited us to afternoon tea. We caught a bus to Bellbird, just a little way out from Cessnock. I was expecting a little place in the country with the sound of bellbirds in the trees. From the bus I saw Nissen huts. They were built for the English migrants working for the Bellbird coal mines. Cessnock and all towns in the area were known as The Coalfields.

Aunty Miriam's house was a picture, with a lovely garden and a picket front fence. Aunty met us at the front gate. She said, "I'm pleased you came, Terese. Welcome to my house." Stepping inside, I could sense the warmth and love in this cosy home. The coffee table was ready with cups and plates. Aunty went out to the kitchen, and Betty followed. As we sat down on the lounge, Aunty brought out a sponge cake, and Betty carried the silver tray with the teapot, milk and sugar. We spent the afternoon talking. The dear lady was eager to ask me questions. She wanted to know what the European people thought of the Australian country and people.

I said, "It's strange to us people from Europe. The countryside, the wild animals and the trees are different in this country. The summers are hot, as hot as it was when we crossed the Suez Canal and the Red Sea. The strong winds in the summer are hot. Australian shops don't sell food that European people eat. There is a lot of bush between towns, and not many houses. The cicadas on hot days drive me mad."

Aunty Miriam laughed. I went on. "We lived in displaced people's camps in Germany. Some of them were near forests, but when we lived in a camp close to a town, we were able to walk about and see the houses in town. They are not different from the ones I see in

Australia. There were flowers growing in the front garden, just as they are in this country. I can remember seeing roses, fuchsias, daisies, bleeding hearts, carnations and gladiolus in the front gardens. In the back yards, as it is in Australia, were vegetable gardens. That is all I can tell you. We were invited by Father's workmate to his garden. As we walked past the house, the man told me that I could pick some gooseberries to eat from the gooseberry bush. The bushes were growing in a straight row in the back yard."

Betty turned to Phyllis and said, "I haven't seen a gooseberry. What do they taste like?"

"The fruit looks like a long white grape,' I said. 'It is a lovely sweet taste, much nicer than a grape."

"You make my mouth water, Terese."

When it was time for us to leave, I thanked the sweet lady and said, "Spending the afternoon with you was a pleasure. The sponge cake was very nice."

Aunty Miriam said, "I enjoyed your company, Terese. You are so open in what you say. It's refreshing to hear an honest talking girl."

It had been a lovely day.

Some months later, I was again invited by the girls to their home. It was the weekend of the Cessnock Show. The girls thought it would be fun for us three to go together, and they knew from previous conversation that I hadn't experienced much of Australian culture. Going to The Show would open a little of the Australian world to me.

I was excited when we walked into the showground. There was so much to see. The girls first walked into the agriculture pavilion. I was familiar with pigs from my earlier years, but this was the first time I had been close to other farm animals. They were washed and brushed, and looked to be in top shape. I had often seen them from a distance, grazing in paddocks. I took a particular interest in the fruit and vegetable section, and the way it was arranged. It was an artistic work creating a picture. I was impressed at what could be achieved.

Walking through the poultry pavilion, I was fascinated to see the strange hens. There were common big black hens, and brown hens, and unusual white hens with fluffy pompom heads. They were not usually seen in people's backyards. There were some unusual looking ducks, and different kinds of pigeons. Some of the fantail pigeons looked to me as if they were deformed. Some pigeons were as big as a small hen. Looking at the big pigeons, I thought that my Dad should have bred those big pigeons and sold them as pheasant for the table.

I was also interested in the handiwork, needlework, knitting, and decorated iced cakes. The work on them was to be admired. They were beautifully presented. We went on to see the artwork and photography. The furniture stores brought out the best of their beautiful furniture. Rooms were created, and the furniture arranged as if it were in a house. White goods, farm machinery and domestic sewing machines were also on show.

The girls and I enjoyed some of the rides we dared to get on. We spent a lovely day together. Sadly, this was the last time we were together. The girls had often spoken of spending their holidays in New Zealand. They took the time off work for the trip to New Zealand, and while they were over there, they joined a religious ministry, and didn't come home.

I had been working at Style Master for over twelve months, and changes were happening. Just before Easter, painters came to paint the building. One of them was a young part-time actor and singer. As the painters came nearer to our bench, the radio was on as usual, playing the song 'Swannee'. The young man couldn't resist. Using his paint brush as a microphone, he sang along with Al Jolson, bending down on one knee and acting the part from the movie, high up on the plank. The girls stopped work to watch the young man on the plank. It was quite a comedy.

Just as the song finished, Mrs King came into the building, yelling at the girls over the noise of machines. "Never mind watching him! Get on with your work!"

Her voice rang out again. "Young man up there on the plank! I don't pay you to entertain! Get on with your job!"

Coming back to work on the Tuesday morning after Easter, I saw remnant material stacked on the far table. Mrs King announced we could buy the remnants. "On Friday,' she said, 'this building is to be sold. You will be working in the main factory."

The day before we moved into the main building, my girls presented me with a gift of boxed handkerchiefs and a big bottle of 4711 cologne. The next day my girls were scattered on different benches. I was put on as a machinist next to Margaret, making belt loops to be sewn onto the trousers. This was not a permanent position for me.

I was feeding the material through the machine when my finger slipped. Two needles went through my index finger. The woman working opposite me fainted. I stayed calm and asked Margaret to get Stan. He was our machine mechanic, and he attended the boilers. (Not the old boilers working on the machines!) He also ran the steam presses, and was our first-aid man. Stan was in a dilemma: which one of us girls should he attend first? But he needn't have worried. Mrs King was running over behind him with smelling salts in one hand and sal volatile in the other. She attended to the woman and revived her with smelling salts.

Mrs King put a few drops of sal volatile into a glass of water for me to drink. It calmed me down while Stan released my finger from the machine and pulled the needles from my finger. It didn't bleed much. Band-Aids were wrapped around my finger, and I continued working, feeding the material through the machine with my middle finger. This kind of accident happened now and then. There was no time off for compensation. I was put to work on the other side of Margaret, sewing canvas.

Margaret and I walked together up Hunter Street to Civic Station every day. When I could afford it, I bought clothes and shoes. I remember buying a pair of sandals made from raffia. When I took them home, Mother put her hands to her head. "Shoes made out of grass!" she cried. She told me that when she was at school she had read a book of prophesy. It had predicted the end of the world, and said, among other things, that shoes would be made of grass, and that people would walk into shops and take things off the shelves, and clothes off the hangers. "How people are going to pay for that, I have no idea," she said. (Within two years of this rare conversation, a modern grocery self-service shop was opened in Beresfield, at the end of our street.) The book had also said that there would be killing and murders on a big scale, and distinguishing male from female would be difficult.

One day Margaret was sick, and I walked up Hunter Street by myself. Winter clothes were on display in the store windows, and my eyes were drawn to a beautiful watermelon red coat at Cox Brothers' store. I could see myself wearing this lovely half circular fitted coat with a big collar and big black shiny buttons. I rushed into the store and quickly tried it on for size. I didn't have time to take a good look at the coat. I had to get to the station, and the shops shut at five o'clock. I put ten shillings down on the coat to hold it until pay day.

On the Saturday morning after pay day I dressed in a straight grey skirt, a tomato red twinset, and my black patent leather shoes. I walked to Tarro station to catch the train to Newcastle. Keith, a local boy I knew, was also waiting at the station. He was dressed in good casual trousers and a sports coat. He had a haircut like Elvis, and he looked very smart. We sat together on the train. He asked me if there was a special reason I was going to Newcastle. I told him I was going to pick up a coat from Cox Brothers'.

He insisted on coming with me. I gave the sales lady the deposit docket, and she went to the backroom. When she brought out the box, I asked if I could try the coat on again before taking it. I put it on. Keith gave me the approval with a whistle, and said, "You look as if you just stepped out of one of those fashion magazines."

"It is a perfect fit,' said the sales lady, 'and it looks good with your black shoes." The sales lady was a manager in the clothing department. She asked me if I would be interested in modelling clothes.

"I would like to,' I said to the lady, 'but my illness prevents me. I am not reliable."

I said this because I was constantly getting sick from the dust in the main building at Style Master. My eyes were often swollen. As it got worse, my tongue and throat swelled up as well.

I loved my red coat. I wore it over full dresses on cold nights when going to dances by train. I wore it over my gown when I made my debut at the Tarro Catholic Ball.

On Saturday evenings, movies were shown at the Tarro Hall. Several times there, I met up with a young man named Keith. Before we sat together to watch the movie, Keith would order a taxi to drive us home after the movie. We got out together at my house, and Keith had only one block to walk to his house.

One Friday evening, Keith asked me to go to Newcastle with him the next morning. I had no plans, and I said I would be glad to go along. We met the next morning on the station platform. I was wearing my red coat and black shoes. We got off the train at Wickham Station, and walked up Hunter Street until we came to a motorbike shop. Keith said, "I'll just take a look in this shop." I went across the street to look at some furniture in a shop window.

About ten minutes later, I heard a motorbike close beside me in the gutter. It was Keith. He said, "I just bought this! Get on the back. I am taking you on a trip."

I hopped on the bike, thinking we were going home. But we passed Beresfield, and Maitland. Keith rode the motorbike all the way to Tamworth! We arrived in time for a late lunch of hamburgers and Coca-Cola in a milk bar. Keith had friends there, and we listened to music on the juke box. We didn't stay long. We said our goodbyes, and rode home.

Half way between Muswellbrook and Singleton, the bike sprung a leak. Oil squirted out, all over my lovely red coat. Keith pushed the bike up the hills and along the flat road. We sat on the bike riding down hills until we reached Singleton. Keith pushed the motorbike to a property where the house was close to the highway. The farmer was finishing his day's work. Keith approached the man and asked if he could leave his bike in the farmer's place for a day or so. The farmer didn't mind, but said that if Keith didn't pick the bike up by the next weekend, he would sell it. Keith agreed, and assured the farmer he would arrange to have the bike picked up within days. We hitched a ride in a car to Maitland and came home in a taxi. Luckily for me, Father was working afternoon and evening shift.

Keith usually came to see me at home on two evenings a week. On one of those evenings, he told me that he had joined the circus. He said there was a job for me as a mermaid sitting in a big bowl of water in the tent, waving to spectators. On my next day off, I rushed into town to buy a swimming costume at Cox Brothers'.

I was again asked by the sales lady to consider modelling. She said, "We badly need a girl with a figure like yours for bathing costumes. I want you to consider modelling."

"No,' I said to the lady. 'I am not always well, and there are times I can't work."

I came home and thought things through. I was in a secure environment at home. If I needed help, a doctor and hospital were close. If I left home to become a mermaid, I would be in a strange place, not knowing where I was going to live. I didn't want to be in some strange place with Keith. I was not ready for travelling all over the state. And I remembered that I didn't like my skin to be constantly wet. Keith went off with the circus by himself, and no doubt he found another mermaid.

PIECES IN PLACE

In January 1956, we had been living in the house for just over twelve months, and I was still in my first year at Style Master. It was a Saturday afternoon. Father had already left for work. It was a good day to be enjoying the life outside, so Mother and I were working in the front yard. Baby Peter was with us, asleep in the pram. Mother and I were planting the white arum lilies that neighbours had brought over that morning when they came to see the baby. Mother was only too pleased to accept plants.

We heard Mrs Murray's voice coming from the direction of the track. She and Eileen were walking across the street towards the house from one of many tracks cutting through the bush from the train station. Mrs Murray called out, "Every time I see you Anna, you got your head down and your rear up working!"

Mother stood up and said, "Mrs Murray! Good that you come to see us!"

Mrs Murray was a big woman in her forties with grey hair and health problems. She was diabetic and her legs were always wrapped in bandages, which restricted her activities. On good days she managed to walk a short distance, as she had on this day.

"Here I am, at last, to see you and your baby," she said, looking into the pram to see Peter. She said how he looked like Dad. Eileen looked at Peter and said, "He is beautiful." Then she said, "I'm getting married later in the year. Then I will be having a baby of my own."

"That is good,' said Mother. 'You are young woman, and make good mother." Mother turned to Mrs Murray and said, 'Come, sit in house. You sit; your legs are sore standing. You walk a long way."

Mrs Murray sat in the bulky lounge that took up most of the room. The conversation started with Mrs Murray saying, "I am impressed! You have done well. You have saved hard for this house you and Paul. That was a big task to take on, building a house on your own. And you speak English much better since I saw you last."

"Yes, it is hard work,' said Mother. 'We must learn new things."

"I noticed most of your people did the same – building a house for yourselves."

"Yes, when we live in Germany, Pawel say when we come to Australia, we must have house for us to live. It is most important," said Mother.

"The work you have done in the short time since you came to Beresfield is incredible. How long is it since you came to Australia?" she asked.

"Three and half years in Beresfield, Five years in Australia," Mother said.

"The life you lived in Europe must have been tough in the years of war,' said Mrs Murray. 'It must have been difficult to leave your country and come to make a home in a new country and to learn a new language. If you don't mind I want to ask you, did you leave your country to escape the war?"

At that moment, Mother spoke to me: "Terese, see the baby is alright."

"Yes Mum. Peter is fine. I will take care of him." I wheeled the pram into the kitchen, where there was some ironing to do. Eileen followed me. Mother was a modest woman. She had difficulty talking about life during the war years when I was in the same room.

Eileen played with the baby while I did the ironing and listened to Mother telling Mrs Murray of her experiences. I wasn't going to miss the chance of getting to know what had happened when I was a baby. I felt that I had the right to know.

I heard Mother say, "I tell you Mrs Murray, if you want to know. You are my friend."

"Oh yes, I am interested in what you tell me," said Mrs Murray.

"I not say this to people before," said Mother.

"I would be glad to hear your story," said Mrs Murray.

"I tell you Mrs Murray. I am twenty-one years, with my baby in my country, Poland. Adolf Hitler, he makes war on Poland. The German soldier comes to my village, knocking on door. He say to me in German, with his hands he show me, "Pack bag." He says, "One bag." I say to him with my hand, "I not want to go, I stay." He says I go and leave my baby. I make trouble to him. I not want to leave house. I pick up my baby, my Terese. The German soldier pushes me. He say, "Get bag ready. Leave baby in house."

"I know what he say. People say this before in my village. Me with my baby, by myself. My Pawel was gone some time. He not come home to me for some days. I wait every day. He not come back. I do not know were my Pawel is. German soldier take people from my village. Soldier say with hands, "Leave baby in house."

"I do with my hands to say, "She come with me." The soldier he say, *"Aus, aus! Schnel!"* This say "Out, out! Quick!" He push me with my Terese into street. People already walking. Some more still come, more from house in village: older mans, women, children's come. Many young people. They take my friend Jusza, too. Me and Jusza good friends for long time. We live in same village, go to same school. The soldier, he say we must walk. He push with gun on back of us. He say, *"Schnel! Schnel!"*

For long time we walk. I get very tired carry my baby and bag long time. I not know before I leave my home I have baby coming. I say to Jusza, "I want to sit for little time, Jusza." She say to me, "Anna, you must go on. You see what German soldier do to people that sit down." Mrs Murray, I telling you, soldier shoot people that sit and not get up to walk."

I could hear mother sniffle, using her hanky.

"It must have been terribly frightening for you to see people being shot," said Mrs Murray.

Mother continued, saying, "It was upsetting people. Mothers and children crying. We walk long way. We walk little slowly. The German SS, he come to me. He hit on my head with gun. I see all black in my eyes."

"Oh! Them bastards!' cried Mrs Murray. 'Hitting a woman carrying a baby!"

Mother continued. "My friend Jusza, she carry Terese for time. The soldier make me sick. My head, she go boom boom."

Again Mrs Murray said, "Oh, them bastards!"

"We have to walk long way. I sick with bad head. We walk fast. My head, she goes boom boom. We walk to cow train waiting for us, not on station. How you say? No houses."

"A cattle train in open fields," said Mrs Murray. She was helping out with words Mother was not able to say.

"Ya, ya. It was sun coming down," said Mother.

"Sunset," said Mrs Murray.

"Ya, ya,' said Mother. 'Germans make us go in cow train. Many peoples in one train. Door shut. All black inside, no place to sit no place to feed my baby. All women tired. No water to drink, no toilet. Women frighten, crying. Frighten children crying. SS lock us up in train. No good for peoples, no fresh wind."

Mrs Murray interrupted, saying, "Fresh *air* is the word you want to say."

"Mrs Murray, I myself frighten too," said Mother.

Mrs Murray couldn't hold herself back. "Oh! Them bastards!"

Mother stopped talking. She wiped her eyes and blew her nose. When she was ready, she continued: "I young woman, never leave home before, not know where we going, not know what happen to us. We stay on train maybe one night, one day. I not remember. Head go boom boom all time. After some time train stop, door open. Sun strong in eyes. Guards shout, "*Aus! Aus!*" Some women and men not see outside, the sun too strong, fall off train."

"Blinded by the sun,' said Mrs Murray.

"Ya, ya," Mother replied.

Mother used her hanky again, saying, "I am sorry I cry."

"That's alright Anna,' said Mrs Murray. 'These memories must be painful for you to talk about. My brother was a soldier in the war. He served in New Guinea. When he came back he could not talk of his experiences, he would say nothing at all. The war was a waste of so many people. Our Australian boys were fighting the Germans overseas in Egypt, and fighting the Japs in New Guinea."

"Pawel and me, we not know New Guinea. We know countries of Europe. Egypt, Japan, Holland, Arabia, America, Africa, Argentina countries Pawel and me know."

Mother continued her story. She told Mrs Murray that the train stopped and the door opened. The SS soldiers stood outside with big dogs so no-one could escape. There was a lot of confusion. The people were shoved and pushed. The women, children and the old were pushed to a building and told to take off all their clothing for showers, and to leave their clothes, suitcases and shoes tied together. Mother's friend, Jusza, was of German origin and could understand what the guards were saying. She told Mother not to undress. Another woman in the line overheard this, and stayed with Mother and Jusza, not undressing. This other woman was a doctor.

"My baby Terese already undress,' said Mother. 'She not moving, not breathing. I got frighten,' said Mother. 'Woman doctor say, "You must take baby out from here, she is poisoned."

The children were taken away from their mothers. Some were already limp, and not breathing. The women screamed with fright and grief that their children were dead. They had been poisoned from the gas fumes lingering in the building from the last unfortunate souls who met their death in the showers. "We next go in," said Mother.

Again I heard Mrs Murray say, "Oh them bastards! Killing women, babies and children! That was murder of innocent people! Oh, them bloody bastards!"

There was silence for a moment.

Then Mother said, "All confusion. Juzsa say, "Wrap baby, stay close to me.""

Mother told how Juzsa then stepped forward to the door, and said something to the young guard. He opened the door just enough for them and the woman doctor to dash out into the open into the air. Outside the doctor made the baby vomit and bring up the poison. "My Terese breathe, come to life"' said Mother. The doctor told her that babies are like canaries, that they detect gas fumes before adults.

"Many people, all confusion,' said Mother. 'A man come with suitcase. He open it and say "Put baby in here." I no time think. I put my baby in, take suitcase. The man he walk away. We stand with people for farm work. Jusza know German. She go to farmer and ask him we do farm work. She say to him, "We have baby."

Farmer say, "No. No babies." Jusza beg him take us for farm work. Farmer say yes. He ask, "Where is baby?"

"I tell him in suitcase. He say, "Give it to me" and he pull suitcase from my hand and he say, "Come, *schnel*."

"I tell you, Mrs Murray, I frighten,' said Mother. 'My heart stop. A chill came on my body thinking where he take my child? Is he report to guards? Will we going back to shower building? I thank God he walk to truck. The farmer open door of truck and say, "Get in. Take baby out, keep quiet." He put empty suitcase back of truck and get more people for farm work. Peoples stay living, working on farms."

Mother explained that because I had been sick from the poison, she left me in a room on the farm all day while she worked in the fields with the other women. "When Terese she get better, I take her out with me, put her on potato bag and drag her with me. I work sunrise, sunset. Boss get pram, much better for my Terese.' Mother paused. 'SS come to farm, look for children. Boss say to SS, no children on his farm. Boss tell me he save my Terese from *kraut kopf.* That mean "cabbage heads". Boss not like SS troops coming to his farm."

The SS troops were sent to farms and factories randomly looking for children who had been hidden by their mothers in the confusion. The SS were to take the children from mothers so they would be cared for in the kinder centre to relieve the burden of the working mothers. That was what they said to the farmer, the man Mother called "boss", but the farmer knew what happened in the kinder centres.

Mother told Mrs Murray how the farmer saved me from the SS. "Boss say to me, 'Anna, I save Terese from kinder centre. This place not good for children. SS take children, mother never see her children again. You must keep Terese in room.' The boss, he tell me children in kinder centre play balloons with poison gas. Balloon break, children die. Boss tell me himself.

"Coming on winter is hard living, always raining, clothes wet. Hard walking in mud, very cold digging up vegetables before ground freezing. I leave Terese in room by herself. She crawling. She sitting in wet nappy on floor. I come from work and hear Terese laughing. I look in through crack in door before open. My Terese she sitting on floor, try to catch rat, catch tail, when they come close. She not move. Terese wet nappy and bum freeze to floor. I get shovel, put under nappy, get my Terese free. It is shame this way we live. I go to boss and ask him give me room upstairs in sun where he keep chickens, hoping there no rats in this room."

There was silence in the room; no words from Mrs Murray.

"You know, Mrs Murray, working in the cold was hard. My feet wet, cold. My hands crack and sore. My body ache. I very tired and cold. I want lie down, go to sleep. I cannot. I must get food, bring it back to room. I wash and feed Terese, put her to sleep. After eat, I wash nappies, iron dry. Iron wet clothes for work in morning. I put fat on my crack fingers to stop pain. My feet and legs ache. Hard working in mud all day. When I go sleep, it time for me get up for work. Every day same, working in fields. It hard working in wet clothes, and shoes sticking to mud. And new baby coming, no-one to help. Many times I think I will not wake in morning."

As I listened to all this from the kitchen, I said quietly to Eileen, "My life is like a jigsaw puzzle. I pick up different parts of my life story, listening to Mother speak to her friends. Today I learned about my early life. Mother never told that part of life to anyone before."

Time was slipping away. Mrs Murray and Eileen had to start walking back to their home. As they said goodbye, Mrs Murray said she would come back soon to hear more of Mother's story.

Mrs Murray came back the next Saturday to listen. Eileen didn't stay. She went shopping and said she would come back later for her mother.

Mother welcomed Mrs Murray into the house. After a little friendly chat, I left the lounge room and stayed with little Peter in my room, leaving the door open. Mother continued telling Mrs Murray her story where she had left off.

"You know, Mrs Murray, winter in Europe very cold. The ground freeze. Animals bring into barn from cold. We work in farm stable and barn, take care of animals, feed animals, change straw, and keep stable clean. Boss, he have good farm. Barn and stable always clean. Many things to do get ready for work in spring. In spring, boss say I stay in house and clean, not work in field. I have baby coming, I must stay hide from SS. The boss he say bring work from house to my room. I stay with my Terese more.

'One day my Pawel come to farm to see boss. I not believe my eyes. It is him! He working for same boss at different farm. This first time I see Pawel since he leave our village. He too shocked: I big woman, baby coming. We so happy – see together."

"Happy to see each other," said Mrs Murray, smiling.

"Ya – yes,' said Mother. 'Boss say Pawel stay for little time. He walk long way go back before tea. Easter coming. Boss say to Pawel he come to see family for Easter Sunday, but not stay night time. My Pawel come see family, stay little time. He walk back same day where he work."

Mother cried. "You know, Mrs Murray, it is very hard."

I have worked out that Mother had her baby, my little brother Wladek, probably in the early summer, in June. Father would have had to wait until the following Christmas to see his new son. The farmer had said that my father could visit at Christmas, as he had done at Easter.

When she stopped crying, Mother continued. "I have two children. Boss give me job closer to my children, milk cows, feed chickens, pull feathers off goose for make eiderdown. I feed my baby. Life better in summer. Days warmer and longer, nappies and clothes dry overnight. When baby is one year, I work in fields. I make little things for baby to feed, show Terese to put in bowl of milk, give to baby. Terese look after baby until I come back from work."

A wedding party in front of the house at Schwabisch Hall where we had a room in the attic.

Me aged 6, looking all the better for Mother's cooking while we lived at Schwabisch Hall.

Dad in a US Army jeep at an airstrip. He helped the Americans with bomb disposal.

Me, aged 7, with Dad at Ludwigsburg. I have lost weight through sickness and camp food. I am wearing the shoes made for me by the cobbler while I was ill.

The Polish community of Luitpold Kaserne camp, Ludwigsburg. Father Bonkowski is the priest in the foreground.

Religious procession at Ludwigsburg. I am in front, in the middle.

Marisha, Renia and me. Our play area is in the background.

Mother and me on the day of my First Holy Communion.

The classroom at Ludwigsburg after the first Polish teacher arrived. I am in the front.

The altar of our Polish church at Ludwigsburg.

School game in the snow at Ludwigsburg. I am on the right wearing my big fur coat.

Mother and Father with the twins at their baptism, early 1948.

Dad (left) with the camp commandant (middle) of Ludwigsburg, in front of the main gate to the camp.

The wedding of Czesiek's godmother. I am the flowergirl.

A Sunday outing with friends at Wildflecken. I am between Mother and Father in the middle, Czesiek is on Father's lap.

Czesiek and me in late 1949, shortly before we left Ludwigsburg.

The ship Skaugum at Port Melbourne.

Our house in Beresfield that Dad built with Mother's help.

Eileen and me dressed up for a concert. Mother did the beadwork on my vest when we lived in Greta camp.

Maitland High Street flooded.

The Long Bridge after the flood. I walked across this to visit Mother and my new baby brother Peter.

Cecil's confirmation. Dad with Father Hanrahan, and me in my grey suit with the red rose.

Our wedding, January 1962 at St Bridget's Church, Raymond Terrace.

Bryan and me, with Karen and Anthony in the pram, at the Botanical Gardens in Penang.

Mum and Dad with my brother Peter at his wedding to Krystina in 1980.

I remembered Mother showing me how to feed my baby brother. I remembered the time I tore Mother's blue blouse, and that Mother gave me a beating. I remembered living in that room, watching the blossoms scratching against the window.

I heard Mother say, "It near two years we come to farm. SS guards not come so much. Maybe they fight in war. It spring again. Pawel come on some Sundays. Boss say I let my children out of room into fresh air on Sunday, but I must watch for SS still might come."

I remembered the day I was let out from that room. It had been like a prison for me and my baby brother. I will never forget that beautiful day, looking out at a paramount view. It was breathtaking for a little girl to step outside for the first time.

Then I remembered the whistling game with the boss. I was given strict instructions many times by Mother that I was not to scream or cry or to make any noise. I was to stay in that place until I was let out. If I played up I would not see her again. Instinct played a part in this. When you are constantly threatened with losing your mother, you sense there is something wrong and you learn to obey. Many years later, I was watching a war movie late at night. The Allies were chasing a German submarine and the German sailors inside it were singing the Germen anthem. I hummed along with them. I wondered how I knew the tune. After some time I realised that it was the tune the boss whistled to warn us that the SS were coming.

"One day, Mrs Murray,' said Mother, 'boss tell all women we must leave, it not safe at farm. Airplanes come from sky shooting at us working in field."

As Mother spoke, I remembered a day when Wladek and I were sitting in the pram under a tree, bullets flying around us.

"Boss say bombs coming soon. We always hear bombs – bang! bang! – far away. Boss take all women in wagon, take us to mountains. A long way. We leave in morning and come in late afternoon. We stay in horse stable, very clean."

As Mother spoke, I remembered arriving in the late afternoon.

"This where we sleep,' said Mother to Mrs Murray. 'We don't work next day. Maybe it is Sunday. Workers not work on Sunday. I put my children to sleep again at night. SS troops come in night, tell me I must go with SS to labour camp with my children.

I tell you, Mrs Murray, that camp bad. SS men put me and my children in hut. Night is cold. One blanket to cover me and my children. I frighten. Women in hut, some cry, some sick. This bad place, Mrs Murray. In morning, I try to find water to wash my children. SS they take my babies away. I try to hold them, but SS beat me. I have to let my babies go. I frighten I not see my babies."

"More like terrified, I would say," said Mrs Murray.

"Yes," replied Mother.

After a pause, Mother said, "The people in camp, they sick, very skinny. Food is brown water, piece of bread. Not much flour in bread, mix with wood dust."

Mrs Murray interrupted, saying, "You mean they make you eat bread made with sawdust?"

"Yes, dust from wood mix with flour,' said Mother. 'Work hard all day, we have no wash. We get one plate soup; most is water, some grass. Maybe small piece of potato, or little piece of cabbage leaf come on my plate, or fat for my sore fingers. All part of my body paining. Women all sleep together on wooden bench like dogs.

I ask women where they take my children. Women not talk – frighten guard see them. Guard beat people with whips; hit them on face, on arms. One woman she sleep with me, she tell me her little girl in same place with my children. We make plan to see children. We let out from camp to work on digging. We sit for lunch. No food, just drink water from small river. When women get up, we stay down. We hide, crawl under bushes with tools when no-one looks. We go to see children in hospital. We climb tree and jump on balcony to room where my Terese is."

There was silence for a moment, then Mrs Murray said, "You were very brave, risking your life to see little Terese."

"Only little time,' said Mother. 'Oh, Mrs Murray! I see my poor Terese. She is little girl! Her face and body all swollen, she cry all the time. Terese, she put up her hands for me to take her. My heart is breaking into pieces to see Terese sick and not take her with me.

The nurse come, find me, and other woman too. We not taken back to labour camp. They take us to death camp. It was Hell we walk into. Smoke all around the camp. Smell is very bad. People that go in death camp are forgotten people."

I heard Mother cry.

"From frying pan into the fire," said Mrs Murray.

Mother hadn't said the name of the camp they had escaped from, and I don't remember her saying the name of the death camp they were now being taken to. Mother said that they were ordered to strip off naked in the open, in front of all the people and the SS guards. They had to walk towards the officer sitting at the table. He looked up and down at every young woman, and pointed with his finger. The young healthy and strong went to the right; the sick looking and the old went to the left. The women sent to the left were not worth feeding. They were sent immediately to be put to death, murdered in the gas chambers and into the crematorium ovens.

"I learn from whisper that officer sit at table is "Angel of Death". I have no knowledge of him. Later I know he is Doctor Mengele. In labour camp, you learn quick, who are important people, especially Doctor Mengele. We frighten every day. SS troops come and take young women, take them to Doctor Mengele. They never return. I try to hide three girls – only young – when SS come."

Mother broke down, sobbing. I had never heard her cry like this before. I felt the grief that she carried all those years and had never spoken of. Her friend, Mrs Murray, was willing to listen to what Mother had to say. Maybe I should have gone out to comfort Mother, but I didn't want her to know that I was listening.

After some quiet moments Mother continued with her story. "We must stand completely still for roll-call until SS ready and count us all. Then we have food. One slice of bread and brown water for coffee. At night we have soup. More like dishwater with grass. Soup is in large drums like we feed pig at farm. We line up for soup. Most want to be first, fight for that position. If lucky, you might get piece of vegetable in grass. Even grass gone at the end. If you are slow, nothing left – you are hungry.

We always have pain of hunger, always in pain from hard work and beating. Not able to sleep on boards. Night is freezing. The clothes we wear not keeping us warm. Camp is dirty. We wash our face and hands in water on ground. Dirty water, smell bad. Smoke from chimney all day, all night, make air and water bad, and make us sick.

'You know, Mrs Murray, we sleep with our shoes on our feet or under our arms so not to lose them in night. Women steal anything they could. Women are so hungry they take bread from your hand. No rules in this place. My feet and hands have blisters, my head and my teeth ache. We work and not think what is happen to us. It is better not feel anything, just stay alive for one day for my children, hope they are somewhere living."

Mother had come to end of her story for Mrs Murray. "The American and English soldiers come to Germany. We are free. You know, Mrs Murray, I am not the same person that my Pawel knew when we are married."

Over the years, I listened in on other conversations like this. Mother's Polish friend, Anna Lesien, occasionally came to visit. One day I was at home from work, sick. It would have been at the time I was suffering allergies from the dust at Style Master. Mother opened the screen door to let Anna into the lounge room. Anna saw me lying on the lounge. As I coughed, Anna looked at me and said, "Terese, you got the flu?"

Before I could open my mouth to answer, Mother spoke to Anna in Polish. "From the time Pawel carried her from that horror hospital in Germany, the dreaded cough has been her constant companion. It has been annoying her all these years. When she is sick, the cough gets worse. That worries me."

Knowing that Mother would open up to Anna more if I wasn't in the room, I got up from the lounge and walked into my room. I left the door open so I could listen to the conversation, hoping to learn more of her story.

Mother talked to Anna. "The doctors in Germany said there was damage to her lungs causing the cough, but there was nothing to worry about, that she would grow out of it in time. But my Terese is a grown woman, and that cough is still with her. '

I am telling you, Anna,' said Mother. 'I am still living on edge. I am trying very much to forget, but I am hounded by dreams at night. What I have been through and seen in those camps. The cruelty and hunger that turns a human into a savage dog that does terrible things like stealing your piece of bread from your hand, informing on one another for that extra piece of stale bread to survive to the next day. I tell you the people in those camps were not treated like a human people. Humanity ceased to exist. Those monsters made the camps worse than Hell. I would rather face the Judgement at the end of the world than go through that kind of living misery again.

I saw women guards, well dressed in leather jackets and leather boots. They had armbands with the word KAPO printed on them. I saw one of them use a whip on the new arrivals, urging them to hurry up. I was among them. I was disgusted at what I saw. Women and men dressed in prison clothing, their faces were that of a skeleton, pulling heavy carts loaded with dead bodies. In the distance I saw chimneys polluting the air with dark smoke. The smell in the camp was rotten; the air we had to breathe was putrid. Straight away I was pushed to help with one of the carts of dead bodies. I asked one of the women, "Where are we going with these bodies?"

'She looked around to see where the whore with the whip was. "We are taking them to the crematorium," she whispered. "Be careful who you speak to and don't volunteer for anything."

Mother talked about how dehumanised she had felt. "The time we were ordered to strip completely naked in the open in front of everyone – I could have died from embarrassment. Can you imagine, Anna, how you would feel standing there in the nude, with young men looking at you! I wished the ground would open and swallow me. It was humiliating to be treated like that."

I can appreciate that Mother was uneasy talking about this when I was in the same room. Women in those days were of modest and virtuous behaviour. That was the way of life, and these values were important to women like my mother.

"Some of us were sent to the right,' she said to Anna. 'Anyone who was too old and sick, who did not please Mengele, was sent to the left. "Soon it will be my turn," I said to myself. Mengele looked me up and down like he was choosing a pig for a roast dinner and waved me to the right.

'We lived in constant fear. First thing in the morning, the overseer of the barrack start shouting and ordering us out into the open. Even the dead were dragged out so the numbers were complete. That was followed by roll-call that every woman dreaded, fearing that you may be the next victim taken for experiment. One morning after roll-call we were marched into an open space. We were lined up for Mengele's inspection and he selected a group for hard labour and the rest remained standing for the rest of the day. Until evening we stood, waiting to be ordered to go into the barracks. Many collapsed, including me. I was wakened by the sound of shouting SS men and women. They counted us and then marched us off."

Mother told Anna about the time we had to leave the farm. "It was too dangerous. The boss got the message that the farm was to be attacked that night. We left the farm and were taken to an orchard in the mountains. We slept overnight in the stables. We were there for two nights. The children were already asleep on the second night, when the SS came to take me and the children. There was nothing I could do.

'The SS and German troops stood with the guns to my children's head. "If you resist," said the SS monster, "I order the soldiers to put a bullet in their head." What could I do? I surrendered. We were taken in the night to that filthy dreadful camp. You know, Anna, if I had known how difficult life for us was to be I should have resisted and let the children be shot."

There was anger in Mother's voice, and then there was silence. Not a word was said. I heard Mother crying for a while.

When she spoke again, she said, "My children would not have had to go through the horror, only to die in the end when the monsters were finished with them. It would have been best for all of us if I did resist and we got shot. The monsters took my children away from me, to use my Terese and my Wladek as guinea-pigs for experiments."

At that moment, I felt that I knew what I needed to know.

Only once did this story come up in conversation between Mother and me. It was several years later, and I was at home on a rostered day off work. By that time, we had bought a television, and Mother and I were watching the six o'clock news on TV. We saw a story about a farm house on fire.

I said to Mother, "That looks like the burning farm house you pointed out to me in Germany when we were in the wagon leaving the farmhouse. We were passing a farm where the house was on fire, and I remember you saying to me, "Look at the house. It's burning. Keep watching; don't take your eyes off it. You will see it fall soon." Then one of the women on the wagon said, "That is what war is: bombing, shooting and burning". I didn't know what that was all about."

Mother looked at me. She said, "I am surprised that you remember. You were only a toddler. I don't even remember how old you were."

I was going to say that Wladek was already walking, but a feeling came over me that I shouldn't mention Wladek. She had never said his name after we left the house in Schwabisch Hall. I didn't want to bring back the bad memories of those dreadful years, but I wanted to go on. I wanted to say "Yes, I remember." I wanted to know what year that happened. I wanted to let Mother know how I missed my brother Wladek very much.

But Mother ended the conversation quickly. "All that misery we suffered has come to an end for us,' she said. 'Thank God for that."

Most times when Mother and I spoke it was only small talk. Real conversations were rare. One of them began when, again, I was at home from work because I was sick. I lay on the lounge listening to new LP records on my new radiogram in stereo, the new sound in music that had just been released on the market. I was listening to songs from the movie *The Student Prince,* and Mother was in the kitchen. When she heard "The Drinking Song", she came out to listen. She was enchanted with the voice, and said, "This man, he sings very nice. He has a very good voice to sing this lovely song."

"Yes,' I said, wanting to talk with her. 'The man singing this song, his name is Mario Lanza. These songs I am playing come from a movie I saw last year, *The Student Prince.* The story is of a young prince sent to the University in Heidelberg—."

"Heidelberg,' said Mother, interrupting. 'That's in Germany."

"Yes, the Prince is Prussian. He stays in the hotel and has fallen in love with Cathy the barmaid. She lives and works with her uncle, the owner of the hotel on the river Neckar. The romance for the Prince and Cathy is short because the Prince has to leave Heidelberg and return to his sick grandfather, the King. After the death of the King, the Prince has to take over the duties of a King and marry a princess."

"Life is not like the way you dream it to be,' said Mother. 'Ludwigsburg is on the river Neckar. A lovely city, it has many beautiful palaces.

"Yes,' I said. 'I remember some of the places we went to in Ludwigsburg. Maybe one day the movie of *The Student Prince* will come back. I will take you into town, and we will see the movie together."

Some years later a festival of classic movies was shown at the Civic Theatre in Newcastle. One of the movies was *The Student Prince*, starring Anne Blythe and Edmund Purdem. Mario Lanza's voice was used to dub the singing. I took Mother to town to see this movie, and *The Ten Commandments* starring Charlton Heston. Mother saw the two movies in one week. That was more than she had seen in her life time. Mother was rapt in the love story of *The Student Prince,* and amazed at *The Ten Commandments.* It was the first time she had seen colour films on a full screen. The parting of the Red Sea was a spectacular scene. Mother said, "It was something of a miracle!"

Father didn't speak of the war either. One time, however, I was outside, and I heard Dad talking over the fence to a Polish neighbour on the subject of searching for families. I stood a little distance from them and strained my ears to hear to what Dad was saying.

Dad told the neighbour that he had been searching for our family through the Red Cross. He said that Mother's family had not been found. He and Mother had always presumed that they hadn't survived the war. However, my father's parents and his two sisters were found still living in the village of Byble, where Father had lived.

Dad said that he wrote a letter to them asking if they were in any stress and did they need anything to make their life a little easier. A letter came back. It said that his two sisters were alive, and that his mother was as good as could be expected. Unfortunately, his Father was ill, but they said they didn't need any help from Dad. The sisters said they had everything they needed. One sister's son was in the military, and he was well paid. "Thank you for your letter,' they wrote. 'It is no use writing to us. We only speak Russian and can't read your letters."

Dad said to the neighbour, "That letter was strange. It was not written by my sisters. They would not forget how to read and speak their Polish language. I can't write and send letters to my family! Sending letters to my sisters will cause them trouble"

Father never attempted to write to his family again, fearing that they may be punished. Under the Communist regime, people were not permitted to live or talk freely. They had to be very careful what they said; it was best to say nothing.

"Even if I could afford to go to Poland,' Dad said, 'it would be no use. That part of Poland where we lived is behind the Iron Curtain. Under the Soviet Union regime, we are not permitted to visit that part of Poland."

Father never heard from his family again.

IN LOVE

Newcastle was a busy place in 1957. People from all around the area came to shop in Hunter Street, to see specialists in Bolton and Church Streets, or to have x-rays at the Royal Newcastle Hospital. Young people came in to the beach. It was so easy to walk the short distance from Newcastle Station to the streets at the top end of town and to the beach. The streets were busy with working people as there were a lot of industries in Newcastle. There were the Victor's and Peters' ice-cream factories, Rundle's Men's Tailoring, a shirt factory, Chanel's factory making dressing gowns and bed spreads, and the vegetable markets in Steel Street. The Co-op Store employed many workers. Cafés, restaurants, ladies' dress shops, menswear shops, department stores and jewellers lined Hunter Street from the Co-op Store at the west end all the way to Newcastle East.

On weekends, Hunter Street was alive with young people. Newcastle was the centre for entertainment. There were six picture theatres, and the Palais Royale and the Town Hall held '50/50' dances on Saturday nights. A '50/50' dance meant that the style of dancing was divided between old time dances, like "The Pride of Erin", and newer dances, such as the jive and the jazz waltz. Small dance studios held classes in ballroom dancing during the week, and held a dance on Saturday evening. There was a hotel on practically every corner of Hunter Street. There was the Great Northern and the George Hotel in Scott Street, across from the railway station, and one in Church Street across from the Court House. The Gold Sands and the Esplanade Hotel faced the beach.

On Saturday afternoons, men liked to listen to the horse racing on the radio, and many ordinary people liked to put on a bet. I remember the grandparents of an old school friend talking about the races as they drove my friend and I home from work one Friday afternoon. The grandmother, Mrs Brown, said to her husband, "Ted, the news of the day is that the flying squad will be about tomorrow. You must keep your eyes and ears open."

"Don't worry Mum,' said Mr Brown, 'we'll have the cockatoo on the post looking out."

I was curious listening to this language I didn't understand. I thought for a moment and said, "Excuse me Mr Brown for interrupting, but how would a bird know the RAAF flying squad from other people?"

There was a roar of laughter in the car. Mr Brown said, "This is race talk. The cockatoos are men watching out for police in plain clothes. They come from another area raiding the hotels looking for SP bookies."

"We call them the flying squad," said Mrs Brown.

Mr and Mrs Brown seemed such nice people. I spoke out, saying that I saw a movie on horse racing and gambling. "That is not the kind of life I want to live," I said.

"Well dear,' said Mrs Brown, 'Ted and I, we look forward to a little flutter on Saturday afternoons. At our age it gives us a bit of excitement and enjoyment."

After two years at Style Master, I had to leave the company because of my allergies. Sometime after that, I had tests with specialists in Sydney. It seemed that I had an allergic reaction to most things. I was prescribed very small tablets to take three times a day. It helped keep the swelling under control, but I was so lethargic I could hardly lift my head off the pillow in the morning. I had a new job by that time, but working under those conditions was impossible. I could fall asleep standing up! This went on for months. I changed doctors.

The new doctor looked at my tablets and told me they were sleeping tablets. He was surprised that I even went to work every day under those conditions. This doctor prescribed antihistamine tablets. He then suggested that I write down everything I used and ate. "That is the only way you will learn about your allergies," he said.

I took his advice and stopped taking the sleeping tablets. I only took an antihistamine tablet when I felt the swelling coming on. That was better, but I was still lethargic, and found life hard to cope with.

After leaving Style Master, I found work in various cafes and milk bars, but I didn't like the late hours. Waiting alone at the railway station at night was risky; some odd people caught trains at that late time. Eventually, I found a live-in position as a housemaid and waitress at Macquarie House, a boarding house on the corner of Watt and Church Streets.

One Saturday afternoon, when I had finished work for the day, I hurried down Watt Street to meet up with my old friends from Style Master. The girls and I were going to the Westminster Hotel in Hunter Street where some RAAF boys were waiting for us.

On the way, I saw two men standing close to a building on the corner. One of them was lighting a cigarette. Just as I approached, he turned and stepped out, not seeing me. I bumped into him, knocking the cigarette from his hand. It happened so quickly, but I noticed the blue eyes in his tanned face, and his brown wavy hair. I apologised to him abruptly.

"There is no need for an apology,' he said. 'I like young girls practically running into my arms."

I was in a hurry and kept walking, not looking back. The girls were waiting for me outside the hotel. At seventeen, I was well under-age, but the other girls were older. I was well-developed for my age, and I was quite sensible when talking to people. As a group, we were well-behaved. We didn't play up, we didn't bother other people, and we never got drunk, so our age was overlooked.

When we walked into the lounge bar, we sat with the RAAF boys at several tables joined together. The jukebox started to play the current hit "Patricia". The boys ordered and paid for our drinks of lemon squash and brought them to the table. We spent a wonderful afternoon dancing to Bill Haley's rock and roll, and Johnny O'Keefe's songs. We then parted and went our own ways. The girls were catching a train to Toronto; they had to be home before midnight. I had to be back at Macquarie House by eight pm. That was my usual curfew, unless I was going to the pictures, and had told the proprietor. On those nights, my curfew was midnight.

We always looked forward to Saturday afternoons with the RAAF boys. Some of the boys didn't always turn up because they had weekend guard duties, but there were always young men to dance with. There was no dating with any of the RAAF boys at that stage. We were just a group that included the two sisters, Christine and Patricia, and a friend, Vivian and a young Italian man, Antonio. The sisters loved Italian men. Antonio and I got to know each other better at the Saturday meetings.

Through the weekdays I often walked into Hunter Street, window shopping on my few hours break. I enjoyed the stroll. It was no surprise to see Antonio wandering about in Hunter Street as he worked shifts in one of the factories in town. We became friendly over a few months. On one of his days off, Antonio greeted me in his usual charming way. He kissed my hand, which I thought was a lovely way for a young man to greet a woman. It was the custom in most European countries. Antonio greeted all the girls in the group in this manner.

"Come,' said Antonio, 'I will buy a milkshake for us."

I didn't want to be rude, so, as a friend, I accepted. We walked to the top of town and sat at the table in the milk bar. We sat and talked for a little while, and he told me that he lived in Hamilton. I didn't pay attention to the name of the street. The reason I remembered Hamilton was because my Dad had wanted to buy a house at Hamilton. I knew it wasn't far from the west end of Newcastle.

I had made the mistake of accepting Antonio's offer to buy me a drink. In an instant it was as if he had put a gold band on my finger. He tried talking me into going with him to his place. He was going to cook Italian meat, entertain me with a glass of wine and serenade me playing his musical squeeze box. I said, 'I am sorry to say this to you Antonio – the answer is no. I am not going with you.'

From that time on, whenever I was in the street, Antonio persisted in trying to convince me to go with him to his place. He wouldn't take no for an answer. Antonio was moving into my space, closing in on me. It made me feel uneasy. He insisted on walking me to the place where I worked. I couldn't get him off my back, so I let him walk me to a hotel on the corner of Bolton and Church Streets. I knew that I could walk through the hotel and out a door way that led into the back of Macquarie House. I pretended that I worked in the hotel, and asked Antonio not to follow me in, telling him that the boss didn't like men hanging about asking about his staff. I left Antonio in the street, and walked into the hotel and out the other door to the lane behind Macquarie House. It was the only way I could get away from him for the day and keep him away from the place I worked.

I stayed away from Hunter Street for a while. When Saturday was my rostered day off, I went home to Beresfield on the Friday evening to be with my family for the day, and returned to Newcastle on Saturday evening to start work on Sunday morning. I didn't go back into Hunter Street until one Saturday afternoon when I arranged to meet the girls. Antonio was not with them as he was working afternoon shift that weekend.

The girls and I walked into our usual hotel lounge. I recognised two men standing at the bar. It was the man with blue eyes I had bumped into in the street, and his friend. He walked over to the jukebox, put in the money and chose a song. He walked back to where his mate was standing and the song "Mona Lisa" by Nat King Cole began to play. It was my favourite. The man looked across to where we were sitting and nodded his head with a smile. I didn't acknowledge him. I wasn't sure if the greeting was for me or one of the other girls sitting at the table. After a short stay, the two men walked out into the street.

The following Monday, a young man named Herbert came to stay at the boarding house. He worked at BHP, and he was waiting to move into a house that was not yet vacant. He was a good hard working young man and we got on well together. He asked me to go to the movies with him, and I accepted. The movie we saw that evening was a comedy starring Dean Martin and Jerry Lewis. They were good at playing their parts. Everyone in the theatre laughed all the way through the movie, and walked out in a happy mood. Herbert and I enjoyed the short walk back to Macquarie House. It was our first night out together. Herbert kissed my hand to say goodnight before we stepped inside.

The next evening, after I finished my shift, Herbert and I walked to the beach. It was safe in those days. There was no violence. People were civil to one another in the street and the beach people were friendly. Everyone went on with the business of being happy and enjoying themselves. Herbert and I walked on the beach with our feet in water, singing songs from *The Student Prince*. I was happy. I felt like I was walking on a cloud, my feet not touching the water. It was a lovely evening for us.

But my happiness was not to last. Herbert was a German immigrant. He had come to Australia with his parents just like me and my family. When I went home on the weekend, I told my parents about Herbert and how happy we were in the few days we had gone out together. Father said that I must stop seeing Herbert before a closer relationship developed between us. It was a direct order, no ifs or buts; it was Father's final word on the subject.

My parents didn't want me to marry a German. I told them Herbert was a good man. Father got very angry. He couldn't hold back his emotions. "I put my life in danger to save your life from those monsters! Your mother and me we came to Australia to start a new life, with our family, and now I have to swallow my pride and tolerate working with them!"

I was shaken by his anger.

"Terese,' he said more calmly. 'Remember this: I am not saying that all German people are Nazi. I just don't want the slightest chance of one of the SS to become part of my family. Give us some credit and let the boy go. I am sure there are plenty of Australian young men that you will keep company with in time."

Mother was crying. "Terese,' she said, 'the SS Nazi skinned the flesh from the people that were imprisoned in the death camps. These SS monsters made lamp shades from the human skins and used human fat for making soap. Believe me, Terese, I saw these things. The Allied soldiers liberated us from those horror camps and these soldiers made the SS guards put the soap and the articles made of human skins on display in the camp. Allied soldiers brought the town Burgermaister and all the dignitaries and the townspeople to see what had been happening in this camp. I can tell you, Terese, it wasn't pretty. To think that one of those SS could be in my family would break my heart. To think you would do this to us, it would be unforgivable, unbearable. I only lived and suffered through that horror for my children. If not for you and your brother, I would have died in that stinking rotten hell of a place!"

Mother had never spoken so openly to me about how she had suffered in the war. It didn't affect my feeling towards Herbert, but I had to stop seeing him. My parents still felt the pain of those dreadful years. I had to show respect to Mother and Father. I could not hurt my parents for my own selfish happiness.

When I went back to the boarding house, Herbert had left. He phoned me a few days later but I didn't give him a chance to speak. I told him that I could not see him anymore, that I was seeing someone else. I never saw or heard from Herbert again.

The following Saturday I met with the girls. Antonio was with them. The RAAF boys suggested we go to the Esplanade Hotel for a change. Antonio came along. I stayed most of the time with the girls. Antonio wanted me to leave the crowd and go with him to the movies.

I got angry. "Listen to me, Romeo – 'I said.

"My name is not Romeo," was his reply.

"You don't understand do you? I will put it this way: leave me alone! The word is 'No' Antonio! Compendia?!"

At the same time I looked around to see how I could break loose from him. I saw two men sitting at a table. One of them was the man with blue eyes I had bumped into. Here was my chance to lose Romeo. I imposed on the two men and asked if it was alright to sit at their table for a little while. The man with blue eyes smiled at me. "No problem, honey,' he said. 'Sit with my friend John while I get the drinks. My shout. What will it be?"

"A squash please, I said to the man with the blue eyes.

I sat with the two men drinking squash. Antonio was annoyed and walked out. I said to the man I knew, "I would like to apologise to you for the day I bumped you. I was in a rush and spoke to you in a rather abrupt manner, do you remember?"

"How could one forget the figure of Lana Turner?" said his mate John.

The music began to play. It was loud; we couldn't hold a conversation. I sipped my drink and excused myself before the music stopped. I walked to where the crowd was standing together. It was time for us girls to leave. We all walked outside and said our goodbyes to the young RAAF men.

"We will meet you next week at the usual place,' said one of the young men. 'This place is too crowded and noisy."

Before I left, one of the boys, Robert, said to me, "I hope you will be with us next Saturday."

"Yes,' I said, 'I will be back next week."

The next day, a Sunday, the streets were quiet. People didn't venture out into the streets in the winter. I was hoping that the girls might be in town for a few hours. I walked up towards the T & G Building. I saw a man sitting on the steps of the Newcastle Post Office. He stood up and walked across the street, approaching me with a friendly smile. It was him, the man with blue eyes.

He introduced himself as Bryan. He asked if I was free and would I care to have a drink with him.

"I have a few hours,' I said. 'A drink would be nice, thank you."

"And what shall I call you, young lady?" asked Bryan.

Oh, how I loved the way he spoke to me! It was the first time I had heard his enchanting voice away from noise and crowds.

"Terese is my name," I said shyly.

"Terese. That sounds a good name. It suits you well, Terese. You have a mysterious smile."

We walked up to the milk bar at the end of Hunter Street near the beach where the widgies and bodgies, with their strange hair styles and strange clothes, hung about on their motor bikes. I felt a little uneasy sitting in the milk bar, but Bryan seemed to fit in with the surroundings. We finished our drinks and walked to the esplanade and to Fletcher Park. We sat on a bench facing the sea and talked.

Bryan told me he was once a milk-bar bodgie. He had owned a Harley-Davidson motorbike, and when he was in his teens had ridden the bike all the way from Sydney to Queensland, to his grandmother's sheep station, Giddy Giddy. While he was at his grandmother's property, he rounded up the sheep on his motor-bike and his granny didn't like it. She said it frightened the sheep. Bryan said his gran didn't like the old ways changing. That was in 1947. He told me how he got a job as a cattle drover in Queensland, and how he spent his 21st birthday on an island with the cattle, his boss and two drovers, surrounded by flood water.

Time got away quickly. I stood up to excuse myself and say goodbye. Bryan stood up and asked, "Do you come to this park often?"

"Yes, nearly every day,' I replied. 'I live and work not far from here. The boss' daughter and I come here to spend some time in the sun during my break after lunch."

Bryan held my hands and commented on how soft they were.

I said, "I enjoyed talking to you."

"Likewise, I am sure.' He kissed my hand and said 'I hope to see you again."

I walked away from him without turning back to look.

As usual the girls and I met the same crowd at the hotel on Saturday. I had to leave early. I excused myself and said I had to go to work.

"Oh,' said Robert. 'I was hoping I could ask you to go out with me to the pictures tonight."

"I finish work at eight," I said.

"It will be too late to go to the pictures then,' said Robert. 'We can go to a dance, if you show me the way.'"

I met Robert at the bus stop in Hunter Street, and we caught a bus to the Palais Royale. We sat at the dance hall without moving a muscle, just listening to Jack Spearing sing, and watching the young people dance. Robert didn't know how to dance the ballroom steps and didn't want to try. The floor was crowded. Robert checked the time on his watch and said he had to leave. We walked to the Bank Corner, and said goodbye. He walked to the station to catch a train back to Toronto.

After that night, Robert and I met once more. Away from the crowd, he was a quiet man. The only conversation between us was that Robert told me he came from Queensland. He came to Newcastle as a recruit in the RAAF, and was based at Rathmines. There was nothing more he could say. We had nothing in common to talk about. I couldn't respond to a person who had nothing to say. That meeting ended with the words "See you around." I walked off to work.

The Saturday coming was a rostered day off. I went home to my family and spent the day with my little toddler brother, Peter. He was so much fun to be with. Children are adorable at that age. They are eager to learn. He was inquisitive and imitated his older brother, Cecil. I loved spending time with Peter. He was a little darling.

On the Sunday morning, I went back to start work and another week of the same routine. I hadn't seen Bryan for a few weeks. The thought crossed my mind that maybe I was too young for him. I was only seventeen. I thought no more about him.

After lunch on that Sunday afternoon, I walked down Watt Street, hoping that some of the girls might be in town at the same time, and hoping that the little Italian friend Antonio was not with them. Every time I was in Hunter Street he latched onto me. He would serenade me while walking in the street. This all was very nice if he was the man for me. Tony was a good boy, but he was over possessive. I felt uncomfortable with him.

I walked around the corner into Hunter Street, and Bryan stepped out of a car. He said, "John is buying a car." I saw John sitting in the car. "We are testing this one out, taking it for a drive,' said Bryan. 'Are you meeting anyone?"

"No, just taking a walk," I said.

"Would you like to come with us for a short drive about town?" Bryan asked.

"Yes, that would be nice, but I must not be too long. I have to go back to work in two hours," I told Bryan.

"It won't be a long drive, just to New Lambton. John's girlfriend works for a family that deals in cars. This is one of their cars'" said Bryan.

John wanted to drive the car to where his girlfriend was working to show her the car. He drove to an exclusive street in New Lambton Heights. The houses were beautiful, with lovely gardens and trees. John stopped the car in front of the dealer's house. It was something one would see in a movie star magazine. John went to the side door of the house. His girlfriend, Lynette, came to the door for a quick look. She couldn't talk to John because the boss had guests. She had to attend to their afternoon tea.

When we arrived back in Hunter Street, Bryan opened the car door for me to step out. He kissed my hand and said, "I'll be seeing you." He was different from most young boys. Bryan was a gentleman.

I walked up Bolton Street to the hotel back door and was back at work in plenty of time.

Some weeks passed. Not many people came out on Sundays like I did in the winter. Walking was my favourite past-time. Sunday afternoon was my day for window shopping. There was no one in the way blocking the store windows. On the other side of the street, I saw a man in a uniform leaning against the Post Office wall. He stood up and gave me a friendly salute as I went past. I was rather flattered that a soldier in a uniform would salute me. I smiled at him to say thank you, and kept walking, unaware of things around me and wondering if the girls were in town. I had walked a little way when a hand grabbed my arm from behind. I turned to look. It was Bryan, in uniform.

"Oh!' I said, 'I see it's you!"

I hadn't recognised him from a distance with the cap on his head.

He looked at me with his friendly blue eyes and a kind of cheeky smile, and said, "In a hurry, are we?"

I felt like someone had pulled the strings of my heart. My knees went weak and buckled. I felt like I was falling to the ground. His strong arms held me up for the few seconds until I pulled myself together and said to him, "You frightened me, grabbing my arm!"

"I didn't mean to,' he said gently. 'You were walking fast and I was trying to catch up to you. I only wanted to slow you down."

I wasn't expecting to see him again and didn't know he would be waiting for me there.

"Are you working this afternoon, Terese?" Bryan asked.

'It's my afternoon off," I told him.

"Will you spend the afternoon with me? I have a surprise I want to show you."

Bryan took my hand and walked me around the corner of the street to where a small blue Morris utility was parked. We walked towards the car and he opened the door for me to step in.

"A car with a radio," I said.

"Yes, we must have music. I bought the utility last Friday," said Bryan.

A radio in a car was something of a luxury in the fifties. To have a radio fitted was expensive; the radio itself was expensive.

"I am taking you for a drive to Rathmines,' he said. 'That is where I am stationed."

"I must be back by seven-thirty." I informed Bryan.

"We have plenty of time. It's about one hour's drive to Rathmines," Bryan said.

Bryan drove through Toronto and up a steep hill, and onto a gravel road through the bush at Rathmines. At the camp gate, the guard acknowledged Bryan with a salute. Bryan had to show his ID card and the guard checked it. He stepped back to attention and saluted again. The gate opened. Bryan drove through to the camp and parked the car in front of the canteen building. He asked me to sit in the car. He brought out a lemon squash for me and a schooner of beer for himself. I held the drinks while he drove down to the lake where the Catalina planes floated on the water.

We drank our drinks, and talked. Bryan said "I sometimes work in the canteen behind the bar, and two nights a week at the movie theatre."

He continued, saying the camp was too far away. "The closest town is Toronto. Living in this camp, it's essential to have a car."

I liked listening to Bryan talk. He spoke well. His modulated voice was clear and pleasant. I didn't say much about myself.

We sat for a while listening to songs and a serial on the radio. Then he asked, "Did you come from England?"

"No. Why do you ask?" I asked.

"When you speak, some of the words you pronounce sound slightly English. That sounds like you may have come from an English family."

"I came from Europe as an immigrant in 1950," I said. That was all I was willing to tell him about myself at that stage.

Bryan said he was born and lived in Sydney. His first job was working for AWA assembling radios. He said that he saved the company money by suggesting that left-handed men be put on the opposite side to the right-handed men on the assembly line. "That way,' he said, 'both sides work at the same time." Bryan himself was left-handed.

He said that he saved his money and bought his Harley-Davidson motorbike for eighty pounds cash. His mother had suggested that he buy land, as it cost a lot less than a motorbike. "But,' he said, 'at the age of eighteen, I had my heart set on moving around and going places."

It had been a lovely afternoon with Bryan, but it was time to go back to the boarding house.

We didn't spend much time together. Working broken shifts, I was only free for two and a half hours during the day. By the time I finished work in the evening, it was too late for me to go out, and Bryan worked some evenings. There were no dates made. Our meetings were by chance. Sometimes it would be three weeks before we saw each other.

I hadn't seen him for some weeks when we met and he said, "I have some news to tell you. The word is that Rathmines is going to close. The Catalina's are obsolete. They will not be flying for the RAAF anymore. I don't know when that will happen. It's only a word, not official as yet."

"What will happen when the time comes?" I asked.

"I will be posted to another camp, or maybe over to Singapore or even to Malaysia," said Bryan.

I let him carry on with the conversation. He was good at talking and always had something to say.

"I have to go wherever I am posted,' he said. 'I've signed up for the next six years. I've not long been back from a posting in New Guinea." That explained the tan he had that first time I saw him on the corner of Watt and Hunter Streets.

Later in the evening I thought about what he had told me. It would take a piece of my life away if he was posted overseas. Bryan had treated me well, not showing any aggressive nature. I did not have to fight him off. Whenever we parted, there were no threats, and no pressure put on me. I liked that kind of friendship. I was too young to be going steady with a permanent partner, and I needed time for myself.

Working in the boarding house was the only pressure I had. I shared a room with a woman worker. She was jealous of my youth, and of how I got on well with the men in the boarding house. She was a single lady in her early fifties. She was nice to my face, but tried to get me sacked by giving me her work to do, and not passing on messages to me from the lady of the house. Thanks to her efforts, I lost my job there and had to go back home.

It didn't worry Bryan when I told him I had to return home. He was rather pleased. He had a car and I was free to be with him. He came to see me at our house. It surprised me that Father was civil to Bryan, and let him stay overnight when we came back from the movies at Rathmines. Bryan had a happy personality. Mother liked him, and he was liked by my family's friends.

I needed work. Again I found myself knocking on the doors of industries and cafés in Newcastle. Within weeks, I found work at the new restaurant at the Oak factory at Hexham. It was hard work, but it was close to home. On the evenings I had off at weekends, Bryan and I spent most of the time at Rathmines camp. There were many parties and balls before the camp closed down.

I worked shifts at odd hours of the day, and it felt like I spent more time catching trains than working. The day shift was good; I had no worries catching a train during the day. The afternoon shift was the worst. I finished at night, and had to walk some distance to Hexham train station, sometimes in the rain. I often missed the train by about five minutes, so had to wait for about an hour in the dark by myself for the next train.

The manager wanted to cut back on the budget. He brought in a chef from the Hilton Hotel in Sydney, and drew up new shifts for us workers. The work changed, and I was working two different shifts on more days. The first shift started from eleven in the morning to eight at night. The next shift was from twelve-thirty pm to nine-thirty pm, but in the kitchen we never finished before ten. We went without pay for that last half hour. I was not at all happy working at this place. It was a dog's life getting home from work at eleven or twelve o'clock at night, washing my uniform before I went to bed and getting up at seven in the morning. By the time I had breakfast and ironed the uniform it was time for me walk to the station to catch the nine o'clock train, which was the only train to get me to work before eleven.

The courtship between Bryan and me was rather slow. When Bryan was sick and confined to the camp hospital, he gave me the car to drive until he was well again. I saw more of Bryan in the two weeks he was sick than I did before. Having the car made a difference. I was able to drive to Rathmines to visit Bryan before the late afternoon shift and on my days off. We grew closer. Bryan got well, and I was again catching trains to work.

Rathmines camp finally closed. There was no more social life for me. My rostered days off were mainly on weekdays and often I worked those days as well. The married women working in the kitchen took days off for one reason or another. With two wages coming in they could afford to take time off work. My life had changed. Not able to go into town, I lost contact with my girlfriends in town. Bryan was posted to Williamtown. It was his second posting there. Bryan helped to make my working life a little easier. He lent me his car through the week and met me at the weekend when I finished the shift. I relied on him more and more.

With the shift work I was doing, we never got the chance to go out for entertainment. It was a blessing when television arrived. Bryan and I sat in the car watching the TV in a Beresfield shop window. I remember watching James Dibble reading the news of the little boy, Graham Thorne, who had been kidnapped ten days earlier for a huge amount of money. The boy's body was found in the boot of a car. I cried when the news came over the TV. My body shivered and went cold all over. I had trouble sleeping. The nightmares and fear recurred more vividly in my sleep from then on. It was something I had no control over.

Mother could see how I relied on Bryan. Perhaps she could see the future of us getting married. My plan was that before I was to be married, my future husband and I would have a house of our own to live in. Until I had a house to walk into, there would be no marriage for me. William, Moore and Randall had just released a new subdivision in Beresfield Heights, on the other side of the highway. Mother insisted that I put a deposit down on the land. She said that in time it would go up in value and I would have a deposit for my house.

Bryan and I had been going steady for over two years when he was sent to Darwin for twp weeks. It was early 1961. A confrontation was looming between Indonesia and Malaysia, and Australian forces were preparing to support British troops in Malaysia. Bryan returned from Darwin unexpectedly and came to see me at work to tell me that it was a matter of days before he was to leave. He didn't tell me where he was going, just that the forces were preparing for the worst.

Bryan was a reserved man. He did not usually show his emotions in public. He held me close in his arms and kissed me with my work mates around us, like it happens in the movies. My boss gave me a wink, meaning I could go outside for a few minutes.

On the back porch of the restaurant, Bryan said, "While I was away from you, I realised that I really and truly love you. I want you to be my wife."

There had been a change in Bryan. For him to show his love for me with people about, I believed he did love me. The gleam in his eyes said he was in love with me. He wanted us to be married before he went away.

Of course I said yes! How could I resist this romantic proposal on the back porch of a restaurant?" My dream was that one day my fiance' and I woul be dressed in our Sunday best, sitting on the front veranda, having dinner in a fancy restaurant, with the sound "Romance" in the back ground, as he asked me to marry him. But that was only a dream seen in the movies. In reality this didn't happen. Men like Bryan weren't romantic. But it had happened: a proposal was made to me on the porch at work, me in my kitchen working uniform and Bryan in his RAAF uniform, against the background sounds of pots dropping into the sink! Bryan's modulated voice asking me to be his bride was the music to my ears.

While Bryan was making arrangements for us to get married, fortunately for Australia, and for many lovers like us, the conflict eased, and Bryan returned to Williamtown.

The next weekend, on my rostered day off, Bryan and I went to Sydney. A diamond ring was to be especially made for me by a friend's brother. The diamonds were laid in front of me on a black cloth. The brilliant diamonds sparkled on the table and I felt like I was an important person having the pleasure of choosing the diamond of my engagement ring. After leaving that house, we celebrated our engagement with a dinner at a hotel in Sydney. I wanted to order the chicken-in-a-basket for our meal, but we didn't know how to tackle the whole chicken sitting in a basket, so we ordered roast turkey that was served in slices on the plate. We thought that would be easier than struggling with a chicken stuck in a basket!

Now that we were engaged, Bryan and I drove around for months knocking on the door of every bank in Maitland and Newcastle trying to borrow money to buy a house. As we could not borrow enough for a house that was already established, we went to see Ellis Brothers' Building Company to see how much money we would need to have a house built. We showed Mr Ellis a rough plan I had drawn up. After some discussion, Mr Ellis agreed to build a two-bedroom house, and arranged the loan for us.

There was no landing on the plan, just steps to the front door. Before we signed the papers, I asked Mr Ellis if we could have a small balcony put on the house outside the dining room door, telling him how lovely it would be to have a balcony to sit on in the cool of the evening after a hot day.

He looked at the plan again and thought for a few minutes, drawing something on a pad. He said, "I will build you a veranda that will be a joy forever in your heart!"

There was one drawback: we had no money for a deposit. "Well what are we going to do?" asked Mr Ellis.

"I don't know,' said Bryan. 'I have sold the car to pay the rest of the money owing on the land."

Mr Ellis said, "If you want the house built, I may be able to help. I have to ask you some personal questions."

"That's OK," said Bryan.

"What wages do you and your fiancée make monthly?" he asked.

We told him. He added it up and said, "Is there any way you could save some of the money from your pay?"

"Yes,' said Bryan, 'we could save so much a month now that the land is paid for."

"Well then,' said Mr Ellis, 'I will loan you the deposit and you can pay me back. When the deposit is paid, I will start work on your house."

We agreed on that arrangement. The house was finished nine months after Bryan and I were married. A few months later, Mr Ellis passed our place and saw us painting the house. He stopped to ask why we were painting the house after such a short time. We explained that the pine timber had popped the notches out and we had filled them in. This was no fault on

Mr Ellis' part. It was my choice to have the pine log timber on the house; it was the modern thing in those days.

Mr Ellis pulled out his wallet to pay for the paint and for the work we were doing. He was an honourable man, and perhaps didn't want his reputation as a builder tarnished. We were as poor as church mice, so we accepted the money. Mr Ellis was a great help to us and the job was done well. He was a good man, a gentleman true to his word.

Our wedding was put back for some months, a request from my parents so they could save for our small wedding. We were married on the 20th of January, 1962, before a few friends, and some of Mother's friends. The Mothers' Club of Tarro Catholic School catered the reception. They made meat salads with ham and corned beef, and for sweets we had fruit salad and cream. There were other cakes on the table. One of Bryan's mates made the wedding cake, and we paid for the ingredients. Another mate covered it with plain icing. I found some little sugar roses and pasted them around the edge for decoration.

We spent our honeymoon travelling up the coast to Lismore, where Bryan had spent some of his youth. Our wedding night was spent at Bulahdelah. We had stopped at the only hotel-motel in the town for a drink and some information. Bryan asked the publican about where might be the best place to stay in Taree. The publican told us that Taree was all booked out for an Aquatic Carnival that weekend. Even the houseboats were all hired out. He suggested that we stay at Bulahdelah for the night. Bryan got into a conversation with the locals and asked about entertainment in the town. There was no picture theatre, and no television. The publican said they couldn't pick up the Sydney channels, and a local chap said it was because of the mountains.

There was no point going any further. It was too far to Port Macquarie, so we agreed to stay in the hotel-motel. We sat in the hotel lounge until six o'clock closing time, and then had hamburgers for tea.

At the next stop, Port Macquarie, the Museum had opened that day for the first time.

We were the first people to sign the visitors' book. That is where I signed my name as a married woman for the first time.

After that, we stopped at Byron Bay. We looked around the lighthouse, and then spent the afternoon on the beach. I was not a beach lover, but it was a lovely day. We took our shoes off and walked along the edge of the crystal clear water. The ocean was a beautiful blue and the sand was clean.

In Lismore, Bryan showed me around. We visited St John's College, where he had gone to school. He spoke to the Headmaster and asked permission to show me around the grounds. He showed me other places around Lismore where the boys would go swimming in the creek. He showed me a rosewood tree still growing not too far from the creek. He thought I would like to see what the tree was like before it was cut down to make furniture. He knew I loved furniture made from rosewood and cedar because when I had worked for a time at a Hamilton cafe, every day I passed a workshop that made beautiful furniture. In the shop window there had been a big piece of rosewood timber on display, along with a finished cabinet and a bedhead.

Driving between Lismore and Grafton, Bryan turned off the highway to take me to a place where an Italian timber-getter once lived. We drove into the bush some miles. Bryan told me that the area of New England had been rich in cedar trees, and he wanted to show me a small historical church that was built of cedar. It was still standing, but dilapidated. The huts in the surrounding village had been built of the same timber, but the families there were hit by an epidemic that wiped out the village. All that was left of the place was a big empty field. Not far from the church, I saw timber house piers still standing. There was no other trace of the village.

In the first two years of our marriage I continued working. I worked overtime, double shifts and rostered days off because the normal wages were not enough to save for a big thing like land or a house. The years were not stable for many young people like us. At the time there were many strikes. People I knew lost their homes, unable to make the payments. Women who had stayed at home and did voluntary work at schools had to go out and find work to keep food on the table for their families. Many young families on one wage lost their homes. I counted my blessings that Bryan was in the Air Force. At least he was getting regular pay, no matter how small. We lived under constant threat of the bomb, especially after the threat of missiles in Cuba. Bryan and I lived moderately while I was working, always putting money towards the house.

Two years after our wedding, I became pregnant. That was when trouble started. I had bad morning sickness. Oranges were all I could eat. Compared to all other food, they had a beautiful taste, and they had to be navel oranges. At first, we bought bags of oranges, and then Bryan brought home cases.

Unfortunately, I became constantly sick, needing extra medication and spending time in hospital. One wage was not enough to cover the bills. Bryan mowed grass on weekends to earn pocket money for himself. There was no overtime pay for working on weekends in the forces. Bryan was given a posting to Malaysia, but at the same time, I suffered a miscarriage. Bryan took compassionate leave to take care of me, and the posting was cancelled.

In the hospital, I was miserable watching the hospital staff. How happy and cheerful they were. I asked myself why I couldn't be happy like those people. Why was this dark cloud hovering over me? I could see nothing but darkness in my mind. How could I get rid of this dreadful feeling and get well? I was exhausted just sitting in a chair. I was always sad, but I didn't want to be. This was not the kind of life I wanted to live. I didn't know at the time that I was suffering from depression. I came home from the hospital, but, after two days at home, I haemorrhaged and was back in hospital for an operation. I came home again, but a day later I was taken back to the hospital, this time with septicaemia.

After treatment, I recovered and was able to go to work. As soon as I was on my feet, but not completely recovered from illness, I went back to work. I went back to Style Master where I had worked as a teenager. The debts had accumulated during the time of my pregnancy, and we were in financial trouble. The bank manager covered our overdraft, helping us by holding back the cheques for a few days until the next pay. Gradually, bills were paid and I felt better.

Not long after that, however, I started to feel tired and unable to cope. I told my doctor, and asked him to prescribe something for me so I could go on working. "After miscarriage, women feel the loss,' he said. 'Pull yourself together and stop feeling sorry for yourself."

For a while I was alright, but then it hit me again a few months later. Depression set in. I couldn't stop crying all day at work, and at home. The girls at work could see that I was sick, and advised me to see a doctor. Bryan loved me; he did try to help in his way. He would bring me a cup of tea in bed, and try to do the washing. He took me out for a drive to help me lose the terrible feeling, but it made no difference. It was with me all the time. When I was a little girl, I couldn't cry; now I couldn't stop!

Then, one day, Bryan said he had had enough. If I didn't stop crying, he would leave me. It was as if he had slapped my face. The shock worked. I stopped crying, but that didn't change the lethargic feeling. The black cloud hanging over my head wouldn't go away. I felt guilty for the loss of my pregnancy. Perhaps it was a punishment. Perhaps the medication I had taken for morning sickness had caused the termination of my pregnancy.

At about that time, some people came knocking at the door, and spoke about free lessons on the Bible. I was willing to listen and let them have their say. They said the Bible lessons would be given in my own home at any time suitable for me. I thought for a few minutes. Maybe through learning and understanding the Bible, I might learn to solve my problems and cope better with life. I took the chance. Those good people from the Bible studies picked me up in their car so I could go with them to the Sunday services. The Bible studies helped a little to settle my mind, but I still felt lethargic.

The flu season came. I was sick several times through the year. The flu affected my allergies. My eyes swelled, and sometimes my tongue swelled, and I had a constantly sore and swollen throat. Cold sores continually appeared on my lips. The doctor put me on antibiotic medication and I felt much better for some time after.

In early 1966, I fell pregnant again, and, once more, I was constantly sick. My neighbour knew I was pregnant again when she saw Bryan bringing in a case of oranges. My boss at Style Master said I must leave work. I had only worked there for nine months. I stopped the Bible studies. I lived with the threat of miscarriage, and the black cloud hovering over me once more. Extra visits to the doctor and the hospital put a strain on our marriage.

Happily, our daughter Karen was born in October. It was the year of a heat wave, and the Hunter Valley was gripped by drought. Young Australian men were fighting in Vietnam. I remember crying after the birth. It should have been a joyful day for me, but I couldn't stop myself crying. I thought of the young fathers killed in war, never seeing their babies. I cried for the young widows who would not see their husbands, and the children who would never know their fathers.

The doctor in the hospital talked with me. He said that this happens with new mothers, and that in a few weeks I would adjust to being a mother. But the feeling didn't ease; I was still crying when I left the hospital with Karen in my arms. How would we live through this uncertain life together? If the worst came, would I be as strong as my mother had been in the time of crisis, defending my child as she had defended me?

IN PENANG

After Karen was born, Bryan was again offered a posting to Malaysia. We were both excited. We went through the routine of injections, x-rays and passports. Everything was ready, except my passport. For some reason it was held back. The day before we were to leave, a car stopped at the front of the house. It was followed by a RAAF car, driven by Bryan. A woman stepped out of the first car and walked into the yard, and waited on the front veranda for Bryan. The woman introduced herself to us both at the front door: "I am a Sister from the Royal Newcastle Hospital."

"Yes,' said Bryan. 'I was informed at work that you were coming."

We went into the lounge room. The Sister said, "I know you are leaving for Malaysia tomorrow. The x-ray shows some abnormality on your lungs, Terese. Can you explain what that might be?"

"Yes,' I said. 'That is a scar from when I was child. I contracted tuberculosis during the war. Is there something wrong?"

"No. Now that we know what that is on your lungs there is no problem," she said.

"Thank goodness you are alright!' said Bryan. 'I was frightened that you may be sick."

"No, there are no problems,' said the Sister. She walked out to her car, saying, 'I wish you a pleasant journey."

But there was a problem: I was leaving home without a passport. Bryan was assured the passport would be at the airport counter the next day. Bryan was worried about that, but there was no need to be. It was at the airport counter the next day, as arranged.

Mother was frightened for us going to another country so far away from Australia.

When something like this happened, she would tell me a few words about her family. Mother told me that her sister was married to a soldier and they were sent over the border to Cszechoslovakia. Then the war broke out and Mother never saw her sister again.

Mother was very upset, and cried when we said goodbye. Our baby Karen was three months old. As we left Australia, I imagined the picture appearing in Mother's mind of the time she was taken away from her homeland, with me a baby in her arms, never to return home.

Father drove us to Newcastle Station. We travelled by train to Sydney and stayed in a motel overnight. In the morning we were driven by taxi to the airport. Bryan's family were at the terminal to see us off. Bryan and I were passengers on a commercial flight departing at twelve o'clock that day. There were only two seats on the plane booked for us. There was no bassinet for the baby, or even a spare seat. We had to nurse our Karen for the long trip. Once the plane was in the air, the day was clear, not a cloud in the sky. The plane flew to Perth to pick up more passengers.

As the plane left the coast of Australia, I looked down. It was a strange feeling to see the land appearing to float on water. The captain announced that we were leaving Australian shores and flying out to sea. I thought how we were on our own. The captain was our guide and we were in his care. As the plane flew northwards, the sun was setting behind clouds as huge as mountains in the heavens. The sun radiated the most glorious colours from behind the clouds. I turned to Bryan and said, "If Heaven is like this all the time, I would never get tired of looking at this glorious sky."

"Yes, it certainly is a pretty picture,' he said. 'It's rare to see something like that."

In a short time this picture faded away and the sky darkened. The plane jerked several times. The captain announced that there was a storm ahead and everyone was to be seated and to fasten their seatbelts. "It's nothing to be concerned about,' said the captain's voice. 'We are diverting the plane to a different route away from the storm."

The plane dropped and I felt my heart left up in the air. I had seen movies like this, where the plane is in trouble but the captain is not saying it, so as not cause a panic. Our lives might have been in danger. We were in God's hands. I prayed to God, asking him to give the captain and his crew the help they needed. The captain directed the plane to a different route and after some time the plane was flying into bright sky.

The plane flew into the sunset again, just as beautiful as before; the same sunset from a different direction. The captain announced that we were special people to see the sun setting twice in the one evening. It was like looking at a miracle. Nobody can really paint a miracle; it's something each person visualises differently. The experience of seeing these two glorious sunsets among the clouds touched my heart. At that moment I thought how it might be the closest I would come to seeing Heaven. I thought I would not be frightened to die.

As the plane flew closer to Indonesia, the captain announced that we were landing at Jakarta to refuel the plane and all passengers must stay on board. As the plane landed, I looked out the window and saw soldiers on the tarmac with guns ready to shoot if necessary.

We arrived at Singapore at 10pm. We were cleared by customs and a taxi driver was waiting for us at the terminal. Looking out from the car window I was so excited. The streets were crowded and I could smell exotic foods cooking. I wanted to know what it was like to walk on the streets of Singapore. We stepped out from the taxi to the famous Raffles Hotel. Two bellboys picked up the suitcases and showed us to a room on the second floor. The door was opened for us to walk into the room. It was like an apartment with an en suite bathroom. We didn't have the time to enjoy this luxury as it was about midnight and we were very tired.

In the morning, there was no time to step out into the street or even the balcony, no time for a cup of coffee. We had to leave early to be at the airport by seven to fly to the island of Penang. Breakfast was served in the plane. Again I had Karen in my arms during the trip. The plane circled around before landing and I could see only palm trees. It might have been a coconut plantation. As soon as we walked on the tarmac I could feel the heat and smell the pungent air.

The RAAF car was waiting for us. I had no idea what to expect, or whether we were going to live in a house just outside the Butterworth Base, or a traditional Malay house. Bryan didn't know. He had not found out about the country or where we were going to live. I had no idea what the country was like; all I knew was that it was some place in the east.

On the way from the airport, we passed rice fields on each side of the road, and a village. The houses looked like gingerbread houses on long piers.

It was a good thing that the driver knew where our house was. The Chinese maid was already in the house waiting for our arrival. Groceries were on the table, just enough to get us through the day and the next morning. The old woman spoke a little broken English. She unpacked the suitcases and hung up the clothes. She had already made up our beds and the cot. There was nothing more for her to do so she excused herself and asked to go home. She said she would be back the next day.

A young man arrived at the door with a catalogue from the store. Speaking in English, he said I could keep the catalogue and order whatever I needed. He said he came every morning to pick up the list, and delivered the groceries in the afternoon. "Ma'am,' he said, 'the Australian and British people use only powdered milk. A small tin of milk is in the bag of groceries, ma'am."

The small house was not that much different from some older Australian brick homes. The main difference was the highly polished red concrete floor, Louvre windows with fancy security bars, and ceiling fans in every room. A heavy iron door at the back of the house was only opened while using the laundry. The English people call these houses 'bungalows'. The furniture in the house was no different to what we had at home, except that the lounge was made from cane like I had seen in old movies. Baby Karen was upset and tired. It was hot and humid, and difficult for her to fall sleep.

Bryan had to start work the very next morning. It felt strange to be left with a Chinese woman waiting for me to give her orders as to what she should do. It wasn't easy for me to give orders to a woman speaking very little English.

"I do washing," said the old woman.

"Yes, that is a good start," I said.

In her way, the old woman told me what her routine was for the day. "If you want different, you tell me ma'am.'"

"Yes, that will be fine," I said.

"I look at your baby ma'am," she asked.

The old amah wanted to take over my duties as a mother. "No,' I said. 'I take care of my baby. You go on with the work."

On the third day, two young Australian women from across the street, Ruth and Leonie, came to welcome me. Their husbands were also stationed at Butterworth. They asked me to join them for morning tea, and asked if there was in any way they could help.

"Yes,' I said. 'I need to see a doctor. I don't know where to go."

There was a telephone at Ruth's house. She phoned the doctor's surgery for me, explaining that I had just arrived and was suffering from heat rash. The doctor made a house call on the way home after he had finished for the day at the RAAF Hostel surgery. He brought calamine lotion and quinine tablets for us all to take, a precaution against malaria.

Malaysia is hot and humid. People new to the country constantly perspire, accumulating salt on the skin which causes a rash of prickly heat on the sensitive parts of the body. I dowsed my and Karen's bodies in calamine lotion, and sprinkled powder all over. Keeping a singlet on the baby absorbed the perspiration and kept her little body cool.

Leonie, Ruth and I all had babies of about the same age. We became good neighbours, having morning tea together nearly every day of the week. In conversation I mentioned to them that things were not working out between the old woman and me. "She has been telling me every day that it's the Chinese New Year and she must leave early for celebration."

"The old woman is playing on you," said Ruth.

I told them how the young man from the grocery store had said the old woman was a malicious old gossip, telling the other amah's about our lives. He had said she was no good.

"You know you have every right to dismiss her,' said Ruth. 'It is true what the boy from the store is saying. I was told the same by my amah: the old woman is trouble."

Before I left the house, Ruth advised me not to buy milk, meat or meals from the food carts in the street. Meals were safe to eat at the hostel centre and at expensive restaurants in town where the business people ate.

Learning from Ruth, I was able to sack the amah. I paid the old woman for the week's work and told her she was finished working for me. The word got around quickly. On Monday, a new amah was at my door step. She was younger and could speak much better English. She told me she worked mainly for the army people. The military were strict with the servants so I took a chance on her to work for us.

Ruth was a help to Leonie and me. It was Ruth's husband's second posting to Malaysia. She was experienced in living in an Asian country and passed on some of her knowledge to us. I had to learn to work out how to convert Australian dollars to Malaysian dollars so I had some idea of the price of things, and how to barter for things. But there was no bartering at the food store; most of the food there was imported from Australia and Britain and we paid the set price just as we did at home.

I told Ruth and Leonie that I didn't like bartering. Ruth said, "I love bartering when I go to town."' A suggestion was made that the three of us go shopping for children's clothes at the market when the babies grew a little bigger. "Yes,' I said, 'I look forward to that day."

On Saturdays, Bryan and I took a short taxi trip to the RAAF Hostel. Bryan liked his beer from a tap at the bar. He didn't like bottled or canned beer. The RAAF Hostel was a centre for British and Australian RAAF and military forces living in Penang. It was a place where new RAAF and Army personnel and their families stayed for a day or so if a house was not yet ready. It was also the centre for the RAAF doctor, a dentist's surgery and chemist shop for personnel and their dependants. The grounds of the Hostel also had a bar, a restaurant and tennis courts. All kinds of sport were played, and movies were shown. It was a place where personnel and their wives could socialise.

Occasionally a small wedding reception was held at the Hostel restaurant. Young soldiers fell in love and married their sweethearts in a very short time. The restaurant was ready for such occasions with a wedding cake at short notice. A cardboard box was beautifully decorated as a wedding cake, and a slit was made in it for a knife. This decorated box was put over a fruit cake and the bride and groom cut through the slit in the box to the real fruit cake. After the photos were taken, the decorated wedding box was lifted and ready to use for the next wedding. It's sad for me to say that some of those young RAAF and Army men didn't return home.

Bryan worked at the Butterworth Base for only a short time. On his promotion to sergeant he was given a position as hygiene and pest inspector on Penang Island with three local men working for him. They worked on all the service personnel homes on Penang Island and Butterworth Base, as well as the Hostel, the Officer's Club and the Penang English Military Hospital. Most of the work was on Penang Island.

Working on Penang, Bryan met business people from New Zealand, England, Canada and America. An American woman in her mid-thirties arrived with her child at the Hostel. Bryan extended the hand of friendship and asked her to join us at our table. Bryan always made people feel welcome. The woman introduced herself as Olivia. She was dressed rather casually in very tight shorts and a kind of gypsy see-through blouse showing her cleavage. It certainly would attract a man's attention. To the Malay people it was not acceptable for a woman to expose her body in public in this way.

But the woman had a way with words. Olivia described the house by the sea she was living in: "Every morning I sit on the patio having breakfast as the sun rises from behind the mountains and the perfume of the frangipani trees lingers in the air. I watch the fishing boats and the Chinese junks passing by. It gives one the feeling of romance on this beautiful island." Listening to her talk was like listening to poetry.

Olivia was good at telling stories. She said her husband was an engineer working with the American forces. She travelled through Asian Countries following her husband to be with him on his rostered days off. Listening to Olivia and getting to know her a little better over the few days she sat with us, I wasn't sure if the stories she was telling were just that: stories. In conversation, cracks appeared. I picked up things that didn't connect. But she had ways with words that would make anyone believe her. I didn't question her, and never mentioned it to Bryan; why spoil his image of the woman? She was only passing. She stayed in Penang for two weeks, and then said she was moving on to another country.

Our house was on the main street, Low Pow Heng. It was the only street access to the hill and streets above the RAAF. Doctors and staff from the Hostel surgery lived in streets up on the hill. Low Pow Heng was always busy. Not only were the delivery boys running around on their 70cc Honda bikes delivering groceries, but trucks moved new people in and out of the area. With all that activity, nobody noticed that some of the RAAF families were robbed in the few hours of the day that people were away from their house. No-one in the street would not be wise to the fact that a robbery was taking place next door because RAAF people came and went all the time.

We lived next to a young Chinese family by the name of Wong. They had moved into their house two weeks before we came to Malaysia. Mrs Wong and I became friendly. She and her husband were educated people, and spoke English very well. Mr and Mrs Wong made Bryan and I feel welcome, inviting us to have dinner at their home. During the evening, our conversation covered many different subjects about life in Malaysia and Australia. Mr Wong's father was a senator in the Parliament at Kuala Lumpur. Mrs Wong said that her father-in-law had two wives. 'He is allowed four, but that is twice the trouble!' she said. She insisted that she and her husband be married in a registry office. That way, Mr Wong could only have one wife.

We had been living in Penang for some time when Bryan had an accident. He'd been drinking. Riding his motorbike home, he ran off the road and into a monsoon drain. He dislocated his shoulder, so he had the next two days off work. We took the opportunity to explore some of the island. It was only 300 square miles.

The weather had cooled a little. Bryan organized a taxi driver for us, and the driver arrived at the house in a Mercedes Benz. "Master, Ma'am,' he said, 'you call me Haragah. I speaking English pretty good. I give you a good time Master, Ma'am. I am your driver guide."

Seated in the car, Haragah said, "I take you, Master and Ma'am, first on a long drive to where we have many fruit trees growing. The fruit durian is now ready for picking time." The drive to the fruit orchard was only about twenty miles. To people living on the island, this distance was a long way. The orchard was at the edge of the jungle. The local people picking the fruit stopped and looked at us as we got out of the car. There was a pungent smell in the air. Haragah said, "Come, you must try this fruit to eat."

The fruit growing on these trees was the size of a football. It could save my life if I was lost and hungry in the jungle, or it could be a silent killer if I stood under the tree and the durian dropped on my head! Haragah asked one of the men to pass the durian to him. The fruit and a knife were passed to the guide. The size of the knife was frightening. The thought crossed my mind that we were in the jungle in the hands of a complete stranger. We had put our trust in the driver's hands to do the right thing by us. He could have demanded a ransom for our lives.

The local bush people would have been no help to us, especially the poor working people. They didn't exactly like us being in the village. We were not welcome, but we were not as unpopular as the British. The local people believed communism was going to give them everything. My Chinese amah told me, "Communism good. Give plenty money and no have to work hard."

Haragah cut the thick skin of the huge pungent fruit. Under the hardy shell were sections like that of an orange. Haragah took a piece out and ate it. He cut a small piece, and came closer to us, handing the fruit to me.

"Ooh!' I said. 'This fruit is on the nose. It smells. No, no! I am sorry; I don't want to offend you. The smell of this fruit is bad. I can't put that in my mouth!"

Haragah put a little pressure on me saying, "If you not try, ma'am, I will not take you back home."

I looked at him with a very serious look on my face, not knowing if he said this as a joke or not. He saw the expression my face and said "I say this as a joke, Ma'am. You try. This fruit is good to eat."

The local people stood watching us. I didn't want to spoil their day. Being a good sport, I said, "OK, OK, since you insist, I will try this fruit."

I closed my nose with one hand and put the pungent smelling durian into my mouth with the fingers of other hand. The local people laughed hysterically at my reaction to the fruit and the expression on my face. Surprisingly, the durian was nice to eat. It's like thick, smooth banana custard. This durian is good food; it's the pungent smell I don't like.

"You like Ma'am?' asked Haragah. 'Want more?'"

"No, thank you," I replied.

The guide turned to Bryan and said, "You try, Master."

Bryan said, "No thank you, not me."

I said to Bryan, "It was this smell I detected when I first came off the plane. The smell of this fruit dominates the island."

"You are more sensitive to the smells than I am," said Bryan.

The durian smells like garbage, or mouldy French cheese, or rotting fish. In a local English newspaper at the time, a traveller from England said it was "like eating strawberry custard in a smelly lavatory."

Back in the car, we continued to see the sights. Bryan asked the driver if the village people had trouble with snakes. Haragah said, "Oh yes Master, Ma'am. This story I tell you is upsetting. A big snake come to village and eat the baby. Yes Master, is no good. Very sad time for the village. Next time snake he come, he eat baby pig. Oh, he is a very big snake Master! One time I come home at night I see him on the road. I stop the car; wait for him to go past. He come away from the village into the jungle. Is very big snake! We go to the snake temple; you see the big snake in the temple."

On the way Haragah stopped the car at a haunted house overlooking the beach. We stepped from the car onto the beach. Haragah wouldn't go closer to the mansion on the other side of the road on a hillside. He told us that people are paid plenty of money if they can stay in the house one night. "Master, Ma'am,' said Haragah, 'no one stay. This a very frightening house. Bad spirits in there make the house shake. The noise of big banging on walls, many bad spirits in the house."

I looked at the house: windows smashed, the doors barricaded, standing on its own against the hill. "Yes,' I said, 'it does look spooky."

It was while we were looking at the house that an Indian man with a turban on his head passed us. He attracted my attention by saying to me, "You are a cautious woman." There was no "good day", just those words. I looked at him, wondering what he was saying.

Before I opened my mouth, he told me I had one child and one was to come. He told me of my personality and our financial state. He said that because I didn't spend money on frivolous things, but saved for a better purpose, it appeared to people that I was wealthy.

I then realised that he was a man telling fortunes. I immediately thought of God. The man read my mind, and said, "I am not God."

I then thought of a brick wall. He said, "The brick wall is not your future."

This man could read everything I was thinking. He then turned to Bryan and said, "I can't say much about you, Master. You can't handle stress. Your mind, sir, is clouded."

I said to the man, "I am not paying you."

"That's alright, Ma'am. I give you this red stone that will bring you good fortune and good health." He then walked away.

Leaving the beach, Haragah drove us some distance to the snake temple. Bryan and I stood at the door looking into the temple. I wasn't going any closer to those snakes. There were all types of snakes moving around freely. Two huge snakes, just as Haragah had described, lay on the floor in front of an altar. Stretched out they must have been twelve to fourteen feet long, maybe longer. Some snakes were lying on the altar, some were on ornaments. Some were on tree branches that had been stood in big vases for the snakes. Incense burning on the altar kept the snakes calm.

An attendant with snakes in his hand asked Bryan and me if we wanted to handle the snakes, or have them around our neck and have a photo taken. The snakes gave me the shivers. I put up my hands and said, "No thank you, keep the snakes away from me."

Those snakes were poisonous. The Malayan Coral snakes were deadly. I wasn't going to take chances playing Russian roulette with poisonous snakes. Bryan wasn't too keen on handling snakes. Pointing at me, he said to the attendant, "I have this snake to deal with!"

The attendant and our guide laughed. People liked Bryan's facial expression when he made jokes. He was good with the local people, making gestures and joking with the people he was dealing with at work every day.

The next stop was the Buddhist temple of Kek Lok Si in Ayer Itam. The temple is dedicated to the Goddess of Mercy, and is the biggest attraction for visitors to Penang. We had to walk many steps to the pagoda. The view from the bottom of the steps up to the shrine at the top was impressive. On the way up there were several buildings, shops filled with all kind of statues and objects carved from ivory and jade, from very light green to very dark green jade. Haragah said that the dark green stone was considered to be lucky. There was a big pool filled with baby turtles, and a small temple where statues represent different bodhisattvas, or followers of Buddhism. "Each one reminds us of the steps we must take to guard our spirits against the weaknesses of the flesh," said our driver guide.

The next sight was the railway to Penang Hill. The little cable train lifted passengers through the jungle to the top of the hill. On the way to the top, the train made a few stops for people that live on the hill growing roses and orchids. Goods were delivered by this train all the way to the top of the steep hill. Every day, men from the RAAF travelled on this train to the top of the west hill, Bukit Penang, to work on the radar controlling the Penang and Butterworth air traffic. The panoramic view was something to see: the settlement of Georgetown, Penang harbour and the aqua sea all around the island. What a beautiful picture this was.

This was the end of our sight-seeing trip. On the way home we were driven through an avenue of big trees and neglected mansions that were used as store houses. I asked the driver why these houses were neglected, why nothing was done for their upkeep. Haragah said, "Ma'am, after sixty years, the constant movement of clay soil breaks up the foundations, breaking up the walls of houses. Not safe to live in, Ma'am." What a shame, I thought. This was probably where the high class British gentlemen and their families lived in the colonial days, owning plantations and running British industries in Georgetown.

It was late in the afternoon and we had come to the end of our adventure for the day. Although we had not seen everything we would make another trip. Going home, we were driven through streets lined with trees of frangipani and the air was filled with a pleasant smell from the white flowers. What an interesting and pleasant day Bryan and I spent learning about the Island of Paradise, as it's known.

I learned later that the name "Penang" means "Pearl of the Orient". It is an island in the Straits of Malacca, and has an interesting history. In 1786, Captain Francis Light of the East India Company could see the future for the island as a harbour for ships on the long trip to China. The East India Company cleared the jungle of trees and thick undergrowth. To encourage settlers to the island, the port was given a duty-free status. New arrivals were allowed to claim as much land as they could clear. The ships carrying cargoes of tea and opium could stop in Penang to get food and water. People living on the island were now Chinese, Malay and Indian. The city of Georgetown could be mistaken for a Chinese city; the busy streets are full of signboards with Chinese characters.

The time had come for Ruth, Leonie and I to make that trip to the market that we had planned a few weeks earlier. We didn't venture out very often. We preferred to have morning tea together in the lounge room and were happy to stay home with our babies in the cool breeze from the fan. This way we saved money for things we needed, and our growing babies needed new clothes. We met at the bus stop in front of my house. This was my first trip on a bus in Penang.

Getting on the bus, we had to make our way past two goats blocking the aisle. Local people travelling on buses brought their small animals with them. It was the only way they could bring animals to sell at the market. People sat on seats with chickens in a crate next to them. Ruth saw an Indian man sitting on a seat with three flat baskets stacked on his knees, and covered with a small table cloth. He held onto the four ends of the cloth. Ruth whispered to me, "Don't sit next to him. Sit behind. I will explain later."

Ruth, Leonie and I made our way to the back seat of the bus. This was an experience I will not forget. The bus driver broke the speed limit, winding around the narrow streets, missing food carts, bicycles and motor bikes, driving as close as possible to the edge of open concrete drains. As the driver dodged the traffic on the narrow road, my heart was in my mouth. Either the driver had very good judgment, or he was simply a crazy driver pushing his luck. It wasn't long before something on the road was hit. The bus came to a sudden halt. Passengers spilled off their seats, losing their animals. There were chickens, ducks and goats on the loose.

The Indian man let go of the cloth, losing the top basket. It fell on the ground and a frightened snake crawled out from the basket. The driver jumped through the window. The three of us pulled ourselves up, standing on the seat. The Indian snake charmer grabbed and played his flute trying to entice the snake to him. The snake was attracted to the charmer, who caught his snake, put it back in the basket and left the bus.

It all happened so quickly. Luckily for the bus driver, it was another truck that had hit an animal. The bus driver was not to blame. He came back and resumed the journey. After we got over the shock we went shopping at the Paulatikis Markets. Ruth did the bartering for me. She loved haggling over prices. I volunteered to pay for a taxi home. Travelling in the bus was a health hazard. That was the last bus ride for me.

Another time I went into Georgetown for shopping, I brought my amah with me. She did the bartering for me. Like most days in Penang, the day was very hot. The heels of my shoes sank into the melting tar. In the heat, the smell was bad. I am sure I could still smell the blood that was spilt in the streets of Penang over twenty five years ago. My amah told me that the

Japanese had invaded Penang during the war. The people of Penang were executed in the streets. As a little girl, my amah witnessed the brutal massacre and atrocities. She told me that the footpaths were drenched with blood, and that on hot days the melting tar absorbed the blood of Penang people lying in the streets. She said there were many people who lost their heads by Japanese swords.

While we were in the city, my amah took me off the beaten track to show me the way the poor working people lived in Penang. I saw boys as young as ten working in the furniture shops, carving out patterns on coffee and casual tables. They worked and lived in the workshop. It was the same in most of the little business shops employing young boys. In some places we had to walk on the edge of the footpath because big baskets of fish were laid out in the sun for days to dry. This was a delicacy for these people. Some of the eating places in those streets left something to be desired. As we walked along the street, a boy was crouched down washing dishes. He thought it was a good idea to wash his feet in the same dish water, and he carried on washing the rest of the dishes. Walking through these streets, I saw men lying on narrow brick fences having a siesta. I saw families living in big cardboard boxes on the footpath where the street ended. This was the way of life for poor people who had no work.

Back in the main street, my amah and I were standing at a stall looking at material when I felt something on my arm. Thinking it might be a spider, I glanced carefully, and through the corner of my eye I saw very long and dirty finger nails etched into a skinny black hand. The shock nearly made me faint. I turned and saw a creature with a black face and a long grey beard standing next to me. Whiskers covered his chest and his hair was long and grey. It looked like he had put his finger in an electric socket and got a shock, making his long hair stand out in a frizz. He stood with his hand out begging. I had change in my hand and I gave it to him so he would go away. My amah gave me a lecture, saying, "Ma'am, you must not do this. Many will come and want money from you."

Just as I got over that experience, we passed a cake shop. In the window, a wedding cake was displayed. I stopped to take a closer look. As we were about to pass the door, a man from the counter came out. Standing in the door way, he spat out a red substance in front of me. His judgement was good; the spit went over into the open drain at the edge of the footpath. I presumed it was blood. Instantly my stomach churned. I looked for a clean corner of the street where I could throw up. I had seen a small slice of life in the city that day.

Bryan took Karen and me into Georgetown to buy shoes for Karen. He carried Karen in his arms. How proud he was of his little girl. (Now, any time I see a father carrying a child in his arms it reminds me of the tender years when our children were small.) Walking in the streets of Penang, we were both proud of our little daughter. Karen was admired by people. A bus even stopped for a few minutes. Everyone wanted to look at Karen as we were walking in the street. The Asian people loved children with blonde hair.

We walked into the shop. Karen was treated like a princess. The shop owner took her from Bryan's arms and sat her down on a chair next to me. "How may I help you, sir,' said the shop owner.

"Shoes for my little girl," said Bryan.

"May I show you, Ma'am, what we have," said the shop owner. He brought out the shoes, and I pointed out the shoes I wanted. While the shop owner put the shoes on Karen, he asked if we were British, American or Australian. In Georgetown the business people had different prices for each group.

Bryan answered, "We are from Australia."

"May I ask, sir, are you in the RAAF or the Army? You are not wearing a uniform; it is difficult for me to know."

Bryan told him.

"Ah yes, sir,' said the man. 'You speak well, sir. That is why I was not to be sure what country you came from. I have a special price on the little one's shoes today." The man looked at me and said, "How many would you like, Ma'am?"

"Only the one pair, thank you," I said.

"Would you like to buy shoes for yourself, Ma'am?"

I fell for the charming way the man spoke to me. That is the way people in business make a sale. I bought a pair of sandals for myself!

In the months of the monsoon, it rained every afternoon. The morning would be bright and sunny, and in the afternoon I could hear the rain coming. It sounded like soldiers marching down from the mountains. The rain came down in sheets with storm and lightning. I was nearly hit twice by lightning in the house. I had just left the kitchen. Walking into the lounge room, I saw the lightning whizz past me. It only missed by a split second. There was a lightning rod behind the house to stop the lightning hitting the house. Somehow, it didn't work. The lightning hit the rod and went through from the back to the front of the house. Another time I stepped into my bedroom and saw a bluish flash pass me. The storms were frightening.

During the monsoon one morning, I was not feeling well and I stayed in bed to catch up on some sleep. I could hear water running. Thinking that Bryan had left the shower on, I got out of bed to turn the water off. I found it was not the shower, but the rain. It had come down very heavily, causing the hill to break away. The rain had washed the clay soil down the streets of the hill, all the way to Low Pow Heng.

Leonie's mother-in-law came from Perth to spend a few weeks with her son Peter and his family. Their baby had been three months old when Peter and his family left Australia. Babies grow so quickly; Peter's mother wanted to see the baby before the family went back to Australia with a little girl. Peter and Leonie made his mother welcome. Peter owned a car and showed her the sights of Penang. His mother was so impressed that she wanted to see them one more time before she left for home. So Leonie said she would take her mother-in-law through the week when it wasn't crowded.

Leonie asked Ruth and me to join them for the day. The four of us women went to see the huge statue of the reclining Buddha. The size of the statue was unbelievable. It was as big as a two bedroom house, 32 metres long in the reclining position, and covered in gold leaf. The

Buddhist people bought a leaf of gold from the priests who were always present at the site, and put this gold leaf on the statue by themselves, or had the attendant put it on an area up high.

Leaving the site of the reclining Buddha, we went to the other side of the island to the sacred place where Buddha left his huge footprints when crossing the seas to India. The footprints measured about 24 inches and were embedded in cement on a small cliff.

We wandered around the island, taking note of the shrubs and the kind of flowers that grew in the area. There was a lovely collection of cordyline shrubs, all different shapes and sizes, and various colours. Peter's mother took photos of the shrubs and the beach, just over the small cliff. A little further from this spot, there was an open shelter with a floor, fans hanging from the roof, and a bar in one corner. It was popular as a night club, but during the day there was hardly anyone about. The local people tried to make a living from tourists, but there was not much to see at that end of the island.

We walked to the car, ready to move on. The car wouldn't start. "What are we going to do?' asked Ruth. 'I saw a kind of a bar near where we were. Maybe people there could help.'

I said that Bryan was working at Butterworth. "He will be having his lunch at the NAAFI today. He said that if we needed help, to phone him." ('The NAAFI' was the Navy, Army and Air Force Institution.)

We all agreed that may be the best thing to do. The mother-in-law said she would stay in the car to rest her legs. We three went back to the cliff where Ruth had seen the bar. I asked the man if he could speak English. He nodded his head. I told him we had a problem, and could we use the phone please?

"No, Ma'am, no phone here," he said.

"I saw you talking on the phone," I said.

"We have no change," he said.

"I am willing to give you ten dollars to use the phone," I said.

"OK. Do you know the number? I will phone the number, you can talk," was his reply.

He dialled the number and passed the phone to me. I asked if that was NAFFI.

"Yes, the woman answered.

"May I speak to Sergeant Roberts, please?"

"No one here Ma'am," said the woman.

"This is the NAAFI I am speaking to?" I asked.

"Yes, Ma'am, no one here." The woman hung up.

Leonie then said she saw some young Australian men on the beach. We went looking for them, but they had gone. In the meantime, the mother-in-law had been harassed by local boys wanting money and cigarettes from her. She had wound up all the windows, nearly passing out with the heat. The boys wouldn't stop rocking the car and frightening the old woman. When they saw us coming, they turned to us for money.

I saw an old man chopping wood nearby. He saw the boys harassing us. I looked at the old man. If looks could kill we would be dead – that is what I saw in the man's eyes. We got into the car. The boys were still rocking the car.

"I will start the car,' said Leonie. 'Maybe with some luck it will start." Leonie turned the ignition and the car started. The boys stepped aside. Leonie said, "Now I remember Peter saying that sometimes he has to rock the car for the generator to start!"

We went home, not stopping anywhere.

When Bryan came home I told him of our experience and that I had tried to phone him. He said "We have problems with the Malay girls on the switch board. If they don't understand English they simply hang up."

There were many places I wanted to see while we lived in Penang. Mrs Wong invited me to spend a weekend at Kuala Lumpur with her. The journey was to be by train, which I was looking forward to. Unfortunately, I fell sick with a migraine headache. I had my long hair cut to relieve the pain. I was amazed how much lighter my head felt. I hadn't realised that my hair was so heavy.

I was still sick. The pain was unbearable. I was confined to bed and couldn't lift my head off the pillow. The only relief for me was an injection which the doctor was reluctant to give me, but there was no other treatment at the time. After the injection, the headache eased. My head was completely numb.

For three days I was unable to think. I could hear what was said to me, but I didn't speak. I couldn't walk by myself. The injection had made my body weak and had affected my balance. I had to be assisted to walk. I could take care of myself in the bathroom, so some part of my brain must have been active, but that is all I could do. Bryan had to bring in an extra amah for the weekend to take care of our baby. What a relief it was when I was able to think again. I slowly recovered. After that injection I had no headaches for about ten years.

Just as I felt well again, I fell pregnant. The constant threat of miscarriage prevented me from picking up my toddler Karen, and I spent time in hospital.

These were worrying times for Bryan. Through those rough months, Malaysia was not at peace. There was racial unrest. Businesses were mostly owned by Chinese and Indian people, and this didn't go down well with the indigenous Malay people. Malays always held the government positions. Mrs Wong told me that it was always "Malays first". Her father-in-law was a senator in Kuala Lumpur, but he could never be Prime Minister because he was not Malay.

Fighting broke out in the streets of Penang. Bryan was driving me home from hospital when troops stopped the car. A soldier put his rifle through the window. He pointed it at me, only six inches from my heart and with his finger on the trigger while the others searched the boot of the car. It happened so quickly. I remember thinking that if a truck passed by and backfired, the soldier might have reacted, and we would have been history. The search finished and we were free to go home to our baby Karen. She had been left in the house with the amah. Bryan realised he should have let me come home in an ambulance.

On Easter weekend in 1968, I gave birth to our son, Anthony, in the British Military Maternity Hospital in Penang. He was in good health, but I had some problems to overcome and was put into intensive care. I was in the best hospital, in good hands. The doctors and midwives took good care of me and supported me to get well. New mothers in this hospital bathed their babies and, after feeding, took the babies back to the nursery. In the nursery, there were four rows of cots. The first two were for British and Australian babies, and behind them were two rows for Gurkha babies. The Brigade of Gurkhas served with the British from 1962 to 1966 in Malaysia. Their wives and families were given the same medical treatment as the British in the British Military Hospitals.

Bryan told me an interesting story of the Gurkha soldiers. My Bryan was not a strict military person. Sometimes he would lapse on the protocol. Coming to visit me in hospital, dressed in civilian clothes and riding his 70cc motorbike, he failed to stop at the hospital ground checkpoint. He took it for granted that the Gurkha soldiers on guard knew him because he worked at the hospital grounds so often. Bryan said he gave a casual salute as he rode through the gate without stopping. One of the soldiers on guard drew his weapon and chased Bryan, yelling at him to stop.

Bryan stopped. The guard caught up with him and was very angry. He lectured Bryan, saying, "You must stop and show your ID card. I am at liberty to cut your throat for not stopping at the gate. I have drawn my Kukri. I must draw blood before I can put this Kukri back into the holster. It could have been your blood sergeant. But knowing that you and I have just become fathers to new baby sons I will let you go this time." The soldier then nicked his own hand as a symbolic act to draw blood before putting his Kukri in the holster.

On my first day of motherly duties, I was still in a daze. Walking into the nursery for the first time, I walked over to the third row and put my baby into a Gurkha baby's cot. Behind me, a Gurkha woman with her baby was making a fuss, pointing to the cot in front and trying to tell me that I was putting my baby in her baby's cot.

The last time I was in that hospital, in the old building, I had shared a room with a Gurkha woman. Even in that heat, she wrapped herself in a sheet so as not to show any part of her body. When we were having our food, the nurse drew a screen between us two women. This time we were in the new hospital building. It was like staying in a five-star hotel. All the walking patients were served meals in the dining room. As soon as I was able to walk I had to join the other mothers in the dining room for meals. The Gurkha mothers had their own culture and customs. They didn't mix with the English speaking women.

The doctor dropped by the dining room at lunch time. He flirted a little with the new mothers, who were a bit anxious, or suffering from depression. It was part of the rehabilitation to make us feel better. I got a light smack on my bottom from the doctor for being cheeky. Telling jokes meant my health was improving. The doctors made sure the new mothers had all their problems worked out and were in good health before mother and baby were released from hospital.

My memories of the time around Anthony's birth are linked to what we heard on Radio Butterworth. We heard the drastic news of the loss of our Prime Minister, Harold Holt, presumed drowned while swimming in the sea. The bush fires in Australia were burning fiercely, and in America, Bobby Kennedy was assassinated. I remember the songs of the time: '...if you're going to San-Francisco...', 'Galveston', 'Watermelon and Strawberry Wine'. They played every day on Radio Butterworth. When I hear one of those songs now, my memory goes back to the time our son was born.

A memory that stands out was when I walked to the shop with my baby boy one morning. A pale-skinned Chinese woman stood at the counter. Her dress looked expensive. As I stood next to her, she started a conversation with me. She asked me what country I came from. I told her. Then she said, "What a beautiful baby! Is it a boy?"

"Yes," I said.

"Would you sell the baby to me? I'll give you one million American dollars. You are still young and can have more babies. I want to buy your baby son," she said.

"We don't sell our babies," I said. I walked away, thinking how the Ghurka woman in the hospital almost had him for nothing!

In the two years we lived at Penang, we were invited to a Chinese wedding and an Indian wedding. They were two young men who worked with Bryan. The Chinese bride was dressed in a modern western style wedding gown, the groom in a western suit. It was a Buddhist wedding. The Indian wedding was a Christian wedding in an Indian style. The bride wore a colourful Indian sari, and the groom wore a western suit.

Living in the main street I had the chance of seeing a Chinese funeral pass my house. The old man had lived down the street from where I lived. I passed his house many times on the way to the grocery store. I had often seen him working in his garden. It was something to be admired, and he took great care and pride in it. My amah and I watched the old man's funeral procession as it passed. The old man's coffin was huge and heavy and painted in heavenly scenes. It was drawn through the streets by two buffalo decorated with flowers. My amah said he was a rich and influential man to have a big coffin, and to have hired mourners cry for him as he departed this earthly life. He had many friends walking behind the mourners. Almost everyone in the village came.

Some months later, a Hindu procession passed my house. The Indians were celebrating the holy day of their Hindu god, Vishnu. Leading the procession was a young man with an iron hoop resting on his shoulders. Long spikes protruded from the each side of the hoop into the man's chest and back. This represented paying penance for past sins. It was very impressive to be witnessing this colourful ritual. I wondered how a man could walk the distance to the temple with spikes in his body. It opens the eyes of western people like me.

The time came for us to leave Penang. Fortunately, Bryan's posting was to Williamtown. We could return to live in our own house at Beresfield. Before leaving Penang, we took a final trip to the Botanic Gardens so Karen could see the small monkeys. Many times we had gone there on a Sunday. That was when most people went to spend time in the garden and feed the monkeys. The gardens were cut away from part of the jungle and the monkeys lived among the jungle trees. We went to the gardens on Thursday, the day before we left Penang. By Thursday, the monkeys were hungry and behaved differently. As soon as we arrived and got out of the car, we were swamped by the little wild creatures. They got into the car through the open windows and took the bag with the baby's things. They took it into the trees, tossing out nappies and taking the milk bottles, and drinks and sandwiches. It was impossible to stay. We got back into the car and drove to the house. We had to buy new babies' bottles for the trip home.

We had left Australia with one baby, and were now going home with two. This time I said to Bryan, "You had better make sure I have two seats for our children. If I have no seats for the children, I am not getting on the plane, so you'd better make sure our children have a seat each."

We left on a chartered plane, flying from Penang to Sydney, stopping only at Singapore. There, the passengers were asked to leave the plane for one hour, but I insisted on staying. My baby had just settled down to sleep and I was not going to disturb him. The sun was almost setting. I watched out of the window as luggage was loaded onto the plane. I saw two very long military trunks. Beside them were two smaller tin trunks like most of the soldiers have, and written on them was the name and rank of the soldier, and the word 'deceased'. I was a little startled to realise that the plane was carrying two young bodies home.

I said to Bryan, "The plane is carrying two young soldiers' bodies."

"How do you know?" he asked.

"I recognised the tin trunk like the one you have, and their names and ranks are written on the smaller trunks," I said.

"This plane is chartered by the air force. The authorities can bring them back on this plane," said Bryan.

I fell asleep on the plane. I didn't hear a thing through the night, and the children slept well. I woke at dawn. The plane was flying over Australia. When I looked out of the window I saw a giant rock and then smaller groups of rock in the middle of a desert. There was nothing else for miles, just desert.

The plane circled around Sydney. "What a beautiful country this is. "We have come home," I said to Bryan.

"Yes, it is good to be back," I said to Bryan.

COMING HOME

The plane landed in Sydney at about seven in the morning. We went through the customs and found that we were stranded. There was to be a RAAF bus waiting to take us to the train station, but the RAAF had forgotten about us. In fact, there were no buses or trains of any kind. There was a transport strike. We felt like homeless people. Karen was sick; she vomited and was in a mess.

Bryan phoned his sister sister, Alva, who lived at Coogee. We went by taxi to her place to clean and feed the children, and to make some arrangement from there to get home. From her place, Bryan phoned the RAAF base. The RAAF eventually found a tourist bus going north. There were just two seats left on the bus. The bus driver let us off at Hexham, and we went the rest of the way to Beresfield by taxi.

Settling in at home was not what I expected. We had come back to a different Australia. It was the time of flower power, floppy hats and miniskirts. The standards of dress and morality were falling with the younger generation.

I had two babies and no-one to help me. I hadn't realised what a help my amah had been to me. I missed her. In the meantime, a third child was on the way. That would be a caesarean for me. The doctor in Malaysia told me that I should not have any more children, and that I may not be so lucky escaping death next time. I got the flu, and I had to look after my children without help. It was too much for me and I miscarried again. Bryan took compassionate leave to take care of the children and me. Bryan also came down with the flu. All the family were sick at the one time. We took turns in taking care of the children. Bryan attended to the children in the morning, and I did the same in the afternoon. Again this put us in financial difficulties.

I got a job for four hours on afternoon shift for a few weeks to pay bills that were piling up. When the afternoon shifts finished, I was offered full-time work, but I had to leave. I couldn't cope with going to work when the children were small.

When they started school I went to work again, this time at the university. I washed dishes and collected cups and saucers in the cafeteria, starting at ten in the morning, and finishing at seven in the evening. I took the children to school in the morning. In my break, I picked them up from school and took them to my parents' place, where they stayed until Bryan picked them up at six and took them home. It was a bit difficult, but we managed. The kitchen pantry was filled with food; the new fridge was no longer empty. Financially, life was much better. I was able to take the children out to shows. Money was not a concern any more. We even managed to save money.

Our plan was to buy a three bedroom brick house, with one room for each child, but it was not to be. Changes in this modern world brought on problems for me. In the kitchen where I was working, the detergents and disinfectants were changed. It affected my allergies, and I got bad headaches. I had to leave. It had been a job I liked and was able to manage without stress. Our dream faded away.

Bryan had returned to being a corporal driving trucks, which he enjoyed, but times were changing. The officers of the war generation were retiring and young university trained officers were taking up their positions. Bryan was relieved of the work he had been happy doing and was asked to teach the new recruits to drive the big transport trucks, and to reverse planes into the hangars. He wasn't happy. He told me that whenever he showed them something, they'd say, "That's not the way we learned about it." Bryan would throw his hands in the air and said "University kids! I've had it!"

The time had come for him to sign up to the RAAF for another six years. Before he made up his mind, he asked me whether I would leave this house if he was posted somewhere else. My answer was "No".

Bryan decided to leave the force while he was still young enough to start a job close to home. He worked for three years lifting and loading 44 gallon drums on a truck. It was hard work. In that short time, he damaged his arms and fell sick with arthritic pain. He was not able to work.

In 1975, at the age of 45, Bryan was put on an invalid pension. That was a big blow for him. He had no other interests; work was his life. He liked to work on his car but his hands got too clumsy to pick up small nuts. He would blame his eyesight. He was often angry, and gave away working on the car. He tried to play bowls to fill in his time, but that didn't work. He said his hands and arms hurt too much. He would go to the club for social chats and a drink. At first it was once a day. As the months progressed, it became every morning and afternoon.

I, too, was sick, having to battle with allergic reactions and constant lethargy. Many times I was called lazy because I got so tired. I could hardly get myself out of bed. It felt like pushing a boulder up a steep hill and never reaching the top. A television commercial at the time showed a woman climbing a mountain of rocks, and how hard the day was for her. When she reached the top she had earned a mug of coffee. That commercial upset me because it was the way I felt. I didn't want to see things like that.

I finally found relief from the fatigue and depression by simply taking one vitamin tablet daily. I started taking them after they were prescribed for Karen. Until she was five, Karen had a cold sore that wouldn't heal. In desperation, I took her to a herbal bio-chemist. He said it was a virus, and that Karen needed treatment. His suggestion was that she should take a particular brand of multivitamins and mineral supplements. "The cold sore will heal in a short time," he said. He insisted that she only take that brand.

I also took the multivitamins for my cold sores, and when I finished the bottle I realised that my allergies weren't so bad, and the fatigue and depression had lifted. I was feeling much better in myself. When I stopped taking the multivitamins, the black cloud came back.

Looking back, I remember that when we lived in Germany, we were given vitamin tablets in the camps, and they had something to do with me being well. After coming to Australia, we stopped taking vitamin tablets, and perhaps that is why I began to feel lethargic and depressed.

Over the years, I have learned to avoid things that upset my allergies, and have continued taking multivitamins every day. I did try other brands, but they didn't work for me, so I stayed with the brand the bio-chemist had recommended. As I get older, I am taking fish oil to keep the pains and stiffness at bay. It also seems to help keep the flu away. And whenever I have an asthma attack, I take a nip of Jamaica Rum. Ventilin gives me the shakes and burns me, but rum always seems to clear the airways!

Knowing how difficult life is for a sick person, I felt sorry for Bryan, and slowly took over the jobs around the house. It was easier that way. Bryan was not the charming happy man I once knew. He had become a grumpy alcoholic.

I took up ballroom dancing. I was meeting new people and learning new things. Bryan didn't want to come; he said he wasn't able to dance. "Well, sit!" I said. But he didn't want to do that either. We quarrelled often.

We had three serious arguments. On two occasions, I left the house and kept walking for a long time. The third time, the year of the Newcastle Earthquake, I walked out and didn't go back. I was nearly fifty years old. Karen and Anthony were both in their early twenties, so I began living my own life. Within twelve months, Bryan and I were divorced. I lived in a flat for a few years. Bryan wanted to sell the house, so I borrowed money to buy his share. He bought a caravan with the money, and I moved back into the house.

I started dancing lessons at the age of fifty two, when I was crippled with pain in the back. I had fallen out of bed onto my knees, and had to crawl to the toilet in pain in the morning. Thank goodness I had "wheels" so I could drive myself to the doctor. When I spoke to my lady doctor about my problem, she suggested I take up some form of exercise like swimming. That was out of the question. I could not tolerate cold water, and, suffering from allergies, I would be affected by the chemicals in the pool.

"What can you do?' asked the doctor. 'If the pain gets to be unbearable, we may have to operate. It may work, and then you may end up in a wheelchair."

Those were the facts my doctor laid out in front of me.

"I will take up ballroom dancing," I said.

"That's a good start," said the doctor.

I was one of six in a dance group. We met at social dances three times a week. My partner was Jonathon. He was very serious about his dancing. He danced every night of the week, and never tired of it. He read books about it, and bought a collection of CDs for sequence dancing. We called him The Professor. He danced well. His footwork was very good, and he looked good with his partner on the dance floor.

Jonathon and I were asked to perform demonstration dances at the Seniors' Hall. People in the audience told us things like "You look good dancing together', 'Your footwork and timing is very good', 'You make dancing look so easy', and 'It looks like you are dancing on a cloud'. The most important thing they said was, 'You look happy." We were also asked to demonstrate dancing for one hour on a Saturday afternoon at the Club Dance.

Someone in the dance group suggested we spend a week at Port Macquarie. We arranged to rent a three bedroom flat not far from the beach, and took two cars. We pooled our money for petrol and food, and worked out our finances so everything came out even. A few weeks later we met at my place. The passengers chose which car they would travel in, and, in case we became separated on the highway, we decided then and there where we would be stopping for morning tea. We were fortunate to have a good morning for travelling. Not that rain would spoil our day; we were all pleased to be on our way. The traffic on the road was good. There was no tail-gating or over-taking at crucial bends, so our two cars stayed together all the way to Bulahdelah, where we had an early picnic lunch.

As we ate, the boys cracked a few jokes. We were all good company, all of the same mind. We all had a good laugh at the jokes going around from one to the other, always ending with Allan having the last word in his softly spoken way. When we finished eating, we packed away the picnic baskets and decided who would take the next turn driving. The passengers wanted to change cars.

While we were travelling Jonathon put on a dance tape, and we had a little sing-a-long to songs like "Teddy Bears' Picnic" and "The Grandfather's Clock". I was having a wonderful time singing off-key until Allan said, "I should have stayed in the other car! Terese's singing is giving me an earache!"

"I'll stop the car, and let you off," Jenny said with a little giggle.

"I'll help you push him out,' I said. 'Just say the word!"

"Fair go!' said Allan, 'It's a long walk to Port Macquarie!"

Being a good sport, I stopped singing. Little Allan was brave, and had cheek telling me that; I am bigger than he is. I hinted at this, saying, "It goes to show that the small ones puff and bluff, and get their way!"

I turned to Allan and said, "It's OK Allan. I will get my chance to pay you back for making fun of my singing. When we are in the flat, and I am having a shower, I will sing to my heart's content, and take extra time in the bathroom, making sure that I use up all the hot water!"

"That's alright,' said Allan in return. 'I won't be offering my services to scrub your back. Your singing has put a wedge between us!"

Jenny giggled and said, "Well Allan, that sounds like it's the last tango for Terese."

"Not to worry, Jenny,' I said. 'There is always the rumba Allan's good at. He will give you a shove and a push on the dance floor." Allan really was a good dancer. He had a style of his own, especially when dancing the rumba. His hip movement was perfect.

Alan paused a moment, then burst out with "Fair go Terese! You almost had me thrown out of the car, and now you are threatening my dancing! What's a bloke got to do to get on the good side of you?"

"Allan, take it from me,' said Jonathon. 'There is no way you can understand a woman."

"What's there to understand?' said Jenny. 'Just talk sweet nothing, and mind your Ps and Qs. That's all we women ask of you."

"Now,' said Jenny, changing the subject. 'I will give you some trivia on where that saying comes from. Somewhere back in history, in the UK, a publican did not like the patrons leaving his pub drunk. He said to them, "Mind your pints and quarts; I want you to walk out of the pub on your two feet, not crawl out". That's how the saying of Ps and Qs originated."

"Well, there is something one learns every day," said Jonathon.

When we arrived at the flat, we sorted out our sleeping arrangements, and settled in nicely. After our long drive, we stayed in the flat on the first night and played cards.

The old jokes came into the conversation. "Ladies, lock your door. Allan has a habit of sleep walking."

Wilma said, "We have a way to cure you of that habit. When one of you boys steps out from your room, there will be a bucket of ice cold water waiting outside the door. When you put your foot into the bucket, the shock will soon wake you!"

After breakfast the next morning, we walked to the beach, and then walked to town to buy food for lunch and tea. On the days and evenings we went dancing, we had lunch or dinner at the Club. On the other nights, each of us girls took a turn to prepare the food, and the boys set the table and cleaned up. We stayed in the flat playing cards, listening to dance music, stepping out dance steps, and planning the next day's outing.

We planned a trip to the Tacking Point Lighthouse. Jon, who was to drive the next day, was not listening; his mind was on dance steps, and he missed out on what was planned. The next day, when we started the trip, the cars went in different directions, and in the confusion we were lost. One car was looking for the other, and the driver was getting hot under the collar.

"It's like the Keystone Cops, chasing one another in circles!" said someone.

To make things worse, it was raining. We finally got together and went to Laurieton, strolling in the main street, and walking in and out of the shops. Little Allan came across a music shop. It was like finding Aladdin's Cave. The shop had strict tempo dance music on display, and some CDs from the fifties like the Andrews Sisters, Jack Speering, Victor Silvester and others. We all came back feeling happy, stepping out the dance to the CDs we had just bought.

It wasn't long before we planned another dance holiday. Betty couldn't come, but Wilma, Jenny, Allan, Jon and I boarded a train to Coolangatta. We changed seats throughout the trip to spend time with each other. Jon noticed two young musicians with guitars, and asked them if they would play. The young boys were hesitant, and said that they didn't want to annoy the passengers. Jon looked around and asked if anyone minded.

No one objected. Someone said that it would make the trip pleasant. The boys agreed to play if we would sing along with them. That was a great idea, except for the generation gap. We didn't know the songs they were playing. One of the passengers suggested they play Australian folk songs. It was a good idea; everyone knew those songs. After the sing-a-long, the jokes started rolling. Judging by the expression on their faces, two ladies who were travelling to the same resort didn't like some of the jokes. There was nothing bad in the jokes. We put these ladies on the right track, and converted them to having a good time. They started to enjoy themselves. It ended up being a lovely way to pass time, and we had a good trip.

We arrived at Murwillumbah late in the evening. The bus from the resort was waiting to take us to Coolangatta. It was still and hot. Luckily for us, our rooms were in front of the pool. For years, I had never set foot into water, but this was saltwater, not chlorine. As soon as we unpacked our swimmers, Wilma and I were in the pool. Jenny soon followed. The water was quite warm, but it was refreshing after the day's travel. It didn't irritate my skin, and it cooled me down from constant hot flushes. We were in the pool for about five minutes when Wilma saw the notice that the pool was closed for the night. We stayed in the water quietly for a few minutes more, until we cooled off enough to settle down to sleep.

I was the first to wake in the morning. I quietly left the room because I didn't want to disturb my sleeping friends with my coughing and sneezing. One of the boys in the next room liked to sleep late. He was sensitive to the slightest noise and I didn't want to be the one to disturb him. Some of the guests on the first floor were up and having coffee on the balcony. As I walked out the gate, they greeted me with a wave. By the time I came back from my walk it was time for breakfast.

Bus trips had been organised for each day of the week, but on the first day we decided to have an easy day in the pool to recuperate from the train trip and to prepare ourselves for the evening dance.

On the next day, Wednesday, we took a bus tour to see the sites. We went to Bond Private University. The grounds and gardens were designed to enhance the modern buildings and capture the Australian spirit with native shrubs and trees. Then we were taken through a new suburb. The houses, on man-made water frontages, were not quite finished, but the "For Sale" signs were out. These house prices were beyond our reach, but we counted our blessings and appreciated our own humble homes. Morning tea break was at the Reservoir Dam picnic grounds. A slight wind was blowing, and it was a pleasant change from the hot days.

Jenny, Wilma and I stood facing the dam. "There is plenty of water in this dam," I said.

Jenny, in her soft voice, joked, "Enough to drown Jon and Allan..."

"That's a little drastic, Jenny,' said Wilma. 'We need those feet for dancing."

Jon was listening, but saved his response for later entertainment.

The next stop was Mount Warning National Park. The bus wound its way through the ever-changing rainforest, eventually arriving at the viewing point. It was a panoramic view of scenery from the sea to the mountains. Mount Warning was named by Captain Cook as a warning to seafarers of the many treacherous reefs along the coast. To the local Bundjalung people, the mountain is called Wollumbin, and remains an important sacred place. To walk around the mountain takes five hours on average, the last section being very steep to the summit.

On the way back, the bus stopped at a fruit stall. There were various tropical fruits and home-made jams for sale. We bought some fruit to take back for tea break.

Allan and Jon clowned about in the bus. They were natural comedians, like a modern-day Laurel and Hardy. Jon, the big fellow, and Allan, the little fellow, acted out the conversation they heard us girls having at the dam.

"Allan,' said Jon, 'did you hear what was said about us when we were at the dam?"

"No Jon, I didn't hear a thing," said Allan.

"The girls wanted us to drown in the dam, but one of them said that wouldn't be a good idea because they need our feet for dancing."

"That's nothing new,' said Allan with a grin on this face. 'I have been told that by many women over the years."

The two boys throwing jokes at each other had the passengers laughing, and the trip ended with happy people. The bus driver thanked Jon and Allan for entertaining the group on the bus. "That made my day easier,' he said. 'I can't make passengers laugh with my jokes like you two fellows did today."

That evening we were dressed and ready to go dancing. Jenny, Wilma and I sat outside talking to the guests in the pool while we waited for the boys. Jon came out and sat with us. We all waited for Allan.

"What is keeping Allan?" asked Jenny.

"He's been a while,' said Jon. I'd better go in and see what is keeping him."

When Jon came back, he told us that Allan was sitting on the bed in shock. He had slipped in the bathroom and hit his head on the wall, and had a slight lump on his forehead. We all rushed in to see if he needed to be taken to the hospital.

"I'm OK,' said Allan. 'Just give me few minutes to recover." He insisted that he was alright to come along with us to the dance.

The next morning, Allan woke with a black eye. At breakfast he told us he was not going on the bus trip.

"Are you feeling sick?" asked Jenny.

"No I'm feeling OK. It's my eye – it looks bad," he said.

"Can you see alright?" asked Jon.

"I don't have any problem with my sight," was his reply.

"Well, that's good,' said Jon. Terese can cover the eye with make-up."

"Yes,' said Jenny. 'Get your black bag out."

Wilma put in her word, saying, "Work some magic on Allan, Terese."

Allan agreed. I plastered his eye with make-up, and worked on his other eye to make it a little darker. Allan was happy. With the work done on his eyes, we were on the way to Currumbin Bird and Animal Sanctuary.

We entered the gates at Currumbin like big kids on an excursion into Paradise. Our imagination took over. We started with a train ride through the park, watching the wildlife that wandered freely about. Leaving the train, we were off to see animals perform for half an hour. The animals were fascinating, doing everything to the ranger's command. (They were better behaved than some of the children in the audience.) Walking around this paradise for a while, we started to get hungry.

"I may wrestle that crocodile we saw taking a snooze in the pool,' said Allan. 'I'll use my pen knife and have a crocodile stack for lunch."

Jenny said, "I am looking for that possum that was hopping from tree to tree. A possum stew would be good."

"A damper with honey would go down well," said Jon.

"I have set my sights on an emu,' I said. 'A drumstick would be a nice snack for me."

"And I will snack on the bits and pieces that all of you leave behind," said Wilma.

Allan and Jenny gave up on the idea of catching the wild animals. Allan said his knife was too small to tackle the beast, and Jenny said she was too heavy to climb a tree to catch her creature. There were no vines strong enough or long enough to tie Jon and swing him on the tree for the honey, and the emu ran too fast for me to catch it.

"Living from the land is not working out for us,' said Wilma. 'Let's buy our lunch from the food shop. It will save us time and energy for seeing the rest of the park!"

After we finished our lunch we passed some time at the gem and souvenir shop before the afternoon crocodile feeding. Jon had a fascination for crocodiles. He was looking forward to seeing them feed. The lorikeets also came to the park every afternoon for their nibble. They flew into the park from all directions and landed on the heads and shoulders of people who were brave enough to stand with a plate of bread and honey. The ranger told us not to move our heads while the birds were flying because their sights were set on wherever they were landing, and if we moved our heads we might be struck in the face. I am pleased to say there were no accidents that afternoon. By the time feeding was over, we had decided that living in the bush was not for us!

We boarded the bus to go back to the resort. On our return we freshened up and walked into the dining room. Our evening meal was served in a short time. After tea, we made our way to the entertainment room, where there was a Pianola. Jon was the strongest. He took it upon himself to push the pedals. As the rolls turned the written words, we sang along. I had a lovely time singing, but my voice slipped out of key. Allan looked at me, rolling his eyes and pulling faces, making us all laugh. His gesture only made it more difficult to stay in key. Being a good sport, and to not inflict any more pain on Allan's ears, I stopped singing. But I was encouraged by the girls to ignore Allan's pained expressions and to continue singing. It was a shame that the other guests didn't join us. They escaped to their rooms. Our sing-along must have been painful for them; we could hear their doors slamming shut.

Friday's itinerary included a bus ride to the casino. We didn't join in with the rest of the group. I was sure they didn't miss us after the previous night's performance. The five of us stayed at the resort, sitting outside our room and talking to other guests in the pool. The boys decided to go for morning dance lessons, and we girls walked to Coolangatta. After window shopping for a while, we stepped into an antique shop for a browse. The sales lady was rather pushy, giving the impression that we should buy something or leave. I said to my friends, "There is nothing in the shop that I need."

: It must be good to have no need for things, said the sales lady.

I thought for a moment. "Yes,' I said. 'It is good to be satisfied with what one is blessed with." I slowly walked out the door.

We met the boys at the Senior Citizens' Hall for lunch, and then came back for a cat nap. It was a very hot day, and after the other guests had left the pool, we decided to take a dip. One big woman in her seventies had stayed in the water. She was alone at the resort, and had enjoyed our company that week. The woman liked talking to Jon. He had the knack of drawing attention with his boyish flair. He loved fun and was always larking about.

Wilma was the first to go in the pool. She was like a little mermaid, hardly making a ripple in the water. Jenny and I were a little on the big side; when we went in, the water rose slightly. Little Allan ran out from his room to the edge of the pool, beating his chest and showing his biceps, posing as Mr Universe, and making us all laugh before he dived in. He made a big splash. Jon, bigger than Allan, came running, stretched out and dived in a full belly flop like a whale. The water splashed over us girls and cascaded over the sides of the pool. The level of water dropped at least ten centimetres. We all quietened down, and performed water ballet to the dance music Jon had playing on tapes.

The water was a great relief from the uncomfortably hot days. Saturday was extremely hot. We stayed in the pool most of the day. We were having so much fun that one lady in particular spent most of the afternoon with us in the pool. She was another woman attracted by Jon's mucking about and telling jokes. Her neck and arms were adorned with gold jewellery, and on most of her fingers she wore rings encrusted with diamonds and precious stones. She told us stories of the exotic faraway countries and places she had lived in, pointing to the ring purchased in each country. Her late husband was an Air Commodore in the RAAF. She said she had met him on the RAAF base where she worked as a nurse before they were married. Fortunately in her case, her husband had left her financially comfortable and she was able to take a holiday at resorts three or four times a year.

We enjoyed the cool water until it was time for us to get ready for the evening. After we finished eating we were ready for a night out dancing.

On Sunday, the bus took us to Carrara Markets. When we arrived at the markets, the boys went their own way. Jenny, Wilma and I browsed among the stalls, looking for bargains. I stopped at a stall selling vanilla and other essences for cooking. The woman assured me that the essences on the table were not imitation. She opened the bottle for me and I could smell the lovely aroma. The vanilla was rather expensive, but I couldn't resist. Wilma and Jenny came away empty handed. The boys had found a stall selling tapes of music from the fifties and sixties, and music by James Last and Montivanni. Allan and Jon thought they had hit a jackpot to find such treasures!

In our young days, the words were clear and the lyrics of lovely romantic melodies were sung by the soft voices of Perry Como, Dean Martin, Nat King Cole, Doris Day and Rosemary Clooney, just to mention a few. The songs touched every heart, and lifted the mood. The orchestra played softly to complement the singer. Drums did not compete with the artist to drown his or her singing. The drums only came forward when the artist finished the song. The orchestra then put the finishing touch with a few bars to end it. The individual musical instruments came clearly together, making the sound of wonderful music.

Coming back from the market, we rested our feet for an hour. Sitting in our room, I took a closer look at the bottle of vanilla, and I read "Double Strength Imitation Vanilla Essence". We walked from our room to where the boys were sitting by the pool. As we joined the rest of the guests for a final barbecue tea, Allan said to me, "Terese, don't sing!"

Through dancing, I had found people I could fit in with. I felt at home with them. They didn't look to offend people, and they didn't take offence at jokes. They were good company. They didn't drink or smoke. We liked to make ourselves as respectable as possible, and still looked good for our age. There were no jealousies or conflicts. We were good friends.

Dancing strengthened the muscles in my back, and the pain eased. My doctor was happy for me, and said, "Keep doing what you are doing, it is working for you."

Dancing had also been good for another health problem. In 1991, just before I began dancing lessons, I was diagnosed with emphysema. I have had weak lungs all my life from the tuberculosis I suffered as a child, and living all my life with smokers resulted in emphysema.

But when I got very sick with flu, I had to stop dancing. I couldn't keep going with Jon the way he wanted to dance. He found another partner. I still go to the Wednesday afternoon dance, but I don't get up on the floor. I just have a cup of tea and a chat.

FULL CIRCLE

Over the years, Mother's headaches, dizziness and depression steadily got worse. Not long before I left Bryan, Mum began to develop dementia. She didn't know how to do things, like when to have a bath. She wouldn't listen to me tell her because I was her daughter. I wasn't supposed to tell her how to do things. But I went regularly with her to a support group.

It was painful for Father to see his wife's sickness constantly changing her, to watch her drifting away from him. Father begged me, "Do something for your mother, Terese, help your mother!"

I explained that she wouldn't get well, that she would only get worse. He got cranky with me. He was an alcoholic, and had his own dementia.

One day Dad called me and said, "Your mother's gone off her head!"

We took her to Maitland Hospital. The doctor couldn't find anything physically wrong, but said she was mentally disturbed. They recommended that she go to James Fletcher Hospital.

Dad asked me to do something, but what could I do? Mum wouldn't sit. She walked all day and all night. Sometimes she tumbled. I would have looked after her if I could, but what could I do with her? It took specialist people to look after her. We admitted her to James Fletcher.

While she was there, she was attacked by another patient. So the staff found her a place in the Father Maximilian Kolbe House at Sandgate. It was a comfort that they spoke Polish, but they didn't have the staff to look after people like Mum. Eventually, they found her a place in an aged care facility at Cessnock.

When I went to visit her, she was so tired. She was always on her feet, walking. Her body could not relax. She walked all day and half of the night. She couldn't sit during the day or stay in bed at night. She could have broken the world record for the distance walked. I tried to sit her down while I was with her, but she would always get up again.

She said to me, "If I could get rid of this headache and dizziness I could go home. I want to go home!" The dizziness was unbearable for her; she could not lay her head down. On every visit I made, she said, "Terese, can't you help me? I want to go home."

My heart broke when I heard her say that. I could do nothing to help. We were losing Mother while she was still living. My father, my brothers and I were in grief for a long time, losing Mother little by little each day over the five years she was in the institution. I felt so angry and frustrated that nothing I could do would help. I felt numb and gripped with stress. I couldn't even pray.

Just before Mother died, she had a fall and broke her shoulder. The nursing staff found it difficult to keep the sling on her shoulder. A few weeks later she fell face down off the toilet seat and broke her nose. She was in pain until she died.

I know there was nothing I could do to help her, but I can't help feeling guilt. Sometimes now, I walk around in the cold without a cardigan on, and I ask myself why I am doing this. I think I must be punishing myself for the cold my mother had to put up with in the concentration camp. It's good that I now have grandchildren to look after once a week. They take my mind off the thoughts I have when I'm by myself at home.

Only ten days after Mother's death, Father also died. He had a heart attack at home. My brother Peter found him lying on the kitchen floor.

Dad had always said that the only way he was going to leave his house was feet first in a wooden box. That is the way he left on his last journey from home.

Sometime after my parents' death, I drove to Beresfield to visit Mother's friend Anna Lesien. On the way, I passed my parents' house, the house we had all helped to build. I wanted to see the changes made after it had been sold. The old wire fence and the mail box were the same.

The veranda was restored to the way it was when Father first built the house. Over the years he had made some minor changes to the front veranda and closed the end in so Mother could sit in the corner away from the draught.

The garden was still much the same. It was mid-winter and the quince shrub was in full bloom in front of the kitchen window. It had been growing there for over forty years. I had first seen a quince blooming in the garden of the Oak factory when I worked there. I had taken a cutting home for Mother to grow in her garden. It gave her pleasure to see the cutting grow into a strong shrub in her garden. I wanted to give her the joy of seeing it flower through the winter months. The snow drops were also in flower. Bryan and I had brought them from his father's place in Sydney when we first married

The snow drops reminded me of the time we lived in the house at Schwabisch Hall. Mother had needed to see a dentist, and had asked Dad to stay with me while she was away. I was sitting at the window and saw Mother leave the house. I looked across the street and saw the white snow drops peeping from under the snow in the garden across the street. I had the urge to go and pick those flowers. Dad stepped out of the room for a moment, and I went outside. I wore no coat, and no shoes – only socks on my feet. I felt the snow, cold and wet, under my feet. My legs were wobbly and I fell a few times. As I walked back to the house with the flowers in my hand, Mother was coming back from the dentist. She recognised me from a distance and yelled out, "Terese! Go inside quickly!" Mother was angry with Father and gave him a hot tongue lashing. Father said nothing. I had caused this distance between them by sneaking out into the cold to pick snow drops.

Sitting in the car now in front of my parents' house, I howled like I did when they died. Life for them had been difficult and sad. Mother was always hoping that someday she would get well enough to enjoy life with Father in the house they had built. Unfortunately it was not to be.

Now, I take some comfort in good memories of my Mum and Dad. When I look at the geraniums I grow in what is left of Mother's brown pot, I am reminded of the simple possessions that she used in camps during our travels. Mother couldn't manage without her brown pot. Not only was it used for cooking, but also for heating water and soups. Cabbage and potatoes were cooked in this brown pot to keep away hunger when the food from the camp kitchen was spoiled and not fit for us to eat. She also had a pan to fry an egg, or the fresh mushrooms that Dad picked in the fields first thing in the morning, or to make potato pancakes and fried bread. Many times Mother brewed up onions and milk in this fry pan to make the mixture that eased my cough in the winter months when nothing else was available.

Another treasure was her small bathtub. Naturally this tub was used for bathing. Mother shared this tub with the family and people in our hut to have their wash. The tub was also used as a laundry tub to wash our clothes. It was used to carry wood for the stove fire, and when we moved from one camp to another it was used to carry our belongings when we had no suitcases.

The last treasure was the water pitcher. Every evening in camp, Dad filled Mother's pitcher with water and had it standing at the end of his bed. No-one in our hut needed to go outside for water during the night, or on freezing wet mornings, to make a cup of tea. This pitcher carried gallons and gallons of water over the years. Without that pitcher there would be no water for our small bath. This pitcher was also used as a bucket, as we didn't have one. Often the pitcher was used for other things, such as carrying wooden chips for the stove. Now, I use the water pitcher to hold wet umbrellas.

These treasures were the only riches Mother owned. They travelled with her from one camp to another all over Germany, and across the seas and oceans all the way to Australia. They meant everything to her. Without these treasures life in the camps would have been more difficult for her than it already was. Mother guarded her treasures with her life. After each use, she slid them under the bed so they would not be stolen from her. Mother wouldn't swap them for anything, and they never left the hut. These items gave her some freedom.

My father, too, had his treasures. In his travels, Dad used his cigarette lighter to light many a candle and a fire. And many times he kept appointments by looking to the sky, putting his two fingers into the front of the fob trouser pocket and pulling out a round object with a chain fastened to the loop of his trouser band. He would flick the top open with his thumb, revealing the pocket watch.

At times he was the knight in shining armour, saving the day by using his pocket knife to open a can of milk for a mother to feed her baby. Dad had many uses for this tool. He whittled a piece of wood with his knife and made a flute so he could teach me a few notes. On his travels he used the knife to cut a bun in half, and to slice bread. On a journey in the train someone tapped Father on the shoulder asking him if he would lend his knife. When scissors were not available the knife came in handy for cutting a rope or a thread. An oil stone was always in his coat pocket to keep the knife sharp.

Dad always carried music inside his coat pocket. When someone started to sing, he didn't need an excuse to bring out the harmonica. He was deaf in one ear, but that didn't stop him playing a good tune on this small instrument. He always managed to play a happy tune and make our feet start tapping. Now, when I hear the song "Moon River" played on the radio, the harmonica reminds me of my Dad.

One morning in 1998, six years since I'd last seen Bryan, and only three years after Mother and Father's death, I received a phone call from the Mater Hospital at Waratah. The woman at the other end of the phone confirmed that I was Karen's mother before telling me that Bryan had been admitted as a patient to the hospital. "I know you are divorced from your husband,' she said, 'but would you please come? Karen's father is dying, and she needs your support."

Karen had been independent from the time she was a little girl, but now she needed my love and all the support I could give her. I left home in a hurry. In my panic arriving at the hospital, I locked my keys in the car.

Karen, Anthony, and Bryan's sister, Lin, were there. We sat with Bryan until late afternoon. Then I began to worry that I'd left the back door of the house unlocked, and that the cat needed feeding. I decided to quickly go home and come back. As I was walking to the lift, Lin came to tell me that Bryan was gone.

We all stood together at his bedside. Karen said a prayer, and then we said our goodbyes separately.

Karen turned to me and said, "Whatever Dad was, he was still my father, and I loved him." Even now, I cry when I think of her saying that.

Anthony stood behind me and said, "Mum, I have nothing to say at this moment. I am just numb. I cannot believe that Dad has gone."

I blamed myself for a lot of things. Lin said, "Don't blame yourself, it wasn't your fault." A social worker invited us into his office to talk.

Later, when I walked outside to my car, I was struck with grief. With Karen's words still in my mind, tears flowed down my cheeks. This was the end of an era. My thoughts went back to the day Karen was born in this same hospital, and how she was Bryan's treasure. I had cried then for our uncertain future. Maybe I had been frightened of losing Bryan. Life had unfolded and slipped away in ways we hadn't expected. When we were young and in love, and searching for our little house, Bryan was the man I wanted to spend my life with, to the end of our days. We never dreamed our life together would end this way.

On the horizon, a full moon was rising in the east. The moon was so big and bright that for a moment I didn't know whether it was morning or evening. It felt so close that I thought I could stretch out my arm and touch it. I couldn't remember ever seeing it so big.

I had rung the NRMA to come and unlock my car, so had an hour and a half to sit around. The glow of the moon filled me with comfort and warmth. I felt at peace. I couldn't say that I got this comfort from God because I've never seen God. But I saw the moon. It was like a spiritual uplifting. Perhaps it was God-sent.

Sometime in 2001, I received a letter through the Department of Social Security about the German Forced Labour Compensation Programme. More than one and a half million people, in over one hundred countries, were being paid compensation money by the German government for the pain and trauma suffered in those horror camps.

I couldn't fill in the forms myself. Denis, my old dancing teacher, helped me complete and submit the forms. My doctor wrote a supporting letter, saying that my health problems – chronic respiratory problems, multiple allergies, depression and anxiety – could be traced back to being hospitalised as a child in Germany. She wrote that I remembered being subjected to injections with large needles, and being left alone in a room for long periods of time.

In March 2004, I had minor abdominal surgery. When I came home, the doctor advised me to take life easy for a few weeks. I decided to shut myself away from the troubles of the world. The TV and radio news would not be turned on in the house until I was recovered and ready to face everyday living again.

Being the beginning of autumn, the days were still hot. I opened the front door of the TV room to the let in the fresh air and to enjoy the glorious day outside. I sat on my lounge, looking across the veranda to where the vine, with its pretty pink flowers, twined its way through the railing. When Bryan and I had the house built, our garden on the corner block was to be the hobby we would work on together. But, like most of my dreams. the idea of a big garden shrank to the size of our wallet. The pickets went by the wayside. We only managed to get the timber rails across. But sitting there at that moment, I counted my blessings for what I do have.

As I watched the bees and the butterflies floating from one bloom to another, pollinating each flower, my mind returned to my first memory of sitting on the floor looking up at the window, waiting for Mother to return. I had amused myself then by watching the branch covered in pink flowers tapping at the window, and the bees flying among the pretty blossoms.

I heard a magpie and a peewee chatting in the tree in front of my house. I had left a bowl of water in the shade for them, and occasionally they flew down for a drink. I loved listening and watching the birds and trying to identify their sounds. Sometimes, late in the afternoon of hot days, I would see a small blue-wing kingfisher taking a drink. The magpie and the peewee came into the yard frequently, the peewee coming right up to me when I was weeding, and giving me a fright by popping up under my arm.

I sat on the lounge for some time, but had to get up and move. I slowly walked out onto the veranda and down the few steps to the letter box. The magpie was at the bowl drinking. I whistled, and she lifted her head. She looked towards me and yodelled. I picked up the mail and turned to walk back to the house. My friend the peewee landed on my shoulder, as if to say, "It's a lovely day."

I came in and sat at the kitchen table, sorting the leaflets from the mail. Among the letters was a business envelope from the USA, addressed to me. I wondered who would be sending me a letter from America. I looked at it again to make sure that it was my name on the letter. I opened it. It was the cheque from the German Government and the International Organisation for Migration. It had been almost three years since I had sent the form away. It was not a large amount of money, but it was an acknowledgement of what happened to me and my parents, and millions of others, all those years ago.

EPILOGUE

One recent afternoon, I put on a DVD of my favourite movie, *The Student Prince*. I began to watch, but soon fell asleep.

I dreamed about Mother. She was at the back door of my kitchen. I was so surprised to see her, and I opened the flyscreen door for her to step into the house. She was young, her hair was dark, and she wore a dark dress. I gave her a big hug. Karen came out from her bedroom, and I said, "Look, your grandmother is here!" Karen looked at me and said, "I don't see her." I turned to Bryan and said, "Look, Mother is here." He said, "I don't see anyone."

"Can't you see me hugging my mother'" I asked them. It was hard for me to let her go. Her body was so warm.

My dreams are the closest physical comfort I have with Mother. When I woke, the sun glittered like gold between the leaves. I thought about the book I had already started writing. When I finish it, I thought, everyone will see my Mother. My brothers will know about their parents, and my children and nieces will know about their grandparents and why they came to Australia.

In a short time, the sun would be setting behind the mountains, turning the day into twilight. What a lovely ending to the day.

ACKNOWLEDGEMENTS

Book writing is a slow process. When I started to write my book I thought it was a just matter of getting words down on paper and that everything would flow easily and the book would be in print within twelve months. But that was not so.

Writing changed my life. It is demanding work. I wrote during the day, and woke at any hour of the night to write things down. I would lose myself for hours. For days at a time, no routine work in the house or the garden was done.

Over the years it has taken to write this book, I have phoned many people, often long distance. I have travelled to see friends and acquaintances to confirm that what I remembered as a child was correct.

There were times I came to a standstill and couldn't go on. I asked myself why I had started writing this book. My friends urged me on, saying this story must be told. They said, "People must know that you survived the horror of war. You are a witness to the truth of the death camps during the war years. Some historians writing about World War II have chosen to ignore the truth and distort history. This must be corrected."

My thanks go to my brothers, Cecil and Peter, to my sister-in-law Kristyna, and to my nieces, Natasha, Katharine and Melissa, for following up information for me.

I thank my friends for giving me a break from working on my book by inviting me to supper. I thank them for their conversation, which brought my memories to the surface and contributed to making this book that much richer.

Thanks also go to Mr Edward Cahill for permission to quote his account of the

Maitland Flood, and to Mr David Sciffer for kind permission to use images of the Maitland Flood, which he digitised from Jim Lucey's original negatives.

The lyrics to the song 'Portrait of My Love' on page 498 were written by Matt Monro and are freely available on: http://lyricsplayground.com/alpha/songs/p/portraitofmylove.shtml

Extracts of this story were first published in *People of the Valley: Writings from the Hunter*, and my thanks to the editors of that publication.

Finally, my many thanks go to my good friend Jill McKeowen for her skilful and intelligent editing. I met Jill when I enrolled in her creative writing class, and over the last six years we have worked together to shape my raw material into a finished manuscript.

Printed in the United States
By Bookmasters